THE CITY THAT NEVER WAS

THE CITY THAT NEVER WAS

TWO HUNDRED YEARS OF FANTASTIC AND FASCINATING PLANS THAT
MIGHT HAVE CHANGED THE FACE OF NEW YORK CITY

REBECCA READ SHANOR

VIKING

The preparation of this book was assisted by grants from the National Endowment for the Arts and the New York State Council on the Arts.

VIKING
Published by the Penguin Group
Viking Penguin Inc., 40 West 23rd Street,
New York, New York 10010, U.S.A.
Penguin Books Ltd, 27 Wrights Lane,
London W8 5TZ, England
Penguin Books Australia Ltd, Ringwood,
Victoria, Australia
Penguin Books Canada Ltd, 2801 John Street,
Markham, Ontario, Canada L3R 1B4
Penguin Books (N.Z.) Ltd, 182–190 Wairau Road,
Auckland 10, New Zealand

Penguin Books Ltd, Registered Offices:
Harmondsworth, Middlesex, England

First published in 1988 by Viking Penguin Inc.
Published simultaneously in Canada

1 3 5 7 9 10 8 6 4 2

Grateful acknowledgment is made for permission to reprint the following copyrighted works:
Excerpts from documents from the Louis I. Kahn Collection. Copyright 1977 Louis I. Kahn
Collection, University of Pennsylvania and Pennsylvania Historical and Museum Commission.
Excerpts from letters by Calvert Vaux 1860, 1864, 1865, 1894. Reprinted from the Calvert
Vaux Papers, Rare Books and Manuscripts Division, The New York Public Library, Astor, Lenox
and Tilden Foundations.
"Endless Train to End New York Subway Jam," *Popular Science,* May 1951. Reprinted from
Popular Science with permission. Copyright © 1951 Times Mirror Magazines, Inc.

Illustration credits appear on pages 253–254

LIBRARY OF CONGRESS CATALOGING IN PUBLICATION DATA
Shanor, Rebecca Read
The city that never was.
Bibliography: p.
Includes index.
1. City planning—New York (N.Y.)—History.
2. New York (N.Y.)—Buildings, structures, etc.
I. Title.
HT168.N5S53 1988   307.1'2'097471   87-40670
ISBN 0-670-80558-0

Printed in the United States of America by
Arcata Graphics, Kingsport, Tennessee
Set in Sabon
Designed by Ann Gold

To my parents, Constance and Donald,
who uncovered for me distant cities,
and to my sister, Lisa, who will
always prefer the country.

Make no little plans; they have no magic to
stir men's blood and probably themselves
will not be realized. Make big plans; aim high
in hope and work, remembering that a noble,
logical diagram once recorded will never
die, but long after we are gone will be a living
thing, asserting itself with evergrowing
insistency. Remember that our sons and
grandsons are going to do things that would
stagger us. Let your watchword be order
and your beacon beauty.

—Daniel Burnham, 1907

CONTENTS

ACKNOWLEDGMENTS   xi

INTRODUCTION   xiii

STREETS   1

PUBLIC BUILDINGS   35

TRANSPORTATION   81

BRIDGES  115

PARKS  157

MONUMENTS  189

AFTERWORD 227

NOTES 229

BIBLIOGRAPHY 237

INDEX 243

PHOTOGRAPH SOURCES 253

ACKNOWLEDGEMENTS

Piecing together the fragments of New York's un-realized plans often took on the aspect of working on a huge jigsaw puzzle—without the aid of the picture on the box. Many people, in a dozen different ways, helped me finish large portions of the puzzle. I am especially grateful to the relatives, friends, and associates of New York's inspired dreamers who freely shared all they knew about the plans and the histories behind them. Margot Ammann generously lent me books and photographs, and offered personal glimpses into the life and work of her remarkable father, Othmar H. Ammann. Harriet Pattison and Marshall Meyers helped in reconstructing the birth and demise of Louis I. Kahn's project for a Holocaust memorial, and provided invaluable information about its concept and design. Reverend Richard Parker dug out pictures, brochures, and correspondence relating to the abandoned scheme for Broadway Temple, and gave me an illuminating tour of the church's cavernous five-story basement, above which was to have risen the proposed cathedral. The late Hermina Wahle shared with me her childhood memories of Gustav Lindenthal, and Allan Renz, the grandson of the prolific engineer, led me to the vestiges of the anchorage belonging to the ill-fated Hudson River bridge of 1888. From Raymond Rubinow I learned the details of the crucial days in January 1960, when the campaign to save Carnegie Hall was launched. Clifford Speer supplied important information about the rapid transit scheme proposed by his grandfather, Alfred Speer.

Work on this book took me into the worlds of engineering, landscape design, historic preservation, urban planning, and architecture. I wish to thank the people who shared their expertise in these fields: Bill Andrew, Department of Environmental Protection of the City of New York; Ethan Carr, New York City Department of Parks and Recreation; Robert Kahn, U.S. Army Corps of Civil Engineers; Richard Manson, Local Initiative Support Corporation; Deborah Nevins, Deborah Nevins Landscape Garden and Design; Sue Radmer, formerly of the Municipal Art Society; and Anthony C. Wood, J. M. Kaplan Fund.

To libraries, large and small, across the metropolitan area, I extend my gratitude for having preserved the fragments of unbuilt New York. My thanks to Seymour Durst for making available his unrivaled collection of New York City books and ephemera; to Ken Cobb at the Municipal Archives for researching my obscure inquiries; and to Jane Hartye at the Samuel C. Williams Library, Stevens Institute of Technology, for help in selecting illustrations. I am also grateful to the staffs of the New-York Historical Society; the Museum of the City of New York; the New York Public Library (including my frequent haunt, the Annex); the Engineering Society Library; the Municipal Art Society; Columbia University's libraries; the New Jersey Historical Society; the Passaic Public Library, New Jersey; and the Architectural Archives, University of Pennsylvania.

I am particulary indebted to my agent, Al Hart, who understood immediately the intention of this book, even in its raw state five years ago, and to Professor Kenneth Jackson, who lent his support as I embarked on the first stage of research. I owe special thanks to Elliot Willensky, who supplied answers to the thorniest questions I encountered in my research, and who offered sound advice throughout the course of this project. I also wish to thank my editor, Mindy Werner, for her important suggestions for improvement of the manuscript, and Kathryn Court for her early encouragement.

Many friends contributed ideas to the book, cheered me on, and pried me away from my desk when necessary. My thanks to Gary Abernathy, Joan Altman, Mark Curcio, Darlene McCloud, Eileen Mullady, Henry Ng, Bruno Silvestre, Caryl Spinka, Terry Stanley, and Henry Tepper. Thanks also go to my friends Patty Mullady and Adrienne Llorence who helped type the first draft of the manuscript.

When, at times, this project seemed overwhelming, my family put things back into perspective with laughter and good food. Finally, to Richard Troiano, who gave me the courage, time, and space to begin this book, and finish it, my eternal gratitude.

Rebecca Read Shanor
New York
May 1988

INTRODUCTION

Even before Peter Minuit purchased Manhattan from the Canarsee Indians in 1626 with the equivalent of $24, an ambitious scheme had been conceived in Holland by the Dutch West India Company for the small settlement of New Amsterdam that lay at the island's southern tip. Designed and hand delivered to the New World colony by the Dutch engineer Kryn Frederycks in 1625, the plan mapped out some thirty houses, a system of streets, a church, a countinghouse, and a gristmill. The centerpiece of the town was to feature a stone fort, measuring over one thousand feet in diameter, complete with moat and drawbridge, to be built on the site of the present U.S. Custom House.

Frederycks stayed only long enough to plot out the town and the enormous bastion before returning to Holland in 1626. No sooner had his ship sailed out of sight, than the citizens of New Amsterdam, apparently unwilling to summon up the energy to build the large fort, scrapped that portion of the engineer's plan and decided to erect instead a four-pointed bastion of sod, one-tenth the size of the structure Frederycks had designed.

Construction of Fort Amsterdam proceeded at a leisurely pace over a period of several years, and by all accounts the quality of the workmanship was slipshod at best. Not two years after the first earthen ramparts had gone up, they "crumbled away like sand," reported a contemporary Dutch historian. When Peter Stuyvesant, the colony's newly named director, arrived from Amsterdam in 1647, he was dismayed to find "more a molehill than a fortress." What was worse, he wrote to his superiors in Holland, to his unending frustration nothing could induce the townspeople of New Amsterdam into strengthening their dilapidated defense, not even the threat of a daily two-guilder fine. Eventually Stuyvesant gave up trying to rouse the citizens into action and in 1650, with the help of a few servants of the Dutch West India Company, began the job of repairing the fort himself. But only a year later he angrily reported in another letter to Holland that, to his "vexation and disgust," the "new earth works, erected without the community's help [had been] rooted up, trampled down and destroyed by the community's hogs, cows and horses."

Such was the sorry condition of the fort in March 1653, when rumors reached New Amsterdam that British troops had mobilized in New England and were preparing to march south. On Stuyvesant's orders, the ruined defense was hastily repaired and night watch guards were assigned to patrol the ramparts. The fort was, however, neither large enough to contain all one thousand townspeople nor large enough to defend their homes, which lay scattered outside the walls of the bastion. In the face of this dilemma, Stuyvesant instructed "citizens without exception" to dig a deep ditch, twelve feet wide, river to river, at the northern boundary of the town, and to pound in a high wooden stockade along its length. Within a month, four divisions of crews, working in three-day shifts, had constructed the wooden palisade.

Ironically, the British did not attack New Amsterdam for another eleven years, and when they came, they came by sea. The wooden wall proved useless in the battle. So, in fact, did the small earthen fort, which, as was soon evident, was no match for the mighty cannons of the British navy. After a four-day seige, Stuyvesant surrendered to the Brit-

t' Fort nieúw Amsterdam op de Manhatans

ish, and on September 8, 1664, New Amsterdam became New York.

Had the massive fort designed by Kryn Frederycks been built, would the course of New York's history have taken a different turn? Might the Dutch flag be flying today at City Hall? One can only speculate. Certain is that Frederycks's plan, because it was not carried out, indirectly spawned what would later become one of the world's most famous financial addresses. In 1699, the wooden palisade that had been built to protect New Amsterdam was dismantled, and the deep ditch was filled in. The narrow lane that surfaced, between Broadway and the East River, was named Wall Street.

The earliest-known view of Manhattan Island. Date depicted, c. 1626–28. This engraving of New Amsterdam appeared in a book about the New World, published in Holland by Joost Hartgers in 1651. (The view was reversed perhaps by a careless printer.) It is generally believed that the large fort in the engraving depicts Kryn Frederycks's unexecuted plan for Fort Amsterdam.

Kryn Frederycks's design for Fort Amsterdam is only one, thin layer in the stack of unrealized plans for New York. Since the 1600s, scores of New Yorkers, both native and adopted, have picked up pen and paper to delineate their visions for the city. Architects and engineers have pictured it graced with ceremonial water gates, broad boulevards, and marble fountains. Doctors, writers, and farmers have sketched out for it spacious parks, mighty bridges, and dramatic skyscrapers. Designs for ingenious transportation schemes have been put forward by inventors and entrepreneurs. But of the thousands of plans proposed for New York, only a fraction has succeeded in reaching three-dimensional reality. The rest were destined to remain dreams on paper.

At first glance, the city's discarded plans do little more than present a picture of New York that looks at once oddly familiar yet curiously awry. An airport in midtown Manhattan? A racetrack in Riverside Park? The United Nations in *Queens*? But laid out side by side the schemes emerge as having played a dynamic, if sometimes imperceptible, role in the shaping of New York City. Many of the failed plans were stepping-stones that led to projects that are today integral fixtures of New York's cityscape. The George Washington Bridge, for example, is the culmination of several proposals, made over a period of 126 years, to span the Hudson River. Some of the schemes, although abandoned, remained good ideas nonetheless and served as conceptual blueprints to later generations, which, under more favorable political or financial stars, were able to see them through to completion. Such is the

history of New York's subway system, which was conceived in the 1860s but not built until 1904. Still other rejected plans took strange twists and sparked alternate projects that impacted the city in ways that no one could have predicted.

Few schemes for New York were conceived in a vacuum. A partial list of the circumstances that have inspired them would include municipal anniversaries, vendettas, new aesthetic sensibilities, epidemics, and the lure of a quick profit. Most of the plans, however, were prompted by New York's phenomenal growth and its attendant urban ills, some of which still plague the city. Gridlock, the plans reveal, is as old as the horse and buggy. Cries

Project for East River Park, aerial perspective. Venturi and Rauch, 1973. The boat-shaped recreational facility, reached from shore by way of two gangplanks, was to include softball and football fields, basketball courts, children's play areas, a community garden, and cafés. "Towed" behind are a swimming pool and a tugboat. The $5.5-million scheme was felled by New York's fiscal crisis in the mid-1970s.

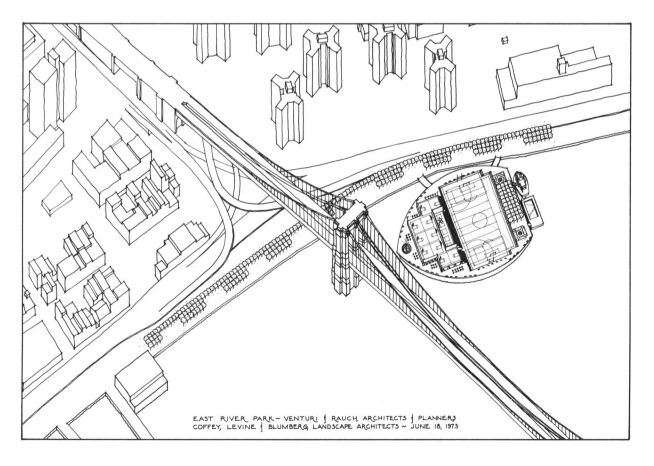

EAST RIVER PARK ~ VENTURI & RAUCH, ARCHITECTS & PLANNERS
COFFEY, LEVINE & BLUMBERG, LANDSCAPE ARCHITECTS ~ JUNE 18, 1973

for increased open space began sounding soon after the creation, in 1733, of Bowling Green, the city's first public park. And the tribulations of traveling by public transportation in New York, commuters today might be somewhat consoled to know, have been endured by straphangers since at least the mid-1800s.

Each era has offered its own solutions to these stubborn constants. Not all of them have been practicable or even desirable. For instance, probably few New Yorkers would care to see lower Manhattan bisected by the monstrous expressway that Robert Moses mapped out in 1940. Nor would many relish traveling to work twenty feet above the street, in windowless cars propelled through iron tubes, as one inventor proposed for the city in 1872. However, among the discarded plans that fall into the category of problem solvers, several hold enduring appeal and merit a second chance. One is the Goodyear scheme of 1951, which suggested replacing the trains on the Forty-second Street shuttle with small bubble-topped cars that would whisk passengers across town on a continuously moving conveyor belt. Another is the plan for a boat-shaped park, proposed in 1973 by the firm of Venturi and Rauch. Although intended by the architects to be "moored" in the East River near the Brooklyn Bridge, the four-acre park could be created virtually anywhere along New York City's 578 miles of waterfront.

Viewed from another perspective, New York's unrealized plans offer insight into the complex process that has built the city. New York did not, as some accounts suggest, evolve effortlessly over the course of three centuries from a humble Dutch village to a confounding metropolis. Nor is it the inspired product of a planning board. (In fact, until the establishment of the City Planning Commission in 1938, there was no permanent body to plan and monitor New York's development.) Rather, New York has been shaped to a large degree by false starts, failed experiments, and lost battles. Cornerstones for monuments were dedicated and skyscrapers begun, only to be abandoned midway because of financial pitfalls. With each technological advancement, architects and engineers scrapped their plans and returned to the drawing board to start anew. On the Senate floor in Albany and on Capitol Hill schemes for bridges and rapid transit prompted passionate debate—and were defeated.

But throughout New York's three-hundred-year history, the most powerful force in the shaping of the city has been public opinion. Lifting their voices in unison, New Yorkers have challenged proposals for in-town racetracks and vapid office towers. They have packed public hearings to oppose plans for superhighways, luxury housing, and colossal monuments. In petitions and on picket lines they have rallied for the creation of public parks and for the preservation of cherished landmarks. They have banded together and campaigned for improved mass transit, pedestrian malls, and tunnels.

Often, they have won.

History has not been kind to New York's unrealized schemes. Their fragments lie rolled up in archives, scattered in miniature on microfilm, and pressed between the pages of books that long have not seen the light of day. Piecing them together can be difficult, and often impossible. Sometimes physical evidence of a plan has survived—that is, an architect's model, a map, or a perspective drawing—but too little information surrounds the plan, and so it hangs in a void, unconnected to New York or even to the era that produced it. Other proposals are described at length and critiqued in newspapers, professional journals, and even diaries of the times, but their renderings have been lost or destroyed. A third group of plans, notably those dating from the seventeenth and eighteenth centuries, are so poorly documented that one cannot even begin to reconstruct them with any accuracy.

In a sense, then, the projects in the chapters ahead picked themselves: enough of their pieces could be recovered to enable reconstruction of their histories, from birth to demise. But the schemes collected here meet two other criteria. While some of the schemes are fanciful, even preposterous, each was intended to be realized, or was at least considered by its author to be wholly feasible. And each, in some way, serves to explain how New York City took shape. Since hundreds of unrealized plans for New York meet these criteria and together would fill volumes, some weeding out was necessary. For obvious reasons, if two or more plans closely resembled one another, the most interesting plan was selected for discussion. Figures such as Robert Moses, Gustav Lindenthal, and John Stevens, whose names and plans reappear throughout the annals of unbuilt New York, are limited here to a maximum of two proposals each. Similarly, periods rich in a particular kind of scheme (as, for example, the 1920s was in proposals for skyscrapers) are represented here by one or two plans. Thus, the plans that follow are but a small cross section of the visions painted for New York.

Readers hoping to find recent schemes for New York in the pages ahead will be disappointed, for, with one or two exceptions, proposals from the 1970s and 1980s are not represented here. They are omitted principally because most of the projects from this period are still in the process of unfolding. In this category belong, for example, the plan to redevelop the Coliseum site; the scheme to build a light-rail transit system along the Hudson River; and Donald Trump's seventy-six-acre dream for the Upper West Side, where he hopes to erect, among other things, the world's tallest building. Even plans from the 1970s and 1980s that show all apparent signs of being dead are, in fact, very much alive. In 1987, for example, Westway, the $2-billion superhighway—born in the early 1970s and killed in 1985—produced an heir in the form of a proposed six-lane highway edged by a waterfront esplanade. The plan to build a tower over Grand Central Terminal, foiled by preservationists in 1978, has taken a quirky turn and may go up, through the transfer of the terminal's air rights, as a colossal skyscraper, larger than the Chrysler Building, on Madison Avenue and Forty-sixth Street.

The outcome of these and other recent proposals will not be known until at least the 1990s. But chances are, most of the schemes will undergo substantial revisions before they take final form, and at least one will end up in New York's pile of discarded plans. Like its three-dimensional counterpart, the city that never was is still far from finished.

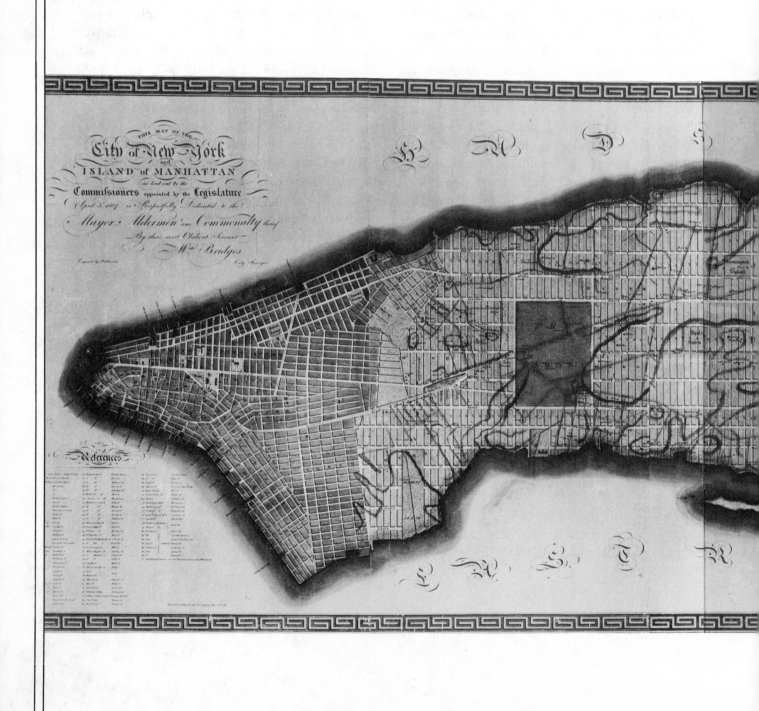

STREETS

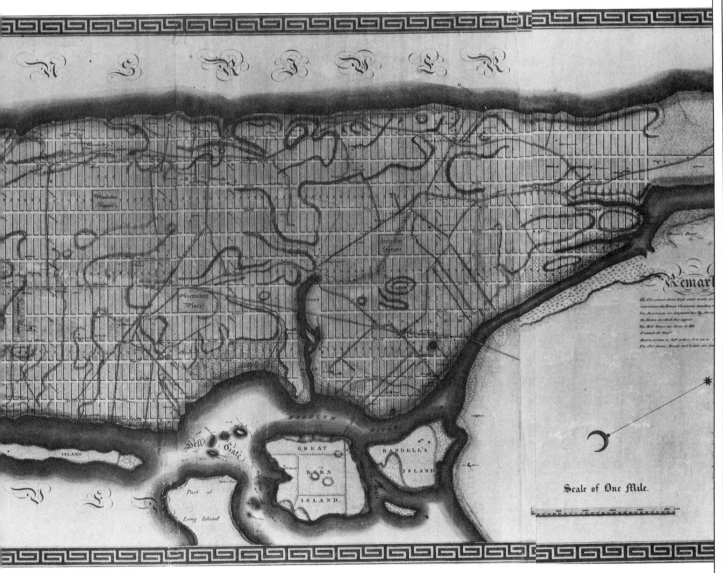

The commissioners' plan of 1811. The dark area at the southern end of Manhattan shows the developed portion of New York City; the undulating lines on the map show Manhattan's existing hills.

In the spring of 1811, while workmen were putting the finishing touches on the facade of City Hall on Chambers Street, inside the building members of the Common Council were excitedly inspecting a newly engraved eight-foot-long map. At last, after years of debate among the city fathers, and despite "the incessant remonstrances" of property owners, Manhattan Island had a street plan. Drawn up by a three-member commission appointed by the New York State Legislature in 1807, the plan was far from imaginative: starting at Houston Street, north of the maze of the city's existing thoroughfares, twelve major north-south avenues intersected with 155 east-west streets, transforming eight miles of the island's rural lands into a tidy grid pattern; here and there the grid was interrupted to make room for public squares. But to those who despaired over the hodgepodge of streets in lower Manhattan, the orderly street plan offered a means by which New York's future expansion could take place systematically and efficiently as the city's population pushed north from below Chambers Street to the upper reaches of the island.

Convenient though the grid looked on paper, it would be decades before it became a physical reality. The commission's deceptively simple design had sliced streets and avenues through farmers' fields, had turned streams and salt marshes into rows of square blocks, and had created public squares where massings of solid rock and dense forest stood. Implementing the plan entailed surveying 11,400 acres of Manhattan Island (work that was superintended by the engineer John Randel, Jr., between 1811 and 1820); compensating owners for land taken (a lengthy and often bitter process where less-public-spirited citizens were concerned); and finally the Herculean task of leveling hills, filling in valleys, and reshaping the island's shores with landfill.

Even before workers had finished gouging out the new mesh of streets

Laying out Riverside Drive, 1879. View is north from West 122nd Street.

with shovel and pick, two avenues were mapped out between the long blocks on the East Side—Lexington Avenue in 1832 and Madison Avenue in 1833—and by the late 1860s most of the parcels reserved for public squares had been carved into thoroughfares. In the years that followed, other new lines were added to the commissioners' plan—among them Manhattan Avenue, Depew Place, and Riverside Drive—and old lines received new names: Middle Road became Fifth Avenue, Bloomingdale Road north of Fifty-ninth Street was renamed Broadway, and Harlem Lane was christened Saint Nicholas Avenue, in honor of New York City's patron saint.

Manhattan's street plan, both above and below Houston Street, has long posed an array of perplexing problems. Its ratio of streets to avenues is hugely disproportionate; its narrow intersections invite gridlock; and its geometry forces traffic to zigzag circuitously around square blocks. A number of plans proposed since the early 1900s have addressed these deficiencies. Schemes for diagonal boulevards attempted to paste shortcuts and some grace onto the 1811 grid; a plan to build a new avenue along the center of Manhattan Island proposed giving traffic an extra north-south artery; and designs for elevated sidewalks offered pedestrians space of their own. But none of these plans made so much as a dent in the map of Manhattan. Instead, the island's street system incrementally acquired a ring of highways, subterranean passageways, and a series of viaducts as it made the transition from the days of the horse and the two-story home to the age of the automobile and the skyscraper.

The White City, a highlight of the World's Columbian Exposition, Chicago, 1893.

In 1893 millions of visitors came away from the World's Columbian Exposition in Chicago intrigued by the African huts and duly impressed by the electricity exhibit, but they left absolutely bedazzled by the White City, which rose from the shores of Lake Michigan in a shimmer of neoclassical architecture, broad boulevards, and azure-colored lagoons. Nobody had seen anything quite like it before—certainly not in America, where the exponential growth of towns and cities in the nineteenth century had left little room for either order or beauty. Home to most urban-dwelling Americans in 1893 conjured up scenes of heavy Victorian buildings, a sky that was crisscrossed with telegraph lines, and manure-littered streets. No wonder the image of the White City—perfectly proportioned, clean, and gracious—lingered on long after the fair had been razed, gripping the nation with an urban fever called the City Beautiful movement. By the late 1890s Philadelphia, Des Moines, San Francisco, and a hundred other cities across the country, large and small, were drawing up grand schemes for public buildings, cascading pools, and landscaped drives patterned after the fantastic spectacle at Chicago's fair.

In Manhattan, City Beautiful enthusiasts surveyed their territory and then rolled up their sleeves. Before them lay a ragged skirt of wharves and terminals, miles of monotonous rowhouses and tenements, and a perfunctory geometric street system. Nothing could have been further from the ideals of the White City, to which they so fervently aspired. But pursuers of the City Beautiful were a determined lot. After the fair a spate of monuments, statues, and fountains sprang up to decorate the city's parks and plazas. Schemes urging uniform pier construction to improve the appearance of the waterfront were put forward. One by one, the imposing edifices of the Metropolitan Museum of Art, the New York Public Library, and Grand Central Terminal were shoehorned between the horizontals and verticals of Manhattan's gridiron plan. As for the sticky problem of what to do with the uncomely street system itself, some people thought a little cosmetic surgery was in order.

The Municipal Art Society was an ardent sup-

Grand Central Terminal, seen from the corner of Forty-second Street and Park Avenue in 1914, a year after the station opened. It replaced Grand Central Depot, which was built on the site in 1871.

porter of this idea. Founded in 1892 by a group of prominent architects and artists to promote the beautification of New York's streets and public places, the civic organization cast a most disparaging eye on Manhattan's rectilinear street system, which, in its view, blocked both traffic and the aesthetic goals of the City Beautiful movement. Wiping out the curse of the gridiron plan would not be easy, the Society acknowledged, but after having given the matter some study, it believed it had found one way to do it: overlay the grid with diagonal boulevards. In 1904 the Society sent its street beautification plan to Mayor George B. McClellan.

The longest of the Society's proposed boulevards began at East Eighth Street and Broadway, near the Cooper Union for the Advancement of Science and Art, and cut a broad, three-quarter-mile-long swath through the tenement-lined streets of the Lower East Side, before terminating at Delancey Street in the vicinity of the Williamsburg Bridge. From Delancey Street another avenue shot southwest, to the Bowery, connecting with the approach to the rising steel skeleton of the Manhattan Bridge, construction of which had begun in 1904. A third diagonal ran from Union Square Park, on the East Side, through Greenwich Village to Christopher Street on the West Side. The Society further recommended extending Sixth and Seventh avenues south several blocks from their respective end points at Carmine and West Eleventh streets, and extending Franklin Street east to the Bowery.

Aside from facilitating traffic circulation of both horse-drawn vehicles and the growing number of automobiles, said the Society's report, oblique thoroughfares offered a host of aesthetic benefits. To begin with, diagonal boulevards fanning out across Manhattan Island would break up the monotony of the grid plan and infuse it with some grace. Moreover, "the irregular shapes of the intersections that such diagonals make with other streets" presented some enticing opportunities for redesigning sections of the city "in a more imposing architectural and artistic manner." For example, the wedge-shaped intersections could be reserved for triangular buildings, suggested the Society, envisioning the Flatiron Building, which had gone up in 1902 on Twenty-third Street at the juncture of Broadway and Fifth Avenue. Or some of the intersections could be given over to plazas and small parks; others could become spacious settings for fountains and monuments. In Paris and London such embellishments had "been to the great artistic improvement of those cities," the Society noted.

Conspicuously lacking in the Society's report to Mayor McClellan was mention of the hundreds of buildings that would have to be demolished when the wide new strips of black macadam were unrolled, and of the hundreds of thousands of people, many of them poor, who would be left homeless by this ruthless quest for order and beauty. But City Beautiful advocates hardly saw the need to justify what they considered to be slum clearance. The *New York Times* in fact outrightly welcomed

The Municipal Art Society's plan for diagonal boulevards and street extensions, 1904.

the devastating consequences that would follow the Society's proposal to extend Franklin Street to the Bowery. "A curious benefit would result from this improvement," the paper mused. "Chinatown would be opened to the public gaze and perhaps destroyed." Fortunately, this "benefit" was never realized, nor were the Society's plans for diagonal boulevards. However, its recommendation for the southern extension of Sixth and Seventh avenues was implemented after the First World War.

A bird's-eye view of Manhattan as it would have looked had the Municipal Art Society's proposed street system been carried out, 1904.

The Municipal Art Society's proposal was just one of many such plans dropped off at City Hall. From 1904 on, the rigid harness of Manhattan's right-angled street system chafed enough New Yorkers to keep grandiose schemes for new thoroughfares coming for several years. But what the Society's report to Mayor McClellan only implied, others pronounced loud and clear. By the early twentieth century, Greater New York, born in 1898, five boroughs and three million people strong, was one of the largest cities in the world and indisputably the nation's cultural, financial, and social leader. There was no need to look westward to the ghost of Chicago's fair now, said proud New Yorkers. Their city was on a par with the great urban centers of Europe, and Europe was where they would seek aesthetic guidance. Certainly for street plans there was no dearth of models on the other side of the Atlantic Ocean from which to choose. Vienna's elegant Ringstrasse, which encircled the inner city, suggested a possible scheme, as did the splay of boulevards cut through Paris by General Haussmann in the 1850s. Crescent-shaped streets, such as those in London's plan, could be attractive additions to Manhattan, as might an Italian piazza or two. Any grand twist, in fact, would lend prestige to the gridiron, which fell so pitifully short of symbolizing either the wealth or the power that belonged to the vast, new metropolis.

The New York City Improvement Commission, appointed by Mayor McClellan in 1904 to prepare a comprehensive city plan, took a long look at European street systems. In its 1907 report, which was peppered with proposals that inserted curves, circles, and diagonals into any available spot within the street plan of the five boroughs, the commission recommended building a regal parkway, 160 feet wide, from Fifth Avenue to the Queensboro Bridge in time for the bridge's opening in 1909. Since the plan would entail acquiring entire blocks between Fifty-ninth and Sixtieth streets at a cost of at least $15 million, the commission conceded it was unlikely that the city would fund the scheme; for its part, however, it believed that building a boulevard to vie with those "of the most beautiful cities of Europe" would be money well spent. The architect

Manicured hedges line the grand approach to the Queensboro Bridge in the plans suggested by the New York City Improvement Commission, 1907.

Louis Jallade agreed. Really, he scoffed, what did Manhattan's street plan have to offer besides a "very ugly system of square blocks" and "long avenues, like Eighth Avenue—that monument of monotony"? If New York hoped to attain the beauty that Paris and London possessed, said Jallade, it would

have to lay out grand drives such as the one the commission had proposed, or to build more diagonal avenues, "like Broadway." Obviously irritated by the public's failure to storm City Hall and demand the immediate revamping of Manhattan's street system, the architect added, "If I might dare suggest, some New Yorkers do not yet see the necessity of any art improvement; they seem to lack imagination."

Jallade wasn't the only one getting peevish about the difficulties of weaving Old World charm into Manhattan's gridiron plan. Referring to the blocks the city couldn't possibly hope to buy for the proposed parkway approach, the commission complained in its 1907 report that "cities in Europe would probably not hesitate to incur" the great expense. Face it, snapped the New York Times, Manhattan's street system couldn't be "corrected by any Haussmannizing process that would be worth its cost." New Yorkers would simply have to put

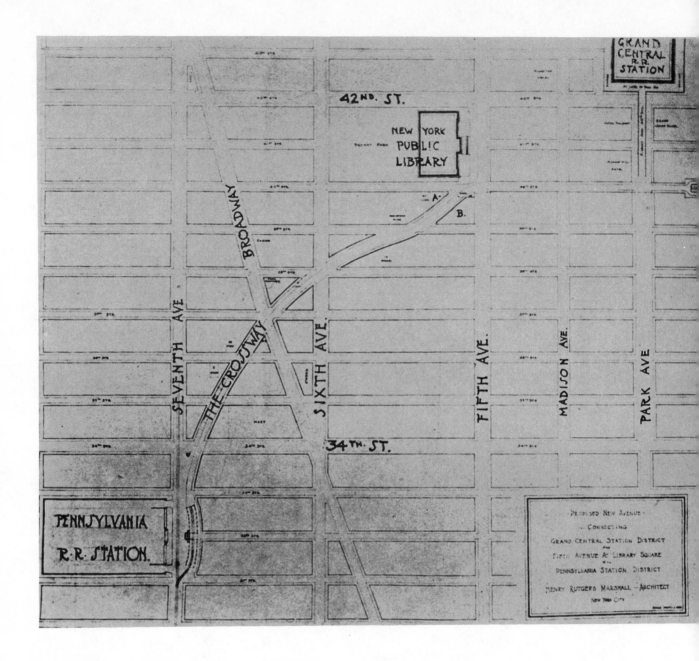

their overblown notions of drives, parkways, and boulevards aside, and learn to live with the "irretrievable mistake" of the island's geometric layout.

If the grid was here to stay, how then, please, could New York show off its magnificent new architecture, asked Henry Rutgers Marshall, referring to Pennsylvania Station, which lay unceremoniously wedged between Thirty-first and Thirty-third streets on Seventh Avenue. The lack of a sweeping view onto the "noble masses" of the year-old railroad station was "a serious loss to the city," the architect declared in 1911. He, however,

Plan for a curved boulevard linking Pennsylvania Station and Fifth Avenue. Henry Rutgers Marshall, 1911.

happened to have just the plan to correct this shortcoming. A curved avenue, gently bending from Seventh Avenue and Thirty-third Street to Fifth Avenue and Fortieth Street, would afford a dramatic view of the station's columned facade from a distance of several blocks. "From the artistic point of view the gain would be enormous," said Marshall. "From Fifth Avenue the vista down the new curved avenue

— 10 —

would be not unlike that of Piccadilly Circus in London." But Marshall's proposed avenue was quickly rejected by the public as too costly and frivolous. New Yorkers, already carping about the crowded conditions on the Broadway Interborough Rapid Transit (IRT) subway line, then only seven years old, favored connecting Penn Station to other parts of the city via a new subway route, not a curved boulevard. And so, at the close of 1911, exactly one hundred years after the unveiling of the gridiron plan, only two avenues skittered obliquely across Manhattan's geometric map: Broadway and the Bowery, old Indian trails that the authors of the 1811 plan had decided to spare.

On January 3, 1910, William J. Gaynor strode across the Brooklyn Bridge from his home near Park Slope in Brooklyn to City Hall in Manhattan. The sight of Gaynor's wiry figure, elongated several inches by a hat that seemed to be permanently attached to his head, was to become a familiar sight to New Yorkers, for the city's new mayor loved to walk. "I walk for health and also for the joy of walking," the sixty-two-year-old mayor said, and he advised his constituents to do the same: "Cultivate the habit of walking . . . and it will keep you in health and make you charitable and forbearing."

During a spring stroll along Fifth Avenue in 1910, Mayor Gaynor found himself feeling somewhat less than forbearing. The pavement, swarming with office workers and shoppers, reduced his brisk step to a shuffle, and the tangle of automobiles, horses, carts, and carriages clogging the street made it almost impossible to cross the avenue. This would never do, declared Gaynor, who was reportedly "horrified" by the scene. New York's most famous thoroughfare would have to be cleared.

By 1910 Fifth Avenue was in full flower. From Washington Square to Andrew Carnegie's mansion at Ninetieth Street, the avenue fairly sagged with posh hotels, clubs, expensive restaurants, and the most luxurious homes money could buy. It was also fast becoming the city's most exclusive shopping street. Since the early 1900s, spurred by the construction of Pennsylvania Station and Grand Central Terminal, retailers in increasing numbers had been leaving their downtown addresses in the "Ladies' Mile" district—located between Eighth and Twenty-third streets, from Broadway to Fifth Avenue—for Fifth Avenue north of Thirty-fourth

Street. Behind the plate-glass windows of Tiffany & Company, Gorham's, the Duveen Brothers, and a dozen other "emporiums designed to delight the hearts of extravagant women," display stands offered diamonds, antiques, and the latest gowns from Paris, tempting well-heeled patrons, as yet unencumbered by an income tax, to step inside and exit with armfuls of prettily wrapped packages. Shoppers whose last names didn't happen to be Rockefeller or Vanderbilt headed for the stately doors of B. Altman's, the first department store to pull up stakes from the Ladies' Mile district and relocate to "upper" Fifth Avenue.

But the crowning glory of Fifth Avenue lay north of Fifty-ninth Street, in a thirty-block stretch known as "Millionaires' Row." This was home to the As-

Mayor William J. Gaynor, 1910.

Double-decker buses, horse-drawn carriages, and automobiles clog Fifth Avenue and the intersection of Forty-second Street, 1910. View is north along Fifth Avenue.

tors, the Goulds, the Whitneys, the Belmonts, and a hundred other families that had made huge fortunes in gold, copper, oil, and railroads. From the early 1880s on, taking their cue from the Vanderbilts, who by 1905 had erected several palatial homes (since demolished) between Fifty-first and Fifty-seventh streets, the rich poured old money and new money into sumptuous residences, each more lavish than the next, and all the objects of envy of passing citizens. As one man put it, "To live and die in a Fifth Avenue mansion is the dearest wish of every New Yorker's heart."

Mayor Gaynor's dearest wish was to free the avenue of congestion. As New Yorkers soon found out, the short-tempered mayor was a man ired by obstacles of any kind, and one who acted quickly to remove them. Several days after his bothersome walk on Fifth Avenue, Gaynor put forward a rather drastic scheme to combat the jam of people and traffic along the avenue, calling for nothing less than a new thoroughfare, one hundred feet wide, to be cut between Fifth and Sixth avenues, from Eighth Street to the southern perimeter of Central Park, at Fifty-ninth Street. The mayor calculated that this improvement would cost $40 million, almost five times what it had cost to build the New York Public Library, which was nearing completion at Forty-second Street, but he believed the project would be willingly financed by property owners whose fallow back lots would suddenly become prime real estate fronting on a main avenue.

"Millionaires' Row," looking north along Fifth Avenue from Sixty-fifth Street, 1898. The château on the near corner, designed by Richard Morris Hunt, was the residence of Mrs. John Jacob Astor.

However, Gaynor stressed, he would make no moves to go forward with the idea until "public sentiment had been expressed in its favor."

The plan for the new avenue was neither cheered nor lambasted. The city's dailies, perhaps numbed by shock, were surprisingly matter-of-fact about the proposed two-and-a-half-mile addition to Manhattan's street system. The *New York Tribune* reported that, of course, the mayor's plan would require demolishing hundreds of buildings, including the New York Yacht Club, the brownstone home of U.S. Senator Chauncey Depew, and the enormous white cast-iron building belonging to Stern

Brothers on West Twenty-third Street. Yes, the messy business of razing buildings was "one of the greatest drawbacks" to the mayor's scheme, remarked the *New York Times* in May 1910, but at least the new Public Library would be spared, and a few days later the newspaper obligingly offered readers a preview of the proposed avenue as it would look from a severed Bryant Park. A benign political cartoon in the *Globe* merely depicted the mayor, shovel in hand, digging out the new avenue.

Reaction from the public was also curiously subdued. Most letters to the editor and to the mayor's office politely offered alternative, less radical schemes to relieve the glut on Fifth Avenue, such as building a tunnel under the street or widening Sixth Avenue. In one of the few snippy notes addressed to City Hall, one man curtly suggested the mayor apply himself first to cleaning up New York's existing

A determined mayor shovels out a path for the new avenue in a 1910 New York *Globe* cartoon.

The proposed path of Mayor Gaynor's new avenue, Eighth Street to Fifty-ninth Street, between Fifth and Sixth avenues, and some of the buildings that construction of the thoroughfare would have destroyed, 1910.

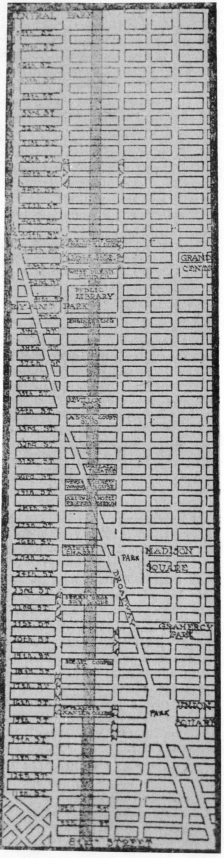

In a 1910 rendering, traffic flows along Mayor Gaynor's proposed avenue across Forty-second Street, and past the rear of the New York Public Library, through Bryant Park.

streets, which were "dirty and out of order," before he began excavating new ones.

While New Yorkers mulled over the proposal, Gaynor put the plan aside and tended to more urgent municipal affairs. In the name of reform, the Democratic mayor set about reorganizing the city's antiquated and inefficient departments, and investigated reports of police brutality. In his campaign to eliminate graft and waste, Gaynor struck four hundred political appointees off the city's payroll, saving New York taxpayers $700,000. Saloons and gambling houses came to expect impromptu visits from the new mayor; and city officials, his brusque, no-nonsense approach.

On August 9, 1910, after six months of long days at City Hall, Mayor Gaynor boarded the *Kaiser Wilhelm der Grosse* in Hoboken, New Jersey, to set sail for a vacation in Europe. As he stood on deck surrounded by family and friends who had come to wish him bon voyage, a stocky man suddenly emerged from the crowd, shoved a gun to the back of the mayor's neck, and pulled the trigger. Although the mayor survived the assassination attempt, the bullet fired by James Gallagher, an unemployed dock worker, remained permanently lodged in Gaynor's throat.

A visibly ailing mayor returned to City Hall in the autumn of 1910. The "fishhook," as Gaynor called the bullet, had diminished his voice to a hoarse whisper and plagued him with a deep cough. Eating was painful, and sleep sometimes impossible. Despite his constant discomfort, the mayor pressed on with his duties and managed over the ensuing years to hammer out complicated contracts for new subway routes, institute an improved system of food inspection, and wage a successful battle against infant mortality. But whether Gaynor intended to revive the plan for a new avenue before the end of his term will never be known. On September 4, 1913, the exhausted and enfeebled mayor boarded the steamship *Baltic* for a rest on the ocean, in hopes that a dose of salt air and a quiet week in a deck chair would restore his health. Six days later, two hundred miles off the coast of Liverpool, Mayor Gaynor succumbed to the bullet he had fought for three years.

◇

Harvey Wiley Corbett, the noted New York architect, picked up the July 1926 issue of the City Club's monthly bulletin, thumbed past the front cover and, beginning to chuckle, settled down at his desk to read eleven pages of pure melodrama. "MUNICIPAL MURDER," announced a headline in bold black letters across the top of the page. "Latest Casualty List From the Skyscraper-Motor Car Front Along the Sidewalks of New York," ran the subheading beneath. "I admit I was puzzled," the architect later joked. "Skyscrapers? Motor cars? Had someone's Buick sedan suddenly gone mad, and slashed some innocent creature's throat with a razor? Was it possible that the Equitable Building had been skulking up Broadway o'nights brandishing a Colt automatic?" Corbett read on:

> Killed 54—Wounded Unknown—This is not a war communiqué of 1918, nor does it refer to American soldiers. . . . It refers to American CHILDREN, who were alive in May and were killed in June . . . [by] the hands of clumped skyscrapers and the packed and pushing motor vehicles that the skyscrapers breed.

Corbett instantly recognized the voice behind this message of doom and gloom. It belonged to Henry Curran, an attorney, a former Manhattan Borough president, and, in 1926, one of New York's most vociferous skyscraper foes. The architect and the lawyer had often locked horns on the tall-building issue, Corbett always siding with the skyscraper, which he staunchly defended as "a splendid thing, an American thing," Curran always arguing that tall buildings caused traffic jams, overloaded the transit system, spewed hordes of workers into the streets at rush hour, and, not to mention, killed children. Look at our city, the lawyer moaned. "We are caught in our own coils—a poor, patient people, skyscraper sick, motor mad, subway crazy. We have become a seething dish of

Harvey Wiley Corbett, 1931.

the Metropolitan Life Insurance Company head-quarters at Madison Square, and the sleek towers of Rockefeller Center, a project designed by a consortium of three architecture firms, on which Corbett served as chief architect.

In 1927 Corbett and Curran met face to face for a public debate to hash out the pros and cons of tall buildings. After presenting the worn-out argument that skyscrapers rob cities of light and air, Curran got to the heart of one of his favorite themes. "All our traffic trouble is due to skyscrapers," he said. "They draw the automobiles and the people in the rush hours and throw them out on the streets again at night." "Nonsense," replied Corbett. Skyscrapers take traffic off the street. "In downtown New York, a business man consults his broker, eats his lunch, sees his lawyer, buys his wife a box of candy, gets a shave, all in the same building. At most he walks a few blocks. Most of the time he travels up and down instead of to and fro."

"Perhaps he does," rebutted Curran. "There may even be a manicurist [in the building] and a haberdasher and boot black as well. This is an entrancing picture of 'home sweet home' in the skyscraper. But how does this business man get into the skyscraper? Is he born there?"

Curran had a point, but it was a little late to be quibbling about the drawbacks of tall buildings. By 1927 Manhattan Island had long taken on a pincushion effect. Hundreds of buildings effortlessly reached up twenty stories, and the tips of the Graybar Building, the Sherry-Netherland Hotel, the Fred French Building, and a dozen other towers poked at the clouds above the thirty-story mark. King of the spires was the Woolworth Building, which had reigned over Manhattan in sixty floors of Gothic splendor since 1913. No, the true culprit of street congestion, Corbett said, was the automobile. Pierce-Arrows, Studebakers, Essexes, Hudsons, and Franklins had downtown Manhattan snarled up in a big ball of lacquered metal. "I notice that Mr. Curran doesn't suggest abolishing the automobile," Corbett commented wryly. "Perhaps he has just bought a new one."

If the lawyer had recently visited "Automobile Row," along Broadway in the Fifties and Sixties

municipal spaghetti." And look at Corbett's record: the thirty-story Bush Terminal Building on Forty-second Street near Sixth Avenue, a fixture on the skyline since 1918, alone had added volumes to this chaos. But Curran hadn't seen anything yet. Corbett was just warming up. In the late 1920s and the early 1930s, the architect's passion for height would produce the Master Apartments on Riverside Drive at 103rd Street, the Art Deco annex to

to plunk down $1,300 for a two-tone green Hupmobile or $1,500 for a Chrysler with a rumble seat, he wasn't saying. But Corbett's point was that, with over half a million motor vehicles registered in New York City and not a single mile of highway to carry them (those would be built in the 1930s), it seemed a little ridiculous to be blaming the skyscraper for the city's traffic ills.

Such was the situation when the Regional Plan Association (RPA) invited Corbett to head a committee and devise a scheme for the relief of Manhattan's street congestion. Although Corbett knew it would be purely academic—the RPA is an advisory body, with no powers to implement its plans—he readily accepted the chairmanship. Let Curran talk on about the detrimental effects of skyscrapers, Corbett thought. Here was a chance to constructively explore how New York's street system might be reconciled with both the skyscraper and the automobile. The subject certainly merited some study. After all, Detroit was not going to "stop building automobiles and we will not stop building skyscrapers," said the architect.

During the first few meetings, Corbett and the committee (whose members the RPA did not identify) discussed the problem at hand. The streets in New York's midtown and downtown business districts, some of which measure barely sixty feet across, were overburdened with cars, buses, trolleys, elevated lines, and pedestrians. That much was obvious. Now to find a solution. Would widening the streets or building new ones ease the crush? No, committee members decided. What about tightening the city's zoning laws? Good idea, they agreed, but that could take years. Besides, even the strictest measures to limit the height and bulk of buildings wouldn't dissolve congestion in districts that were already densely developed. Might taking a portion of the traffic off the streets lighten the load? Yes, of course. Then there's our answer, said Corbett: "Some form of double-decking must be used."

Actually, the final design drawn up by Corbett and his colleagues amounted to triple-decking, for the plan put all rail transport underground, roped off the street primarily for vehicular use, and placed pedestrians on raised sidewalks. The committee admitted it had no idea how to sink the city's elevated and trolley lines out of the picture—transportation experts would have to figure that one out—but it thought it did have a logical two-step scheme for

Before: In a photograph taken in the late 1920s, trolleys and automobiles inch their way through Times Square north of West Forty-third Street, and matinee crowds jam the sidewalks.

After: In the scheme for temporary elevated sidewalks at Times Square, proposed by Harvey Wiley Corbett and his committee, pedestrian and vehicular traffic moves freely. The second part of the committee's scheme called for the incorporation of permanent elevated sidewalks in new buildings constructed at Times Square.

implementing its tiered street system. First, temporary sidewalks would be constructed twenty feet above the street. Then, as blocks were redeveloped—a common phenomenon in New York, the committee noted—arcaded sidewalks would be built into every new building at the second-story level, footbridges would be constructed above the street at every corner, and presto, the city would have another stratum! Pedestrians would be able to move about "out of danger from traffic, protected from the snows of winter and the glare and heat of the summer sun," wrote the committee. "Walking would become a pastime (it is now one of the most haz-

ardous occupations). Shopping would be a joy. The overwrought nerves of the present New Yorker would be restored to normalcy and the city would become a model for all the world."

Meanwhile, below this pedestrian paradise, motorists would have every inch of the street to themselves. And thanks to the space beneath the arcaded sidewalks, they would also gain four new lanes for parking, two on either side of the street. If, over time, even this generous roadbed became saturated with automobiles and trucks, additional lanes for parking could be created by utilizing room within buildings at ground level. "This process can con-

tinue . . . *ad infinitum*," said Corbett. "In fact, it could continue until the entire surface under the buildings is available for traffic, if ever such a condition should demand it, and it is not impossible that it may." Heady with its vision for the future, the committee wrote:

> We see a city with sidewalks, arcaded and with solid railings. We see the smaller parks of the city . . . raised to this same sidewalk-arcade level, public parking space for autos provided underneath, and the whole aspect has become that of a very modernized Venice, a city of arcades, piazzas and bridges, with canals for streets, only the canals will not be filled with water

but with freely flowing motor traffic, the sun glittering on the black tops of the cars and the buildings reflected in this waving flood of rapidly rolling vehicles.

The Regional Plan Association presented the committee's scheme in its publication of 1931, *The Building of the City,* an impressive volume packed with recommendations for the metropolitan area, ranging from housing policy to zoning principles. Fearing readers might misconstrue the purpose of the committee's plan, the RPA hastened to explain that it was offered only as a proposed remedy "for congestion in the intensively built up areas" of

Manhattan, not as an excuse to build "a city *de novo* in places where it is still practicable to have a one-level street system." For its part, the RPA thought the multitiered plan was "interesting" and well worth the expense "where the need is as pressing as in the Times Square district." But it faulted the scheme for placing pedestrians two levels away from underground rapid transit and suggested that subterranean passageways be added to the design, much like the ones Corbett and his associates had newly drawn up for Rockefeller Center.

Readers who leafed through *The Building of the City* looking for cost estimates of the proposal or for architectural specifications drew a blank, because nowhere did dollar figures appear, nor were blueprints prepared by the committee. But it had never been the intention of the RPA or the committee to furnish detailed plans. The primary objective of the tiered street scheme, indeed the RPA's own objective, as it emphasized, was to offer ideas that might stimulate architects, planners, and engineers. "New York will never appear as we picture it," wrote Thomas Adams, the RPA's general director of Surveys and Plans. "Our only hope is that the lines we have drawn will inspire the citizens to express themselves with a greater love of order and a higher sense of beauty in the building of the city."

The tiered city as envisioned by Harvey Wiley Corbett and his committee, c. 1929.

OPPOSITE:
Cross section of a hypothetical street showing six lanes of traffic, four parking lanes beneath the sidewalks of arcaded buildings, and the potential for additional parking space within the buildings themselves.

The trouble with Manhattan's street plan, said Robert Moses, chairman of the Triborough Bridge Authority, as he handed Mayor Fiorello H. La Guardia a map in 1940 marked with a heavy brown line, was its paucity of major crosstown arteries below Houston Street. East-bound cars and trucks roaring out of the Holland Tunnel or off the West Side Highway slowed to a viscous crawl once their tires hit the narrow streets of lower Manhattan. On the other side of town, meanwhile, vehicles spilling off the East River bridges had to buck a battery of red lights, eighteen of them to be precise, to get over to the West Side. Add up the lost man hours and wasted gas, said Moses, and what you had was one of the most expensive two-way traffic jams in North America.

La Guardia smoothed out the map on his desk and scanned the proposed crosstown corridor that ran from river to river just north of Canal Street. On paper, the thick line promised to keep traffic humming smoothly between the ramps of the East River Drive and the West Side Highway, and into the laps of downtown tunnels and bridges. In an accompanying memorandum, dated November 11, 1940, Moses predicted that the road would raise real estate values along the route, bring new business to the area, and give local streets some breathing space.

La Guardia thought the plan was a good one, and so did the New York City Planning Commission, which included the road on its master plan for Arterial Highways and Major Streets in 1941. But, in fact, the highway did nothing Moses had said it would. Instead, the road lived on to plague five mayors over a period of twenty-nine years, generated untold hours of bitter debate, and struck fear in the hearts of thousands of downtown residents and merchants. Small wonder, for the highway Moses had envisioned was a six-lane, elevated, double-decked monster called the Lower Manhattan Expressway, which chewed a path, two and a half miles long, from the Hudson River through Little Italy and the Lower East Side all the way to the Manhattan and Williamsburg bridges.

In 1946, during Mayor William O'Dwyer's administration, Moses announced that construction

Robert Moses, c. 1956.

of the mammoth highway would begin in 1948. This call to the bulldozer was a little premature, however, since the city didn't have the resources to finance the $22-million road. Moses would have to wait out another decade, through Mayor Vincent Impellitteri's tenure and into Robert F. Wagner Jr.'s first term as mayor, before he found the money needed to build the expressway. Meanwhile, ever confident that funding would turn up from somewhere, Moses retained the engineering firm Madigan-Hyland to refine and enlarge the plan, and made sure that New Yorkers reading the front page of the morning paper in the 1940s and the 1950s were periodically treated to updated maps of the phantom road, which, as time elapsed, acquired two additional lanes, sprouted a clover leaf, and was moved north, to Broome Street.

In 1956 Moses got lucky. Under the newly created federal highway program, the road was included in the National System of Interstate and Defense Highways, thereby becoming eligible for 90 percent federal aid and 10 percent state aid. In

The first plan for the Lower Manhattan Expressway. Triborough Bridge Authority, 1940. The view looks east from the West Side Highway (bottom right) toward the Manhattan Bridge (upper right). Two spurs (upper left) connect with the Williamsburg Bridge.

Double-decked traffic roars over Sara Roosevelt Park between Hester and Grand streets in a 1940 rendering of the proposed highway. A spur along Chrystie Street connects with the approach to the Manhattan Bridge (lower right).

The second plan for the Lower Manhattan Expressway. Madigan-Hyland, c. 1960.

1958, with funding secured, Madigan-Hyland made several revisions to the expressway plan, prepared a two-volume study touting its many advantages, and the project went off to the New York City Planning Commission and the Board of Estimate for review. In 1960 the road was approved and officially entered on the city map. With that, Moses was all but guaranteed his highway; only a vote by the Board of Estimate to remove the road from the map, a process known as demapping, could undo the bold line that ran river to river across lower Manhattan.

Madigan-Hyland's reworked version of the expressway plan, which came with a price sticker in the $100-million range, routed crosstown traffic from the West Side Highway and the Holland Tun-

nel along Broome Street at ground level in six lanes. Near Elizabeth Street the expressway became an eight-lane elevated road and veered south, along Chrystie Street, connecting with the approach to the Manhattan Bridge. From the Bowery, a spur east to the Williamsburg Bridge burrowed beneath local streets in the vicinity of Delancey Street. In a report accompanying the plan, the engineering firm estimated that the expressway would displace two thousand families and eight hundred businesses employing ten thousand people. Completion of the expressway was projected for 1966.

At this last bit of news, residents and merchants in lower Manhattan suddenly sprang into action, led by Assemblyman Louis DeSalvio who had vowed to stamp out Moses' ogre. Between 1960 and 1962, while the Board of Estimate repeatedly put off deciding whether or not to condemn the private property that lay along the expressway route, opponents to the highway picketed City Hall, packed raucous public hearings, and voiced their outrage in a barrage of letters addressed to Mayor Wagner, who had come out in support of the expressway. Eleanor Roosevelt sent off a message to City Hall sharply criticizing the administration for having failed to draw up a relocation plan for the low-income residents who would be displaced by the project. Lewis Mumford picked up his pen to warn the mayor that the multilane highway "would be the first step in turning New York into Los Angeles. Since Los Angeles has already discovered the futility of sacrificing its living space to expressways and parking lots, why should New York follow that backward example?" he asked. Congressman John V. Lindsay (little anticipating that the expressway controversy would embroil him as mayor five years later) wrote Wagner to question the logic of ripping a road through the homes and workplaces of several thousand people when other alternatives existed. A less brutal solution to move traffic speedily east and west, the Congressman suggested, would be to link the West Side Highway and the FDR Drive with a route around the southern tip of Manhattan, a scheme the public soon dubbed "Lindsay's Loop."

The expressway debate came to a head in the summer of 1962, when it appeared that a vote by the Board of Estimate on whether to condemn the private property along the highway route was imminent. On June 18, five hundred protestors jammed City Hall for a public hearing that lasted eleven hours. Fifty-nine people testified during the marathon session, but it was Louis DeSalvio's unsparing testimony that made the newspapers the next day. Moses' plan was "a mad visionary's dream," the Assemblyman declared, and a "pork-barreled grab" that would serve only to fatten the bankrolls of contractors and developers. To believe that a superhighway could cure lower Manhattan's traffic ills, raise real estate values, and revitalize local business, as Moses claimed, was "pie in the skyline," he said. Let's "kill this silly proposal to cut the city's throat with this stupid idea of a Lower Manhattan Expressway," DeSalvio urged the Board of Estimate. The Board's response was to postpone its vote to late summer.

In August 1962 hundreds of residents and merchants, whose living rooms and livelihoods hung in the balance, marched to City Hall, hoisting cardboard tombstones and signs painted with skulls and crossbones. Their message was clear, but still there was no word from the Board of Estimate. September passed, October passed; meanwhile, the thousands who lived and worked in lower Manhattan, gripped in cruel suspense, waited out the weeks, never knowing how long they could expect to see a paycheck or have a roof over their heads.

On December 11, 1962, the Board of Estimate finally stirred. Fearing "the effects of economical and social blight in the shadow of the expressway," the Board explained, it had voted not to condemn any property. The decision sent ripples of relief through the lower Manhattan community, although it winced at the irony of the Board's statement. Since the late 1950s the residents and businesses in the path of the proposed expressway had suffered the stigma of occupying an area designated on the city map as soon to be flattened for a highway. Their landlords were reluctant to upgrade property. Insurance companies and banks shunned the area as a high-risk no-man's land, and new businesses looked elsewhere for space. Charging that the paper expressway was causing "economic strangulation" of their neighborhoods, opponents to the expressway demanded that, as a final move, the road be demapped. Traffic congestion was strangling the economic life of lower Manhattan, the City Planning Commission replied, and the expressway stayed outlined on the map.

In 1964 new support for the highway came from the slumping construction industry, which had just finished work for the New York World's Fair, another Moses project. The expressway represented two thousand jobs, a total that was upped by several hundred hard-hat slots after Moses announced plans to garnish the highway with a housing development for 460 low-income families. The figures were absurd, opponents to the expressway argued. For every construction job that the road provided, five would be lost locally. And, presuming that 460 families would want to live in concrete towers adjacent to a major highway, where would some fif-

Cast-iron buildings on Broome Street, between Greene Street and Wooster Street, late 1960s.

teen hundred other families go? Consider the condition of the existing housing stock, responded Madigan-Hyland in a report that suggested that many residents of lower Manhattan would welcome the opportunity to leave the area. "Most of the buildings [along the expressway route] were constructed before the turn of the century. In many cases these old buildings are poorly maintained and are, in fact, dangerous for occupancy."

The buildings certainly are old, boomed the new voice of the New York City Landmarks Preservation Commission. And what was more, beneath many of those shabby exteriors lay some of "the best cast-iron architecture still preserved in the

United States." Seeing the wrecker's ball fast approaching, the commission, created in 1965 after the demolition of Pennsylvania Station, began setting the wheels in motion to designate an area that included Broome, Greene, Wooster, and Canal streets as a historic district. Within the protective embrace of a historic district, the cast-iron buildings would be safe from destruction.

New hope sprang in the hearts of the expressway foes in January 1966, when John Lindsay became mayor of New York. As a congressman and later as a mayoral candidate, Lindsay had often expressed his reservations about decimating lower Manhattan's neighborhoods for the sake of improved traffic flow. But the road seemed to be a disease to which no New York City mayor was immune. In early 1967 the Lindsay administration

— 29 —

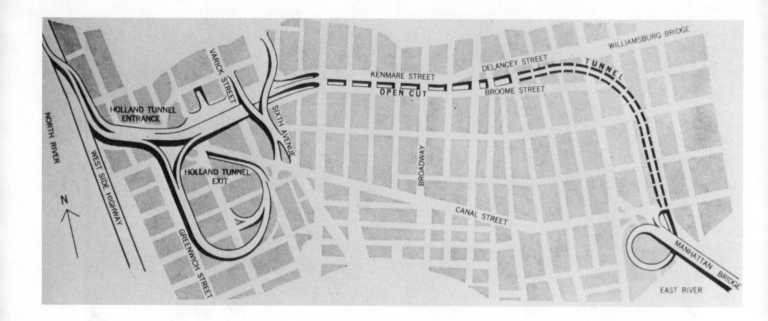

The Lindsay administration's plan for the Lower Manhattan Expressway, 1967.

unveiled a new plan for the Lower Manhattan Expressway. This one wove its way over and under the city's streets, from the Hudson River to the Williamsburg and Manhattan bridges, in a combination of surface-level road, tunnel stretches, and depressed highway. Sweetening the plan were promises to build parks, schools, and offices above portions of the highway, and assurances that the new design would save as much as 85 percent of the area's residential properties and 60 percent of its businesses.

But hardened opponents to the expressway were not easily seduced. "We're not fools. We know it's a version of the old Moses scheme," said Jane Jacobs, author of *The Death and Life of Great American Cities*. "Only the cast is different," commented another observer. "The plot is the same—it doesn't matter who the mayor is."

As it turned out, in this case it did.

In May 1969 Lindsay announced that further planning for the expressway would be suspended because the bill allowing 90 percent federal aid for the construction of the community facilities along the route had been rejected by the legislature. But a more stunning blow to the highway project came in 1969, after Lindsay lost the Republican mayoral primary to Senator John Marchi. Using his en-

dorsement by the Liberal party to stay in the race, Lindsay courted voters who were seeking an alternative candidate to Mario Procaccino, winner of the Democratic primary. Since the overlap of liberal Democrats and expressway opponents was too large to ignore, in July 1969 Mayor Lindsay crumpled up the scheme for the highway, tossed it into the city's discard pile of plans, and proclaimed the Lower Manhattan Expressway dead "for all time." A month later, the Board of Estimate dealt the final blow by voting to demap the road.

Lindsay was re-elected mayor in November 1969. But the long-term winner in the saga of the Lower Manhattan Expressway was the neighborhood that later came to be called SoHo (a shortening of "south of Houston Street"), which holds a treasure trove of nineteenth-century cast-iron architecture unequaled anywhere in the world. Because of the threat of the expressway, SoHo had remained pickled in time for nearly thirty years, bypassed by developers who saw no reason to pour money into new construction in a neighborhood that was slated for demolition. When the expressway plan was killed in 1969, SoHo emerged from under the paper road a little shabby but very much intact. In 1973, finishing what it had set out to do in 1965, the Landmarks Preservation Commission designated a twenty-six-block area as the SoHo Cast-Iron Historic District, thereby assuring the Victorian architectural gems there a protected future.

In early April 1971 Mayor John V. Lindsay announced that, in observance of Earth Week later that month, Madison Avenue between Forty-second and Fifty-seventh streets would be closed to traffic at midday for five days and turned into a pedestrian mall. The idea was a generous show of support to the environment-conscious groups that would be celebrating Earth Week, because no traffic meant less air and noise pollution. But, as it turned out, people didn't have to be fluent on the subject of injurious decibel levels or have to know about the dangers of hydrocarbons to appreciate the rare delight of midtown space reserved for pedestrians. At noontime between April 19 and April 23 thousands of workers poured out of nearby office buildings to amble down the middle of Madison Avenue or to picnic while watching the passing parade of people. In fact, the mall proved so popular that it was extended another week. Afterward, the author and urbanist William Whyte gave the project a rave review: "It lasted only two paltry weeks, was restricted to 12–2 p.m., had a smattering of old benches for street furniture, and the second week it rained. But it was a whale of a success." Encouraged by the public's response to

Picnickers and strollers enjoy a traffic-free Madison Avenue during Earth Week, April 1971.

Mayor John V. Lindsay, c. 1971.

crosstown traffic, which would be permitted to traverse the avenue on intersecting streets. The result: Madison Mall, a fifteen-block hiatus in the midst of Manhattan's noisy, engine-choked, glass-towered tumult.

The OMPD believed that the pedestrian mall would mitigate a variety of problems plaguing the area, not the least of which was "the midtowner-on-foot's daily battle to survive in the streets." Indeed, on weekdays, then as now, thousands of people pounded the avenue's pavement, weaving through an obstacle course of mailboxes, trash baskets, and lampposts, more often than not spilling into the street, where they had to fight a curbside chaos of buses, cabs, and cars. Banning most vehicular traffic would give pedestrians space of their own, said the OMPD report, and, at long last, some priority over the automobile. At the same time, the broad, tree-lined mall would provide midtown's blocks of unrelenting concrete with a verdant oasis, three-quarters of a mile long—an amenity that otherwise would be impossible to afford in a district where real estate (in 1971) commanded between five hundred and one thousand dollars a square foot. Here, away from the din of jackhammers and the turmoil of traffic, tourists, shoppers, and office workers could put up their feet or nibble on an ice-cream cone and restore their frazzled nerves. In short, Madison Mall would make the heart of New York "more liveable and humane," said the OMPD report.

That was not the way some people saw it. Local retailers, hotels, the Automobile Club of New York, and the taxi industry, among others, promptly booed the idea of shutting off one of Manhattan's main arteries to private cars and cabs. Merchants certainly weren't about to buy the OMPD's claim that the mall would send them a "captive audience" of thousands of people per hour on a good day. Remembering the chilling sight of Frisbees whizzing past their elegant shops during Earth Week, the elite of New York's retail world protested that the mall was only sure to destroy "the quiet and dignity of the area and [transform] it into a carnival and street-fair area." Besides which, complained the president of Abercrombie and Fitch, how were pa-

the makeshift mall, Mayor Lindsay asked the city's Office of Midtown Planning and Development (OMPD) to draw up a plan for a permanent pedestrian mall along the same stretch.

The OMPD's report, issued in October 1971 and crammed with statistics, charts, and definitions, beginning with "What is a mall?," made for rather dry reading, but anyone with imagination could see that it sketched out a precious slice of greenery and relative tranquillity for one of the city's most densely developed areas. As the OMPD pictured it, Madison Avenue's sidewalks, some of the narrowest in midtown, would be widened to twenty-nine feet and transformed into a pleasant promenade lined with trees, benches, outdoor cafés, and sculpture. All traffic would be banned, with the exception of city buses and emergency vehicles, which would travel along two middle lanes, and

Design for Madison Mall. View is south from the corner of East Fifty-first Street, showing the rectory of Saint Patrick's Cathedral on the right and the Villard Houses (pre–Helmsley Palace days) on the left. Office of Midtown Planning and Development, 1971.

trons to do their shopping if they couldn't pull up in limousines or taxis to Madison Avenue's curb?

Other opponents to the scheme imagined endless columns of honking cars inching their way through midtown as they detoured around Madison Avenue. "All the Alka-Seltzer in the world would never cure the traffic indigestion the mall would create," snorted one man. The Independent Taxi Owners Council, which represented some five thousand medallion owners, wholeheartedly agreed. Envisioning a yellow blanket of cabs stuck in constant bottlenecks and strangulating traffic jams, the Council officials put down their grievances in a letter and hand delivered it to City Hall. Just in case Mayor Lindsay missed their point, they left behind them several shopping bags stuffed with nooses and Coke bottles.

Others took the legal route. In February 1972, after the mayor's office announced that a three-month run of the mall would begin in the spring to test the waters for a permanent mall, the Fifth Avenue Association retained W. Bernard Richland to determine the legal hurdles Lindsay would have to clear before moving ahead with the project. According to Richland, they were considerable: establishing a mall would require a change in the city map, compensating affected property owners, and expending city funds, all of which were subject to final approval by the Board of Estimate. With this information in hand, the Fifth Avenue Association, Crouch and Fitzgerald, Brooks Brothers, and seventeen other plaintiffs took their case to court. In his decision, handed down in March 1973, State Supreme Court Justice Abraham Gellinoff concurred with Richland's findings, ruling that "monumental changes in the physical and economic existence of Madison Avenue" could take place only after review and approval by the Board of Estimate.

This was dismal news for Mayor Lindsay, who had decided not to run for a third term. The chances of realizing even a trial mall before he left City Hall, in December 1973, were slim, Lindsay knew, for he faced formidable opposition on the Board of Estimate. Nevertheless, he decided to try.

Leading the anti-mall flank on the eight-member Board was the city comptroller and the Democratic mayoral candidate, Abraham Beame. Beame had toughed out two elections, first the four-way Democratic primary, and then a runoff against Herman Badillo. Since the taxi industry had endorsed Beame in the primaries, the mayoral hopeful owed it a few favors. Also certain to cast ballots against the proposed mall were Brooklyn Borough president Se-bastian Leone and City Council president Sanford Garelik, both of whom had announced strong support of Beame during the runoffs, and Queens Borough president Donald Manes, who had many cab drivers in his own political club.

Despite the political odds, Lindsay made a valiant effort. In a series of closed meetings before the Board of Estimate vote on July 12, 1973, the mayor presented the advantages of his proposal once more to the opposition. He debated with Leone and Manes, and he tried to win over Garelik, who a month earlier had put down the plan as "Madison madness." He promised the Independent Taxi Owners Council that he would wield a firm hand on cruising gypsy cabs. Then, as a final concession to the taxi industry, he offered to temporarily abandon another of his pending projects, the closing-off of Central Park during weekdays to cars and cabs.

The mayor's efforts were to no avail. Beame and his allies struck down the plan for Madison Mall by two dissenting votes—and Lindsay knew exactly why. After the tally, the mayor, who, during eight years of office, had weathered repeated strikes by municipal workers, student uprisings, the biggest snowstorm in twenty years, and bitter race riots, turned to the opposition with a final remark: "I want to say to my colleagues if political life depended on what cab drivers thought of you, I would have been dead years ago."

PUBLIC BUILDINGS

Since its beginnings, New York has erected public buildings to stand as proud emblems of the city and its citizens. Each age has had its own expression. New Amsterdam, although numbering few more than one thousand inhabitants by the mid-seventeenth century, boasted the Dutch Reformed Church of Saint Nicholas, a large twin-peaked building that rose several stories above the gabled houses surrounding it. The early nineteenth century produced City Hall, which at its completion, in 1811, was hailed as "the handsomest structure in the United States; perhaps of its size, in the world." Yearnings for civic grandeur after the creation of Greater New York in 1898 culminated in such monumental edifices as the United States Custom House, Pennsylvania Station, and the Bronx Borough Courthouse. In the 1920s the possibilities offered by skyscraper construction shaped the plan for Riverside Church; the new modernism of post–World War II architecture found inspired form in the design of the United Nations complex.

And then, inexplicably, in the mid-1950s an overwhelming mediocrity seeped into many of the plans for public buildings in New York. It is manifest in the vacuous face the Coliseum, the former convention center, shows Columbus Circle and Central Park, in the bland design of the New York Foundling Hospital on Third Avenue and Sixty-ninth Street, and in the squat brick public-school buildings constructed during the 1950s. Worse yet, as mediocre buildings went up in the 1950s, some of the best of the city's public buildings were threatened by demolition or, at the very least, by mutilation. The 1950s, for example, was the era of the attempt to raze Carnegie Hall and construct an office building in its place, and was when the first renderings were published showing Grand Central Terminal adjoined by a fifty-nine-story tower—a scheme that was, in fact, later realized in the form of the Pan Am Building.

The 1960s was not an auspicious age for the public building, either. At the start of the decade the banal box of the Civil and Municipal Courthouse went up near Foley Square, and in 1963 Pennsylvania Station, a Roman classical temple of granite and travertine marble, built at Seventh Avenue between Thirty-first and Thirty-third streets in 1910, came crashing down. The building was replaced in the late 1960s with Madison Square Garden, an office tower, and a new station, reached by a hole in the sidewalk that leads to a warren of ticket windows, fast-food shops, and stuffy waiting rooms twenty feet beneath Seventh Avenue.

In 1965, two years after the demolition of Pennsylvania Station, the New York City Landmarks Preservation Commission was established to designate and preserve notable buildings, structures, and districts throughout the city. To date nearly eight hundred landmarks across the five boroughs have been designated and are thereby protected from radical alteration or demolition. Public buildings that are landmarked include the Brooklyn Museum, Central Synagogue on Lexington Avenue, New Brighton Village Hall in Staten Island, Carnegie Hall, and Saint Paul's Chapel (New York's oldest surviving public building) on lower Broadway.

Unfortunately, however, the preservation of venerable public buildings in New York was not accompanied by a pronounced improvement in the design of new public buildings, at least not in the 1970s. Witness, for example, the State Office Building, the behemoth that invaded Harlem in 1973, or the Family Court building, a grim chunk of black granite erected in 1975 on Lafayette Street in lower Manhattan. Better designed are some of the public buildings that have gone up in the 1980s, such as Public School 234, located on Chambers Street, and the Jacob K. Javits Convention Center. Significantly, both buildings, while unmistakably contemporary, look back to the rich public architecture of New York's past: the exterior of P.S. 234, an attractive red brick structure trimmed with cream-colored detail, recalls school buildings of the late nineteenth century; the convention center—a vast vitrified hall— has antecedents in the Crystal Palace, the 1852 marvel of iron and glass that briefly adorned present-day Bryant Park. Are P.S. 234 and the convention center mere anomalies, or do they herald a new age for public architecture in New York?

The Crystal Palace, c. 1853. Fire destroyed the magnificent building in 1858.

A corner of the galleries at the New-York Historical Society's Second Avenue home, wallpapered with paintings.

In 1860, barely three years after moving from borrowed rooms at New York University into a handsome new home on the corner of Second Avenue and Eleventh Street, the New-York Historical Society found itself rich in unexpected acquisitions and short on space. In the third-floor galleries, bumping gilded frames with the Society's portrait collection, were 79 new paintings and 250 engravings inherited in 1857 from the bankrupt New York Gallery of Fine Arts. Thirteen huge stone bas-reliefs from Nineveh, dating from 650 B.C. and donated to the Society by James Lenox in 1858, occupied the basement. Crammed in glass cabinets, along narrow corridors, and in dim niches of the library was the 1,127-piece Egyptian collection, purchased by the Society in 1860 from the estate of Dr. Henry Abbott, a British physician.

Acquiring mummies and Assyrian artifacts was not the original intent of the New-York Historical Society. Founded in 1804 "to collect and preserve whatever may relate to the natural, civil or ecclesiastical history of the United States in general and this state in particular," the Society had, for more than fifty years, focused on building its holdings of manuscripts, maps, American paintings, and historic relics. But as the institution in New York City that came closest to meeting the definition of an art museum (the Metropolitan Museum of Art would not be born until the late 1860s), the Society was loath to turn away important works that would otherwise wind up in the private galleries of wealthy collectors and thus out of public view. So, when donors and art dealers marched up the Society's steps on Second Avenue, bearing Renaissance paintings, antiquities, and medieval tomes, staff members obligingly scurried about to clear shelves and wall space.

That is, until the arrival of the Abbott collection. After squeezing in the doctor's last parchment scroll, the Society decided it was time to seek roomier quarters and officially establish itself as the institution it was fast becoming: New York's first "grand museum of antiquities, science and art." In 1862, with the authorization of the Board of Commissioners of the Central Park and the New York State Legislature, the Society secured for its purposes the State Arsenal, a spare, four-story Gothic Revival building, erected in 1848 at Fifth Avenue and Sixty-fourth Street as a warehouse for military munitions. Long emptied of all explosives, the arsenal had, in fact, been suggested by Frederick Law Olmsted and Calvert Vaux in their design for Central Park as the eventual home for a museum. Although it was a "very unattractive structure and only tolerably built," the partners wrote in the report that accompanied their plan for the park in 1858, its "external appearance, so far as may be necessary," could be improved "without going to any great expense." The Society's trustees agreed; with "practicable alterations," they reported after touring the building, the arsenal could be "admirably adapted" for use as a museum.

The architect called on to remodel the arsenal was Richard Morris Hunt, a founding member of the American Institute of Architects, an energetic spokesman for architects' professional rights, and the first American to have studied at the famous École des Beaux-Arts in Paris. When the thirty-eight-year-old architect accepted the commission in 1865, he was still years away from creating his greatest body of work—the Tribune Building, baronial homes for the rich, the base of the Statue of Liberty, and the Fifth Avenue facade of the Metropolitan Museum of Art—but, significantly, Hunt's plans for the Society's museum prefigured his fondness for French Renaissance architectural motifs, which he would later slather on the ostentatious in-town châteaux of the Vanderbilts and the Astors, and on his pièce de résistance, the 255-room Biltmore mansion in Asheville, North Carolina.

For the arsenal's alteration Hunt proposed wiping away every trace of the building's fortresslike mien. Gone in the architect's scheme were all eight of the structure's crenelated towers, four replaced by mansard pavilions and the crowns of the others lopped off at the roof line. Carved limestone window trim, balconies, and a striped polychromatic band that ran along the first-story level transformed the naked facade into a richly textured

Perspective drawing of the proposed remodeling scheme for the State Arsenal. Richard Morris Hunt, 1865.

LEFT:
View northeast from the carriage drive in Central Park, toward the State Arsenal and Fifth Avenue, 1862.

surface, and arched portals embellished the unprepossessing entryways. The face-lift, Hunt estimated, would come to about $150,000.

The scheme met with the unanimous approval of the Society's trustees late in 1865, but the Board of Commissioners of the Central Park, who by law had final say in the matter, sent the architect back to the drawing board "with directions to prepare other plans for buildings of more extensive scope and with ample room for the anticipated requirements of this proposed great and noble undertaking." Hunt immediately developed studies for a large complex of somber-looking buildings, topped with mansard roofs, that ringed a pair of open courts. New Yorkers who had recently visited Paris would have instantly recognized the scheme as a close copy of the new wings added to the Musée du Louvre—a resemblance that was no coincidence. After his student days at the École des Beaux-Arts in the 1850s, Hunt had stayed on in Paris to assist Hector Lefuel, architect to Napoleon III, in designing portions of the monumental additions that were tacked onto the former palace. Evidently the young architect saw no reason why New York shouldn't partake of a little French pomp—and of his past labors.

Hunt's design was approved by the Society's Building Committee in January 1866, and earned high praise from the *New York Times,* which hailed the proposed museum as "an appropriate and beautiful edifice" that could be "indefinitely enlarged and extended, without the least detriment to its symmetry as the future exigencies of the Museum may require." However, the plan did not entirely pass muster with the Board of Commissioners of the Central Park, who argued this time that the imposing scale of the contemplated buildings would overwhelm the arsenal grounds and diminish the beauty of the surrounding landscape. If the Society were earnest about carrying out the plan, said the commissioners, the only site they would authorize for the project was the park space lying between Seventy-ninth and Eighty-fifth streets, along Fifth Avenue.

The Society's trustees were furious. Hunt's ambitious design, they reminded the commissioners,

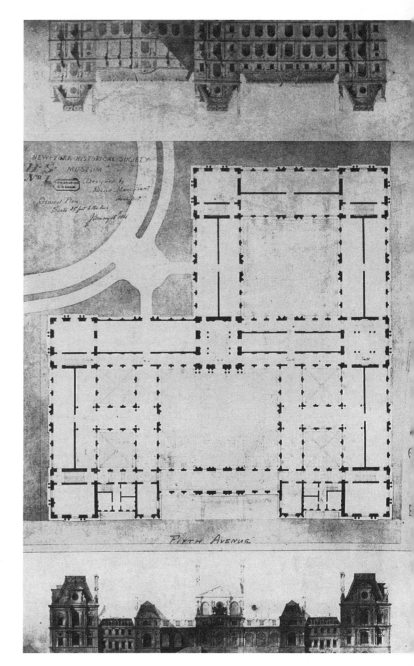

Plan and elevation of the proposed museum building for the New-York Historical Society, Fifth Avenue and Eighty-second Street. Richard Morris Hunt, 1866.

had been drawn up "in compliance with their express wishes." Furthermore, a move twenty blocks north of the arsenal would put the museum in a spot that would hardly be considered by the public as convenient to reach. Why not compromise: the arsenal grounds for a small section of Hunt's plan? But their arguments fell on unsympathetic ears; by

March 1866 the commissioners had begun preparing the paperwork to rescind the Historical Society's right to the arsenal site and to reserve for the projected museum the plot of land between Seventy-ninth and Eighty-fifth streets. The New-York Historical Society soon reconciled itself to the idea of moving farther uptown, and in 1868 the State Legislature set aside for the museum the six-block area Olmsted and Vaux had intended in their design for Central Park to be used as a playing field.

As the Society embarked on a fund-raising campaign to construct a museum at the new site (it is unclear from the Building Committee's reports if the trustees intended to erect Hunt's Louvre look-alike or to commission a new plan), William Holbrook Beard was at work designing a museum for Manhattan Square, twenty acres of rough ground situated opposite Central Park between West Seventy-seventh and Eighty-first streets, at the behest of a Wall Street tycoon named Henry Keep, who had pledged $1.5 million to see it built and stocked with art. Beard, a popular painter of the day, best known for his droll depictions of bears, guinea pigs, and other animals acting like human beings, had never in his life designed so much as a doorstep. But apparently this didn't bother Keep, who had made his fortune slapping down money on bigger gambles than on an art museum, and it certainly didn't faze Beard, who bluffed his way through the architectural commission by pasting Gothic windows onto a large, vaguely Moorish building, capping it with an impressive dome, and then concealing most of the structure behind a screen of fluffy trees.

But the artist was bolder in his treatment of the main entrance to the museum. No grand flight of stairs here, no welcoming vestibule or even a conventional door, Beard had decided. What he envisioned was a cavelike subterranean tunnel, populated with statuary of animals and humans, that burrowed beneath Central Park West, from Central Park to Manhattan Square. Peculiar? Certainly it was, acknowledged John Hassard, writing in *Scribner's Monthly,* but the scheme was "not a mere freak." Beard's plan, he explained, was a care-

William Holbrook Beard, c. 1880.

fully constructed three-dimensional metaphor, intended to edify and entertain the public en route to the museum. For puzzled readers who wondered what ferocious animals and a dark underground passageway had to do with an art museum, Hassard offered the following interpretation.

Approaching the mouth of the tunnel in Central Park, visitors to the museum were to be greeted by "Ignorance" and "Superstition," two hulking stone figures clutching primitive weapons and "barring the avenue to aesthetic culture." Those courageous enough to slip by the brutish duo entered a dim, rustic passageway, "symbolical of the rude origin of art," and made their way past statues of packs of snarling lions and other menacing beasts meant to represent "the difficulties to be overcome before the student enters into the real enjoyment and comprehension of the beautiful." Ahead, in a light-filled antechamber, sat the colossal figure of a kindly old

William Holbrook Beard, *The Bear Dance*, not dated, oil on canvas. Beard incorporated the animal imagery of his paintings in the design he drew up for the art museum at Manhattan Square (see photos on pages 46 and 47).

man, "perhaps the guardian genius of the place"; spotlighted in a niche above him stood famous historical figures. Here visitors found themselves "at the portals of Art," and at the most crucial juncture of the journey. Enlightened persons would turn left to a staircase, which led to a sculpture gallery and into the museum building proper. Those unwilling to enter "the realm of aesthetic culture" were to be given the opportunity to flee through a craggy passage on the right, which would take them into the grounds of the museum and back to the safety of the street.

Henry Keep died in 1869, before the plan for Manhattan Square could be realized, but another movement for an art museum was already in swing, led by members of the Union League Club. On a rain-swept evening in November 1869, three hundred of New York's most prominent citizens turned out for a meeting at the club to hear William

Cullen Bryant, editor of the *Evening Post,* speak on the importance of "taking early and effectuated measures" for founding a museum of art. After assuring his audience that "no rivalry with any other project is contemplated"—a reference to the New-York Historical Society's ongoing efforts to raise funds for its building in Central Park—Bryant launched into an argument he had presented many times before on the editorial page of his newspaper: "We have libraries and reading-rooms, and this is well; we have also spacious halls for musical entertainments, and that is also well," but was it not shocking to think, he asked, that so wealthy a metropolis had no major repository of art, while every European capital boasted a museum "the opulence and extent of which absolutely bewilder the visitor." There American painters flocked to study the stirring canvases of Reubens, Goya, and Turner, but sadly, when they returned home, most were confined to producing "cabinet pictures" for private collectors. If the genius of the American artist were ever to be unleashed, said Bryant, a museum that both commissioned new works and served as

a place of instruction for budding talent would have to be established on native soil.

The idea, enthusiastically received by all present at the Union League Club, was taken up by a fifty-two-member provisional committee, which drafted a plan of organization, elected officers, and petitioned Albany for a charter. On April 13, 1870, by act of the State Legislature, the Metropolitan Museum of Art was born. For the first year of its existence, it had no home nor a single painting to its name.

Meanwhile, the Board of Commissioners of the Central Park were engaged in a game of museum hopscotch. The American Museum of Natural His-

Proposed art museum, Central Park West, between West Seventy-seventh Street and West Eighty-first Street. William Holbrook Beard, c. 1868.

tory, incorporated in 1869, and living since 1870 in cramped rooms at the arsenal, had repeatedly expressed its dire need for more space. The obvious place for the museum's collection of birds, beasts, and bones, the commissioners thought, was on Fifth Avenue, between Seventy-ninth and Eighty-fifth streets, but the New-York Historical Society (still located on Second Avenue) legally retained the right to the property, although its prospects for financing

Detail of the main entrance to the proposed art museum. William Holbrook Beard, c. 1868.

BELOW:
Antechamber of the proposed art museum. William Holbrook Beard, c. 1868.

a new building for the site looked slimmer by the month. Did they dare rouse the fury of the Society's trustees by reoffering them the arsenal? Best not, the commissioners agreed. Then, of course, there was the homeless Metropolitan Museum of Art to consider. How long before its trustees came wandering into the park looking for land, and which grassy meadow to give them? After some deliberation the commissioners decided there was only one solution: the Historical Society would stay put in Central Park, and the Metropolitan and Natural History museums would share Manhattan Square on the West Side. That decision was signed into law by the New York State Legislature in April 1871.

In December 1871 the Metropolitan moved to temporary quarters at 681 Fifth Avenue, between Fifty-third and Fifty-fourth streets, in what had been Mr. Dodsworth's Dancing Academy. Thanks to William Blodgett, a member of the museum's executive committee who on his own initiative had boldly purchased 174 old masters works while on vacation in Europe, the Metropolitan also finally had a few paintings to hang on its walls. After the museum's first public reception, held in February 1872, George Putnam, a publisher and another member of the Met's executive committee, happily reported: "We had a fine turnout of ladies and gentlemen and all were highly pleased. The pictures looked splendid and compliments were so plenty and strong that I was afraid the mouths of the Trustees would become chronically and permanently fixed in a broad grin."

What did not make the trustees grin as the winter wore on was the idea of having someday to double up with the Natural History museum in Manhattan Square. The Natural History museum felt likewise. Early in the spring of 1872 envoys from both institutions met with the Board of Commissioners of the Central Park to consider other alternatives. Luck was with them, the commissioners reported. Unable to raise the necessary funds, the Historical Society had abandoned its plans to build in the park, leaving the grounds between Seventy-ninth and Eighty-fifth streets free for a new occupant. It was the commissioners' opinion that the site would

The first home of the Metropolitan Museum of Art, 681 Fifth Avenue, 1872.

do beautifully for the Metropolitan Museum of Art. Any objections? Frankly, said representatives of the Met, we would prefer building on Reservoir Square at Forty-second Street and Fifth Avenue (now the site of the New York Public Library). Out of the question, responded the commissioners, and so, by May 1872, it was settled: the American Museum of Natural History would go up in Manhattan Square; the Metropolitan Museum of Art would build on the east side of Central Park; and the New-York Historical Society would remain downtown on Second Avenue. Not five months later, Calvert Vaux and his assistant, Jacob Wrey Mould, resigned from their position as architects of Central Park and became two of the busiest men in town: they had landed the commissions to design both museums.

The first section of the American Museum of

Wing A of the Metropolitan Museum of Art, Fifth Avenue and Eighty-second Street, shortly after it opened in 1880. Calvert Vaux and Jacob Wrey Mould, 1880.

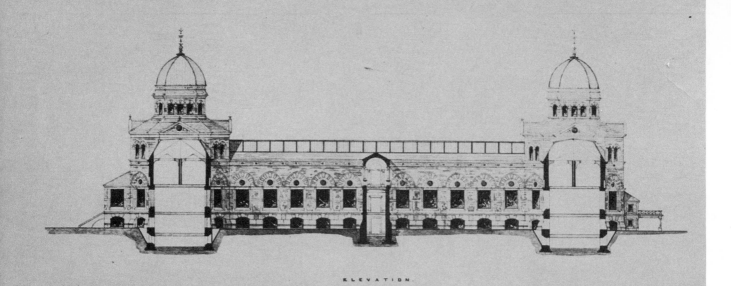

ELEVATION.

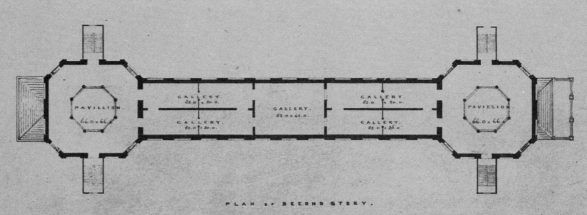

PLAN OF SECOND STORY.

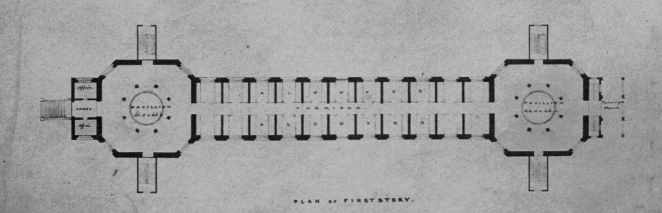

PLAN OF FIRST STORY.

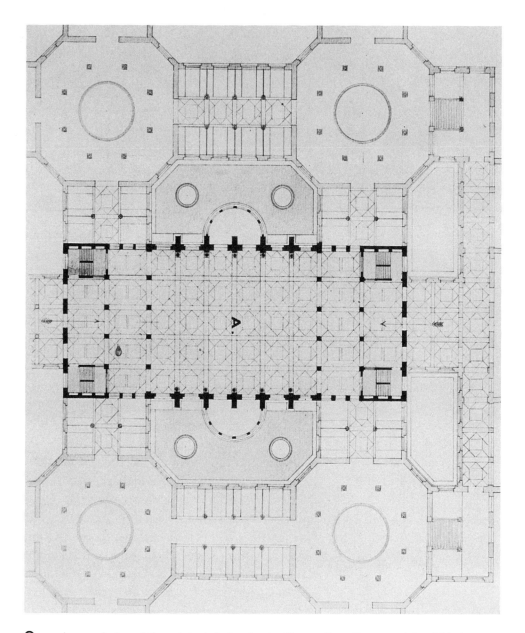

General ground plan of the original design for the Metropolitan Museum of Art, Fifth Avenue and Eighty-second Street. Calvert Vaux and Jacob Wrey Mould, 1872.

OPPOSITE:
Elevation and floor plan of the original design for the Metropolitan Museum of Art. Calvert Vaux and Jacob Wrey Mould, 1872.

Looking north, toward the first wing of the American Museum of Natural History, from West Seventy-fourth Street between Columbus Avenue and Central Park West, c. 1887. The vacant lot on Central Park West, between West Seventy-sixth and West Seventy-seventh streets, would later be occupied by the New-York Historical Society.

Natural History (now all but hidden from view by later additions) was dedicated in 1877 by President Rutherford Hayes. Meanwhile, rising on the other side of the park was Wing A of the Metropolitan Museum, which, when it opened in 1880, was snidely described by one critic as looking like "a cross between a cotton press and a pork-packing establishment with the interior of a railroad station." The building was, in fact, Vaux and Mould's second design for the museum. Originally they had proposed erecting four large octagonal pavilions, connected by long galleries and arranged around a series of open courtyards, but museum officials rejected the plan as much too "magnificent and elaborate." Had they only known! Before 1910 the Metropolitan would grow by two brick extensions to the north and south; by one stately Greco-Roman facade on the Fifth Avenue side, designed by Richard Morris Hunt; and by a pair of graceful wings flanking the main entrance, designed by McKim, Mead & White. Today all that remains visible of Vaux and Mould's handiwork at the Metropolitan Museum is the west facade of their 1880 building, which can be seen from inside the Lehman wing.

Ironically, the last institution in the museum shuffle to find a resting place was the New-York Historical Society. Not until an anonymous donor offered one hundred thousand dollars in 1885 toward erecting a new home did members of the Society's Building Committee head uptown to search for an available site. In 1905, after several years of house-hunting and a protracted fund-raising drive, the Society bid farewell to Second Avenue and carted its treasures to its spacious new building, designed by the firm of York and Sawyer, on Central Park West between Seventy-sixth and Seventy-seventh streets, opposite the American Museum of Natural History, where it remains today.

What turned out to be one of the most bungled design competitions in the history of New York began on September 1, 1893, when the last contestant, pleading tardiness because of a streetcar accident, submitted his drawings just as the bells of Saint Paul's Chapel signaled the noon deadline. The subject of the competition was a large, white marble building that was to replace the not yet one-hundred-year-old City Hall, itself the product of a competition, won by Joseph F. Mangin and John McComb, Jr., in the early 1800s. For the new building, more than one hundred entrants, some from as far away as Liverpool and Paris, submitted plans, each hoping to net first prize, which carried with it the position of project supervisor and a percentage of the building's anticipated $4-million cost. Awaiting five runners-up was a total of $10,000 in awards money.

By 1893 a competition for a large municipal center was fast becoming a perennial event in New York. Unable to stuff another government office into City Hall, the city had been forced for some years to house its overflow in privately owned buildings scattered throughout lower Manhattan—an arrangement that cost taxpayers some $300,000 in annual rent. In 1888, desiring to trim the budget and solve City Hall's space shortage, Mayor Abram Hewitt had invited architects to submit plans for a pair of seven-story wings that would flank the ends of City Hall. The Hewitt competition had come to naught. In 1889 Mayor Hugh Grant sponsored a competition for a new building altogether; it also came to naught. In 1893, barely two months after taking office, Mayor Thomas Gilroy, hoping to save the expense of purchasing a plot of land on which to build a new municipal center, launched yet a third competition. Barring floods or famine, pledged Gilroy, he would see that City Hall was "removed" by 1894 and construction of a new municipal building "worthy of the greatest City on the continent" at last begun.

Removed? What exactly did that mean? asked alarmed citizens. Did the mayor intend to transplant City Hall, one of New York's oldest and most cherished public buildings, to Central Park and turn it into a museum, as had been suggested during the Grant administration? Or was "remove" a euphemism for "demolish"? "I am in favor of whatever the public is in favor of," responded Gilroy, "with the understanding that the new municipal building be erected on the [City Hall] site."

Edward F. de Lancey, a prominent member of the New-York Historical Society, quickly conferred with the Society's trustees, grabbed his hat, and immediately marched over to Chambers Street to enjoin the mayor to call off the competition and leave City Hall right where it was. "The beauty of its architecture, its age, its historic interest, and the attachment of all New Yorkers, native and adopted, to it and the park alike, demand its preservation," declared de Lancey. If any building was to disappear from City Hall park, he said, it should be the "ugly and unwholesome Tweed Court House," which stood several yards north of City Hall on a site more than ample for a new municipal building. But if the mayor was intent on razing the beloved

Mayor Thomas Gilroy, c. 1895.

City Hall's main facade, 1908.

landmark, de Lancey added, the New-York Historical Society was fully prepared to drag City Hall uptown, cupola and all, to a newly purchased plot on Central Park West and Seventy-seventh Street, where it hoped soon to be moving from its home on East Eleventh Street. "The interior of the building would have to be altered almost entirely to fit the objects of the Society," said de Lancey, "but the exterior would be precisely as it now stands in the park."

Hard on de Lancey's heels to the mayor's office was the president of the Tilden Trust, John Bigelow, who administered the $2-million fund left by former New York Governor Samuel J. Tilden for the establishment of a public library system. Once the old Croton Reservoir in Bryant Park was torn down, the Trust hoped to erect a building designed

by Ernest Flagg on the site, but with City Hall apparently up for grabs, Bigelow saw no reason why it couldn't be appropriated for use as a library and moved to Fifth Avenue and Forty-second Street. The mayor liked that idea very much. Imagine City Hall "rebuilt 200 feet back from Fifth Avenue," he mused. "There could be lawns, shrubs, plants and walks in front of it and on each side of it, and the effect would be very beautiful."

Andrew Haswell Green thought differently. In 1894, Green, a former comptroller of Central Park, and later of the city, was occupied with the delicate negotiations for the consolidation of the Greater City—an idea he had advocated, often alone, since the 1860s—but he took the time to write an angry letter to Mayor Gilroy protesting the removal of City Hall from City Hall Park. City Hall "and the ground upon which it stands are memorable in the City's annals," Green reminded the mayor. On this soil, long before City Hall was built, "Alex-

Looking south along Fifth Avenue, past the Forty-second Street reservoir, c. 1895. The huge tank was emptied in 1897 and torn down in 1899 to make way for the New York Public Library.

Proposed design for the Tilden Trust Library, viewed from the corner of Fifth Avenue and Forty-second Street. Ernest Flagg, 1891.

Runner-up, City Hall competition. Edward P. Casey, 1893. Casey was the sole architect among the six winners of the competition who did not use the Hôtel de Ville in Paris as the basis for his design.

RIGHT:

Runner-up, City Hall competition. Rankin & Kellogg, 1893. For reasons not known, John R. Thomas's winning scheme for the new City Hall was never published, but it undoubtedly resembled Rankin & Kellogg's plan, which, like many of the plans submitted for the competition, was patterned after the Hôtel de Ville in Paris.

OPPOSITE, TOP:

City Hall competition entry. H. Langford Warren, 1893. Warren, who did not place in the competition, proposed erecting a Beaux-Arts building, crowned at its center with a Baroque dome.

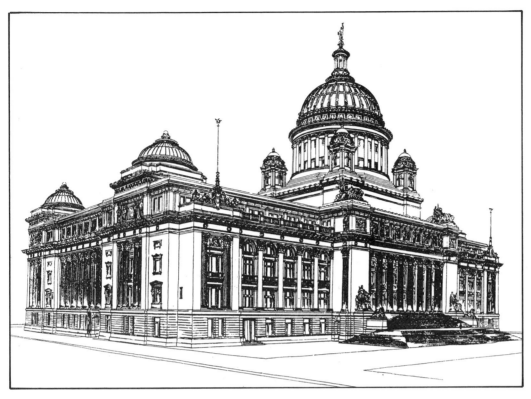

ander Hamilton made his maiden speech on the occasion of closing the Port of Boston in retaliation for the destruction of the tea," and here "the Declaration of Independence was read to the American army in the presence of Washington." At City Hall New Yorkers had celebrated the opening of the Erie Canal and sadly filed past the body of Abraham Lincoln as he lay in state in April 1865. To take City Hall out of the park, said Green, "would be, to state it mildly, little short of wanton wastefulness."

Whether City Hall would be moved to new grounds or demolished was still undecided when the competition results were announced in January 1894. Of the 134 entries received, six "best" had been chosen, reported jury members of the Municipal Building Commission. Unfortunately, they had found none to offer a completely satisfactory design. Where there was a suitable arrangement of the interior space, there was an uncomely facade; where there was an attractive exterior, there was an unacceptable floor plan. And the scheme found to be "least objectionable" would cost $13 million to construct, more than three times what the city was prepared to pay for its municipal building. To salvage the disappointing competition, said the commission, it was considering patching together a design made from the best features of each of the six schemes.

What the jury's report didn't mention were the names of the winning architects. When curious New Yorkers began pestering the commission to publish the six plans and reveal the identities of the authors, embarrassed jury members were forced to admit their ludicrous dilemma: legally, there was no way to determine who the six winners were. In compliance with the rules of the competition, all 134 contestants had submitted their designs anonymously, with accompanying sealed envelopes that contained their names. Since the competition rules stipulated that the jury was not to break the envelopes until it had selected "one successful candidate"—which it clearly had not—the envelopes had to remain closed, and the winners forever a mystery. "We are tied hands and feet by the terms of agreement," said Mayor Gilroy. "In our efforts to prevent collusion we have actually shut out common sense. We cannot open the envelopes without violating the agreement, and unless we do, we can't find out the names of the competitors."

Some people thought they smelled a budding scandal in the air. Why hadn't the commission picked one successful candidate? Had one or more jury members not found a favorite architect among the six drawings? Had some shady deal with a potential contractor fallen through? "The subject appears to be rapidly assuming a political aspect that will . . . disgrace the City of New York," wrote one suspicious critic. But before the commission members were implicated in any wrongdoing, an unexpected turn of events rendered the entire competition moot. On May 8, 1894, responding to New Yorkers' mounting protest, Governor Roswell Flower signed into law a bill prohibiting the demolition of City Hall or its removal to another site. Two days later, a crestfallen mayor conceded, "It is manifest that . . . these plans are now useless."

The messy remains of the competition were inherited by Gilroy's successor, Mayor William Strong, who took office at City Hall in 1895. Who were the winners? cried persistent New Yorkers. And what about the prize money? roared 134 architects. Strong quickly extricated himself from this uncomfortable spot by seeing to it that Albany passed special legislation empowering the city to open the envelopes and distribute the award money. But when it came time to match the envelopes with the six designs, Strong turned a deep crimson: the envelopes were not to be found. "The plans were stored away in an unoccupied room in one of the city buildings," reported *American Architect and Building News*. "As no appropriation had been made for paying a man to look after them, no one looked after them. The six selected plans were put among the rest and the whole collection, numbering 134 sets, was piled together. Moreover, the sealed envelopes, containing the names of the authors of the designs, were piled up somewhere else, but no one knows where."

The envelopes were discovered a year later in a dim corner, bundled up with string, by a sharp-

Proposed civic center, City Hall Park. Henry F. Hornbostel and George B. Post, 1903.

eyed civil servant. Officials sorted through the plans, located the six winning schemes, and paired them off with the newly found envelopes. The names of the winners—but not the plans—appeared in *American Architect and Building News* in February 1896, nearly three years after Mayor Gilroy had announced the competition. The author of the "least objectionable" plan turned out to be John R. Thomas, architect of numerous churches in Brooklyn and Manhattan. Asked by a journalist from the *New York Times* to describe his plan for the public, Thomas confessed that his memory of the scheme was "not quite clear," although he did recall that it was "in the style of the French Renaissance, and somewhat like the Hôtel de Ville in Paris," but "by no means a copy of that building." When the plans were published a few months later, Thomas's design was inexplicably not among them, but the public had no difficulty imagining what City Hall Park would have looked like with a spin-off of the nineteenth-century Parisian building on the site of City Hall because four of the five runners-up—Rankin & Kellogg of Philadelphia; P. D. Weber

of Chicago; Gordon, Bragdon & Orchard of Rochester; and Ernest Flagg of New York—had designed variations of the Hôtel de Ville. So, in fact, had at least a dozen other entrants in the competition. Unoriginal though the plans may have been, each runner-up was awarded $2,000; Thomas received $7,000 for his labors and the commission to design the Hall of Records at 31 Chambers Street, near City Hall.

At the birth of Greater New York, in 1898, the city was still without a large municipal building, and paying dearly for it. The cost of additional office space to administer five boroughs had increased the city's annual rent bill to half a million dollars. By 1903 it had grown to nearly a million dollars. Enough money spent! cried the architect Julius Harder, who proposed consolidating all government offices and the personal residence of the mayor under one capacious roof in Union Square Park. From the Municipal Art Society came a plan to erect a complex of low-rise civic buildings on Chambers Street, west of the Hall of Records, extending to Broadway. The architects George B. Post and Henry F. Hornbostel suggested clearing City Hall Park of all structures but City Hall, building a forty-five-story campanile for municipal offices at the intersection of Chambers and Centre streets, and connecting it with a new, enlarged terminal that would receive the trolleys and elevated trains rolling off the Brooklyn Bridge.

Although none of the schemes met with the approval of the city, the Post-Hornbostel scheme did offer practical solutions to the twofold problem of how to get the maximum number of offices on the smallest parcel of land (build up, not out) and where to site the building (on land already acquired by the city for the projected extension of the Brooklyn Bridge train terminal). Thus, when the city finally did get around, in 1907, to sponsoring another design competition for a municipal building, it was not surprising that the program called for a sky-scraper, at least twenty-three stories high, that would rise on Centre Street near City Hall.

Unlike the Gilroy-sponsored fiasco of 1893, the 1907–1908 competition was well run and speedily concluded. Only twelve firms were invited to participate in the competition—among them Carrère & Hastings, McKim, Mead & White, Howell & Stokes, and Warren & Wetmore—and within a month of receiving the entries, the three-member jury had reached a decision. In May 1908 the firm of McKim, Mead & White was declared the winner. Six years later the forty-four-story Municipal Building, reaching like a white plume above the cupola of City Hall opened its doors.

≡◇≡

On Sundays in 1922 it was Standing Room Only at the Methodist church on Fort Washington Avenue and 178th Street. No droning sermons, no somber organ music here. In the best show in town this side of the local vaudeville circuit, newsreels flickered across a silver screen, acrobats and bird-call imitators regaled the congregation, and onto the rostrum were likely to step baseball heroes, divas, and Hollywood matinee idols to say a few good words about the Lord. New acts, new stars, were featured every Sunday, their names and pictures outlined in blinking lights, and admission to the show cost no more than a modest offering in the collection plate.

The producer behind the weekly theatrics was the Reverend Christian Reisner, a Kansas-born minister who early on in his career had discovered that old-fashioned fire-and-brimstone did not nearly fill pews like a little splashy advertising at the front door and some lively entertainment at the pulpit. (Reisner's own special act was the "Snow Sermon," which he conducted in mid-July from behind a hill of crushed ice trucked in from a downtown cooling plant.) The minister had his share of critics, but to people who protested that a house of worship was hardly the proper place for such antics, Reisner patiently explained that he was merely employing modern publicity strategy "to make the business of religion the success it ought to be." After all, if bright lights and ballyhoo sold chewing gum and automobiles, he said, why not the gospel? Reisner's mix of showmanship and salesmanship proved to

The Reverend Christian Reisner, c. 1925.

be very effective. By 1922, only two years after his appointment as pastor of the church at 178th Street, attendance had soared from eighteen to one thousand loyal parishioners.

Early in 1923 Reisner and his congregation learned that their church building was to be razed in a few years to make way for the long-awaited Hudson River bridge, which was projected to be built from Fort Lee, New Jersey, to a spot very close to their altar. If the news caused distress among church members, to Reisner it came as a sign from heaven to move forward with his plan for "a magnificent advertisement of God's business," the dream he had harbored for ten years—a skyscraper cathedral. By late autumn 1923, with a $100,000 gift from the Board of Home Missions, the energetic pastor had acquired a site on the west side of Broadway between 173rd and 174th streets, commissioned the architect Donn Barber to design the building, and organized a directorate of bankers and businessmen to oversee the fund-raising campaign for the construction of the skyscraper.

The plan for the $4-million church, unveiled in December 1923, embodied all of Reisner's flair for theatrics. It rose from the sidewalk of Broadway, forty stories tall, a sheer cliff of granite and limestone, punctuated at its pinnacle by a seventy-five-foot-high revolving cross that shot rays of red and orange light into the sky. On the tympanum, a gigantic figure of Jesus, arms outstretched, beckoned the masses to pass through the portal below and enter the two-thousand-seat sanctuary, which for unabashed flamboyance vied with the interior of a Loew's picture palace. The five-story basement of the cathedral housed a swimming pool, a bowling alley, and a gymnasium. For children there were nurseries and rooftop playgrounds; for people of all ages there were classrooms, a cafeteria, and a large social hall. Parishioners could even live in the church if they so chose: two twelve-story apartment buildings wrapped the base of the cathedral and five hundred dormitory rooms occupied the tower. Reisner christened his lofty advertisement of God's business "Broadway Temple."

Construction of the cathedral was to be financed through the sale of 5 percent interest-bearing bonds—a financing scheme some straitlaced Methodists thought to be hugely inappropriate, given the nature of the project. "Is profit basically Christian?" asked one critic. "Or 5 percent?" Think of it as "an investment in your fellow man's salvation," responded Reisner, who before long had used his sales skills to sign up D. W. Griffith, E. F. Hutton, John D. Rockefeller, Jr., and other headliner names to purchase $500,000 worth of bonds. The public followed suit. By 1925, $2 million had been pledged in bond subscriptions, enough to proceed with the excavation of the cathedral's foundation and with the construction of the apartment buildings, which, when finished, were expected to generate some $200,000 a year in rental income, and so help pay off the interest on the bonds. Reisner, recognizing an advertising opportunity when he saw one, erected a large eye-catching fence around the construction site, emblazoned with the message: "Ask How to Help."

In answer, gifts poured in from around the country. The president of Warner Brothers promised the church a "modern motion picture booth," as fine as any to be found in Hollywood. Another donor offered the church the largest Wurlitzer organ ever built. The generosity of Charles V. Bob, a mining engineer, bought the cathedral its huge revolving electric cross, which was soon named "Byrd Beacon" in honor of Commander Richard Byrd, the famous aviator. Rockefeller gave Broadway Temple an outright gift of $100,000, even though he had newly committed himself to financing the construction of another cathedral—Riverside Church.

In October 1927 snappily attired doormen, sporting visored caps embroidered with the words *Broadway Temple*, greeted residents at the entrances of the church's brand-new apartment houses. Broadway Temple, however, was nowhere to be seen. Between the apartment buildings loomed a wide gap sprouting unfinished steel work, testimony to the financial woes that had befallen the cathedral's building fund: unanticipated expenses had driven the cost of construction $1.5 million over the original $4-million figure.

Reisner stepped up the fund-raising campaign.

Portal and tympanum of the proposed cathedral, from a promotional brochure, c. 1925.

OPPOSITE:
Proposed Broadway Temple, west side of Broadway, between West 173rd and West 174th streets. Donn Barber, 1923.

BELOW:
The richly decorated sanctuary of Broadway Temple was designed by the firm of McKenzie, Vorhees & Gmelin, after the death of the architect Donn Barber, in 1925.

The Reverend Christian Reisner, holding a rendering of Broadway Temple, and an unidentified man pose in front of the cathedral's future site, c. 1925.

Swimming pool, Broadway Temple. Construction of the swimming pool, which was to be located in the cathedral's vast basement four stories beneath Broadway, was halted at the onset of the Depression in 1929. A tour of the cathedral's basement today reveals the ghostly remains of the poolside balconies and the concrete floor of the unfinished swimming tank.

He flooded the press and popular magazines with subscription coupons, entreating citizens of all faiths to buy bonds for the temple "and let God come to Broadway." In promotional flyers and brochures, cranked out on his office mimeograph machine, the minister urged believers to "say it with Architecture . . . Build!" He lined up Will Rogers to perform at a benefit luncheon, coaxed $50,000 out of James B. Duke, the tobacco mogul, and, to the astonishment of the parishioners, succeeded in getting Commander Richard Byrd to appear at a New Year's Eve fund-raising rally.

Reisner managed to raise $1,500,000 by late 1928, only months before the church on 178th Street was demolished, and built the promised social hall, gymnasium, and bowling alley in the cathedral's cavernous basement. But before the pastor could finish the swimming pool, the two-thousand-seat sanctuary, and the rest of the church, the plan for the skyscraper cathedral was blown asunder by the stock market crash of 1929. In the wake of the crash, Broadway Temple found itself saddled with a $2-million mortgage and a $1-million obligation to bondholders.

It would take the church nearly twenty years to dissolve its debts. In the interim, Sunday services were held in the social hall under the red glow of an electric cross installed by Reisner, who had lost his cathedral but none of his knack for putting on a good show. Bright placards posted outside the unfinished church announced the upcoming appearances of Eddie Cantor, young Jackie Coogan,

Broadway Temple's newly completed apartment buildings frame the construction site of the proposed cathedral, c. 1927.

Broadway Temple as built, west side of Broadway, between West 173rd and West 174th streets. Shreve, Lamb & Harmon, 1952.

the Singing College Girls, and Max Heron, a popular magician. Weekly newsreels spun inside the state-of-the-art projection booth donated by Warner Brothers. On some Sundays there were free roses, bags of flour, and other gifts for the congregation, courtesy of local merchants; in mid-July there was always Reisner's traditional Snow Sermon.

Reisner died in 1940. Although his successor, the Reverend Allen Claxton, did not offer parishioners the entertaining services they had enjoyed since the early 1920s, he cleared Broadway Temple's $3-million debt, raised another $1 million, and in 1952 built a church above the Temple's existing basement. "A Dream Comes True!" proclaimed a flyer that showed a low, modest structure wedged between the apartment houses that were to have framed Broadway Temple's dramatic portal. Reisner's skyscraper cathedral it was not, but the minister would probably have been pleased to know that the small church (still active today) was designed by Shreve, Lamb & Harmon, architects of one of the greatest skyscrapers of all—the Empire State Building.

The headquarters, they had all agreed, would be located in the United States. The question was where. Russia preferred New York City. Great Britain and Norway leaned toward Boston. China fancied the Westchester County, New York–Connecticut area, and Australia opted for San Francisco. The seven-member international Headquarters Committee, on the other hand, was partial to the Hyde Park estate of former President Franklin D. Roosevelt, located in Dutchess County, New York.

So began the infant United Nations search for a permanent home early in 1946. With fifty-one member states to please, a list of stiff criteria governing the choice of a site to meet, and invitations pouring in from cities, towns, and villages across America, the search promised to be a long one. In the meantime, who would put up thousands of delegates until they had found a permanent roof over their heads? After all, there was business to conduct. Among other items on the immediate agenda, a secretary-general had to be appointed, resolution texts for the establishment of the Atomic Energy Commission waited for approval, and the disputed presence of Russian troops in Iran needed to be resolved.

Come and stay with us, we've got plenty of room, offered Mayor William O'Dwyer as he muscled his way past White Plains, New York; Atlantic City, New Jersey; Vassar College; and Burlington, Vermont, which had all volunteered to be temporary hosts to the United Nations. Just say the word, and Radio City Music Hall, the Empire State Building, and City Center are yours, promised the mayor in a moment of enthusiastic munificence.

The United Nations did not end up meeting in temporary quarters quite so grand. In March 1946 the organization was installed in several buildings at Hunter (now Lehman) College in the Bronx. For a few months a "deliciously incongruous atmosphere" reigned at the campus turned world capital, recalls Abe Rosenthal, who covered the United Nations in its early days for the *New York Times*. "There was a document center in the locker room, the Balkan experts met in the French I and II rooms, the press center was a boarded-over swimming pool . . . and where Hunter women had once nimbly leaped over leather horses, the United Nations Security Council met to discuss Franco Spain."

Before registration for fall classes, 1946, the U.N., in need of more elbow room, was moved to the Sperry Gyroscope plant in suburban Long Island at Lake Success ("Everybody loved the symbolism—'war factory' turned to the uses of peace," remembers Rosenthal), and the General Assembly sessions were held in Flushing Meadows Park, Queens, hard on the Grand Central Parkway, in the "dank and drafty" hall of the New York City Building (now the Queens Museum), a holdover from the 1939–40 New York World's Fair. Meanwhile, the Headquarters Committee toured the United States in search of a permanent home. It had in mind a site, preferably scenic, that would accommodate a large assembly hall; offices for the secretariat and the eighty-some organizations affiliated with the U.N.; a communications station; hotels; an airport for "the biggest ships or rockets contemplated now or in the centuries to come"; and an initial population of up to fifty thousand people. Happily, there seemed to be no dearth of places to choose from. Saratoga Springs, New York; Chicago; Boston; and Rapid City, South Dakota, wanted the U.N. So did Princeton, New Jersey; Philadelphia; Duluth, Minnesota; San Francisco; and the Smoky Mountains Invitation Committee. In a late bid, residents of Martha's Vineyard, Massachusetts, telegrammed the United Nations to offer their idyllic island, situated several miles off Cape Cod, as a headquarters site. "The temperate climate, our serenity of scene and the tang of fresh salt air" are well suited for "harmonious living and exchange of opinion," they wrote.

New York was not about to sit back and watch someone else pluck the U.N. out of its hands. At the direction of Mayor O'Dwyer, a distinguished committee that included Arthur Hays Sulzberger, Robert Moses, Nelson A. Rockefeller, and the architects Wallace K. Harrison, Louis Skidmore, and Aymar Embury II was formed to come up with a dream home the United Nations couldn't resist. The committee didn't have to waste time picking an address; Moses, chairman of the committee and

Members of the United Nations Headquarters Committee inspecting the Hyde Park site, 1946. Left to right: François Briere, France; Awny El Khalidi, Iraq; Dr. Shuhsi Hsu, China; Huntington Gilchrist, United States, secretary to the committee; Dr. H. E. Stoyan Gavrilovic, Yugoslavia; Major K. G. Younger, United Kingdom; Don Julio A. Lacarte, Uruguay; Georgii Saksin, U.S.S.R.

city parks commissioner, had already selected one—the northern end of Flushing Meadows Park—and why not? The half-square-mile tract that lay within the 1,200-acre park, created by Moses out of a malodorous ash dump and swamp lands for the New York World's Fair of 1939–40, offered all the amenities desired by the U.N. It was close to major highways, two airports, and mass transit. It was quiet and scenic, with ample room for an assembly hall, missions, and offices. What was more, after some adding and subtracting, the committee decided that New York could afford to give the city-owned property—long since swept clean of most of the fair's buildings—and all permanent improvements, such as utility lines and transit access, to the U.N. for *free*. In round numbers that represented a $27-million gift. The architects Harrison, Embury, and Skidmore were charged with designing the gift.

The committee's proposal was formally presented to Trygve Lie, secretary-general of the United Nations, by representatives of the mayor in October 1946 at the New York City Building in Flushing Meadows Park. The stocky Norwegian warmly thanked the city for the offer amidst a blaze of popping flashbulbs and then ducked into a meeting of the General Assembly; to the disappointment of reporters who trailed him to the door, he wouldn't comment on the plan. But later on, leafing through the committee's oversized prospectus, lushly illustrated by Hugh Ferriss, Lie must have thought he was looking at the far side of the moon, not Flushing Meadows Park. Perpetual night seemed to have gripped the proposed 350-acre compound. Under the cover of darkness, shadowy figures (Spies? Diplomats?) scuttled into the huge luminescent dome of the General Assembly building, one of four principal buildings designed for the site. Other sinister-looking figures lurked among the massive pylons that edged a long moat fronting on Grand Central Parkway. Behind the complex, the vespertine waters of a deathly still lagoon bisected deserted gardens. "Is this a fitting symbol of the brave new world, expressing peace and brotherhood of all mankind?" asked an aghast resident of Sheboygan, Wisconsin, after seeing the plan in the *New York Times*.

Apparently the United Nations Headquarters Committee thought so. By mid-November 1946 it had narrowed down its list of possible permanent sites to Boston, Philadelphia, San Francisco, Westchester County—and Flushing Meadows. But before putting the matter to a vote, an eighteen-member subcommittee was dispatched on a whirlwind cross-country junket to take one last look at each of the candidates.

The delegates received royal welcomes. Their eager suitors, all hoping mightily to win the hand of the U.N., wined and dined them, pulled out their symphony orchestras to serenade them, and escorted them on guided tours of the proferred sites in motorcades, helicopters, boats, and blimps. Philadelphia, the first stop on the itinerary, promised its guests a $17-million donation of a bucolic two-mile tract, half of which lay situated in Fairmount Park. San Francisco gave them their choice of two spectacular properties that overlooked the Golden Gate Bridge and the Pacific Ocean. Over lunch at the Harvard Club, Boston's mayor unveiled three possible sites for the U.N.'s home. The chairman of the Westchester County Planning Commission offered twelve square miles of field and stream in Mohansic Park. If that would not be enough, "We can assign to you twenty square miles," he promised.

In late November, eleven exhausting days and thousands of miles later, the delegates turned in their recommendations to the Headquarters Committee. Boston was out of the running, largely because it was felt the city would not "welcome all members of the United Nations." Flushing Meadows was also struck because, "several subcommittee members," Lie later recalled, "were inclined to doubt the city's contention that large, many-story buildings could be built at the Flushing site, in view of reportedly unstable ground conditions." And

frankly, he added, "There was even some reference to an occasional marsh odor." That left Philadelphia and San Francisco, which the subcommittee held to have "equal merit," as first runners-up, with Westchester a close second.

An uproar broke out at Lake Success. San Francisco? *Nyet!* chorused delegates from Russia, who lobbied to have Flushing Meadows put back on the list of contenders. Out of the question, agreed Great Britain, which started out rooting for Westchester but then turned around and backed Philadelphia. Philadelphia? Unacceptable, protested El Salvador, the Philippines, China, and Saudi Arabia, which considered San Francisco the best choice. Let's just call the whole thing off and think about it for a while, proposed Warren Austin, the United States chief delegate to the United Nations. That's the worst suggestion of all, came the unanimous response.

In Manhattan, meanwhile, on the morning of December 6, 1946, the real estate developer William Zeckendorf, Sr., sat hunched over the *New York Times* at breakfast, immersed in an article on the continuing saga of the headquarters debate. The U.N. and the developer had something in common: they were both racing the clock. The Headquarters Committee was scheduled to present its choice for a permanent site to the General Assembly in less than a week from then. By the end of December, Zeckendorf had to come up with $5.5 million; otherwise he would lose his option to purchase a huge tract between Forty-second and Forty-eighth streets along the East River. He had already shelled out a million-dollar down payment for the seventeen-acre parcel, where slaughterhouses, cattle pens, breweries, and packing plants stood cheek by jowl—hardly attractive property. But one night after a walk near the site, Zeckendorf had concocted a fantastic scheme to demolish the existing buildings and to deck over the entire area with an elevated platform on which would rise a series of apartment and office towers, a six-thousand-capacity convention hall, and a hotel. Scheming on, he had dropped a landing strip for small aircraft, a floating nightclub, and a marina into the East River. Zeck-

The domed General Assembly building, proposed United Nations complex. Wallace K. Harrison, Louis Skidmore, Aymar Embury II, 1946.

View across the moat, toward the General Assembly building, proposed United Nations complex. Wallace K. Harrison, Louis Skidmore, Aymar Embury II, 1946.

OPPOSITE, TOP:
Proposed United Nations complex, Flushing Meadows Park. Wallace K. Harrison, Louis Skidmore, Aymar Embury II, 1946.

BOTTOM:
The New York World's Fair, 1939–40, Flushing Meadows Park.

endorf, the dynamo behind Kips Bay Plaza in New York, Mile High City in Denver, and Century City in Los Angeles, was not a man content to build castles in the air. Before long he had commissioned the architect Wallace Harrison to put his vision to paper. The plan, unveiled in October 1946, was called X City.

But as Zeckendorf recounts the tale in his autobiography, on the morning of December 6, while reading the *Times,* he had another idea. Turning to his wife, Marion, he said, "I'm going to put those bastards on the platform!"

"Which bastards on what platform?" she asked.

"The U.N.—I'm going to put them on the platform over the slaughterhouses." And before the day was out, Zeckendorf had telephoned Mayor O'Dwyer with his proposal, the mayor had contacted Robert Moses, and Moses had called a man who was known both for his bottomless bank account and his generosity.

Four days later, on the evening before the Headquarters Committee was to vote on a site, Wallace Harrison walked into the Club Monte Carlo, where Zeckendorf and his wife were celebrating their wedding anniversary, unfolded a map of the East Side property on their table, and asked point-blank: "Would you sell it for eight and a half million?"

"I'd had a lot of champagne by that time," Zeckendorf admitted, but without making so much as a calculation, he replied he'd sell the East Side property for "whatever they were willing to pay." "They" were the Rockefellers.

The next morning Nelson Rockefeller telephoned the developer at his office. "We've been up all night patching up the details, but it's going to work," said Rockefeller. "The old man is going to give that 8.5 million dollars to the U.N., and they're going to take your property. See you soon . . . Goodbye." Stunned and still fuzzy from the previous night's champagne, Zeckendorf rang the switchboard operator to make sure he had heard the name right. Yes, said the operator, "R-o-c-k-e-f-e-l-l-e-r."

X City, William Zeckendorf Sr.'s proposed East River development, East Forty-second Street to East Forty-eighth Street. Wallace K. Harrison, 1946.

William Zeckendorf, Sr., c. 1946.

RIGHT:
The site of the United Nations, East Forty-second Street to East Forty-eighth Street, as it looked in 1946.

Later the same morning Warren Austin stood before the Headquarters Committee to relay the good news. He held in his hand a short letter from John D. Rockefeller, Jr., which he read aloud. "It is my belief that this city affords an environment uniquely fitted to the task of the United Nations and that the people of New York would like to have the United Nations permanently," Rockefeller had written. "For these reasons I have ventured to obtain a firm offer covering property located on the East River in the midtown area, which should it serve your purpose, I would be glad to give to the United Nations."

On December 14, 1946, only eight days after Zeckendorf's call to Mayor O'Dwyer, the General Assembly voted overwhelmingly to approve the East River site as the permanent home of the United Nations.

The design for the diplomatic headquarters, drawn up by an international team of architects under the direction of Wallace Harrison, was approved the following year. For the six-block complex, the architects borrowed components of Zeckendorf's X City proposal, placing the low-slung Conference Building on a landscaped platform over the FDR Drive, and taking one of the developer's towering slabs for the Secretariat Building. All that remained from the Flushing Meadows plan was the dome atop the General Assembly Building, which for the East River project was whittled down from a gigantic bubble to a small bulge. At the U.N.'s housewarming, on October 14, 1952, Lester B. Pearson, the incoming president of the General Assembly, remarked: "There is, I think, a happy symbolism in the structure of our headquarters; part of it reaching upward toward the heavens and part fixed on the ground. The reconciliation of these features is, I suppose, difficult in the art of architecture." But, he added, "it is even more difficult in the science of politics and in the conduct of international affairs." Indeed, not three days later, in the chambers of the new General Assembly building, delegates faced off in a lengthy debate on South Africa's policy of apartheid.

In the spring of 1887 Walter Damrosch set sail from New York City to his native Germany for a summer of study with the renowned conductor Hans von Bülow. It was a busman's holiday of sorts for the twenty-five-year-old musician, who in the two years since the death of his illustrious father, Leopold Damrosch, founder of the Oratorio Society and the New York Symphony, had become known to music lovers in New York as the baton-wielding figure at the Metropolitan Opera House. Little did the young conductor guess that the summer was also to be the prelude to his father's fondest dream: a great concert hall for New York City.

As fortune would have it, Andrew Carnegie, czar of America's steel industry, was also aboard the steam packer, bound for Perth, Scotland, with his bride to enjoy an extended honeymoon at Kilgraston Castle. Soon into the voyage, the two men were introduced. Having served on the board of the Oratorio Society, Carnegie was well acquainted with the elder Damrosch's lifelong efforts to bring music to the masses, and he commended Walter for having chosen to follow in his father's footsteps. For his part, the young conductor was thrilled to meet the Scottish-born millionaire, whose rags-to-riches story was already legendary; when, a few days later, the industrialist invited him to visit Kilgraston after his summer studies, Damrosch accepted with pleasure.

At the castle the conversation turned to New York City's need for a large concert house. By 1887 the city had outgrown—and grown north from—the cluster of music halls located on or near Fourteenth Street that were managed by the Steinways, the Chickerings, and other piano manufacturers. And, alas, the Metropolitan Opera House, a grand edifice built in 1883 at Broadway and Thirty-ninth Street, was acoustically ill-suited for orchestral performances. More than once during their discussions, Damrosch suggested to Carnegie that he build the concert house New York lacked; to Damrosch's disappointment, the self-made millionaire was not interested in adding a concert hall to his list of philanthropic causes. Carnegie "could understand that a library, a school, or a hospital could not and should not be self-supporting, but I could not convince him that music should fall in the same category," Damrosch wrote. "He always insisted that the greatest patronage of music should come from a paying public rather than from private endowment." But during the summer of 1888, when the conductor was again invited by the Carnegies to Scotland, he had better luck.

In 1889 Andrew Carnegie presented the city of New York with a $2-million gift, still on paper, called Music Hall. The site purchased by the philanthropist for the concert house (renamed Carnegie Hall in 1898) was located on Seventh Avenue and Fifty-seventh Street, near a stretch of vacant lots, coal yards, and scattered rowhouses. Only the Osborne, a gracious apartment house built a few years earlier and situated catty-corner from the concert hall-to-be, foretold the elegant future that

Walter Damrosch, c. 1887.

Andrew Carnegie, c. 1907.

RIGHT:
The Metropolitan Opera House, Broadway and West Thirty-ninth Street, 1900. The building was torn down in 1967, a year after the new Metropolitan Opera House opened at Lincoln Center for the Performing Arts.

Carnegie's "tone temple" would bring to Fifty-seventh Street. In time, art galleries, fine antique stores, piano showrooms, and high-priced specialty shops took their places near Carnegie Hall, earning Fifty-seventh Street the title "America's rue de la Paix."

The architect retained to design Music Hall was William B. Tuthill, a thirty-four-year-old New Yorker who in all likelihood won the important commission by virtue of his reputation as a gifted musician and a fine singer—which, in 1889, far outstripped his reputation as an architect. But he soon proved to be equally talented at the drawing board. In association with the consulting architects Richard Morris Hunt and Dankmar Adler, Tuthill

produced a stolid, six-story Italian Renaissance–style building of reddish-brown brick, which housed a majestic, if restrained, ivory-and-gold 2,760-seat auditorium. But as the opening night crowd on May 5, 1891, discovered when Walter Damrosch launched the New York Symphony into the first strains of Beethoven's *Leonora* Overture, Tuthill's greatest achievement lay in the hall's superb sound. "The acoustics were perfect," raved the *New York Herald* the next day. "There was no echo, no undue reverberation. Each note was heard."

Over the ensuing decades a long list of celebrated figures stepped in front of the footlights of the great concert house, headed by Peter Ilyich Tchaikovsky, who appeared as guest conductor at the five-day

The Osborne Apartments, in an 1885 photograph taken from a vacant lot on the corner of Seventh Avenue and West Fifty-seventh Street, later the site of Carnegie Hall. View is west along Fifty-seventh Street.

BELOW:
Carnegie Hall in 1896. William B. Tuthill, 1891.

Carnegie Hall on opening night, May 5, 1891.

gala that marked the opening of Music Hall. To the concert house came also Gustav Mahler, Sergei Rachmaninoff, Isadora Duncan, George Gershwin, and Camille Saint-Saëns. There in 1900 Winston Churchill took to the stage to expound on the Boer War, and there in 1943 Duke Ellington and his orchestra shook up the walls of the house with a few tunes "especially designed for the super jitterbug."

But in the summer of 1955 a deathly hush settled over Carnegie Hall. The building was up for sale, announced Robert Simon, Jr., whose father had purchased the concert hall from the Carnegie estate in 1925; unless the New York Philharmonic was interested in buying it for $4 million, "the Old Lady of Fifty-seventh Street" would be torn down to make way for a skyscraper. The symphony's board of directors thanked Simon for the offer, but replied that the Philharmonic had plans to move into a

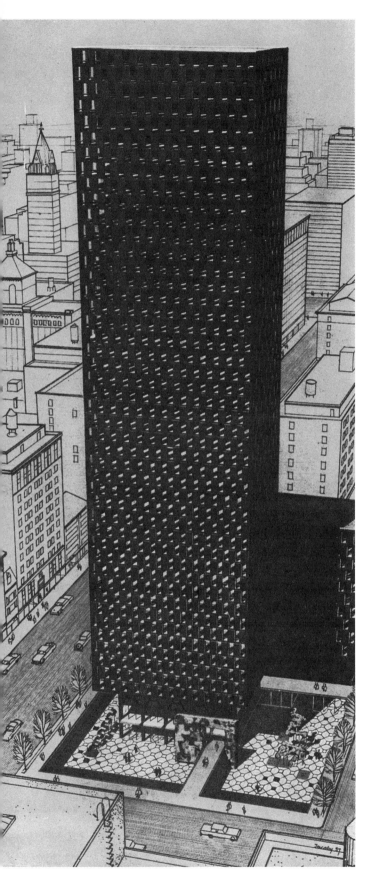

brand-new home, uptown, at Lincoln Center, just as soon as it was completed.

The Philharmonic's response elicited bitter rumblings in music circles about betrayal and high stakes gambling. After all, back in 1892, after a fire had gutted the Metropolitan Opera House, hadn't Carnegie Hall rescued the orphaned Philharmonic in its hour of need? Now, sixty-three years later, the orchestra, Carnegie Hall's principal tenant, was callously going to abandon the concert house in *its* hour of need. And for what? For modern quarters in a proposed performing arts complex, which in 1955 was still in the planning stage with no guarantee that it would ever be built. Given the worst scenario, New York could find itself with a skyscraper on the site of Carnegie Hall, a hole in the ground at Lincoln Center, and no concert house at all. Was it worth the risk?

That summer concerned citizens banded together and formed the Committee to Save Carnegie Hall, electing the baritone Lawrence Tibbett as chairman. Their goal: $4 million. "We won't stand out in history as the community that swapped a Stradivarius violin for a juke box," vowed one man at a public rally held inside the hall. But apparently most New Yorkers had already given up the concert house for dead. A year later only $14,000 had been raised; meanwhile, Robert Simon had upped the asking price of the concert house to $5 million.

He soon found a buyer. In July 1956 the real estate developer Louis Glickman handed Simon a $200,000 check for a two-year option on the property and announced that Carnegie Hall would come tumbling down to make way for an office tower in 1959, when the Philharmonic's lease was up.

The scheme for the Fifty-seventh Street site, designed by the architects Ralph Pomerance and Simon Breines, was released in 1957. New Yorkers were the first to see the proposed $22-million, forty-four story building, in a small photograph buried near the back of the *New York Times;* even in black and white the image was a sobering one. But the

Scheme for an office building proposed for the site of Carnegie Hall. Pomerance and Breines, 1957.

color rendering that millions of Americans saw the next month in the pages of *Life* magazine more accurately depicted the garish slab that was slated to replace the cherished concert house. Rising from thirty-foot pylons above a sunken plaza, a shoe box of a tower flaunted a screaming bright-red skin made of steel panels faced with porcelain enamel. (The choice of color, Pomerance explained, "was an attempt to relieve the sameness of the Manhattan skyline.") Relentless rows of blank windows, set on the diagonal, played off against the vermilion facade, suggesting a giant four-sided chessboard; and at street level, a matching red gateway greeted workers who were to reach the office tower from Sixth Avenue via a footbridge that spanned the sunken plaza. "I've never seen an uglier building," gasped a shocked reader from Toledo, Ohio, in a letter to the editor of *Life*. "It looks like the back of a large cereal box."

Shoe box, cereal box, chessboard—it didn't matter in the end. In July 1958 Glickman announced that the project was off. "It now seems that the Philharmonic will be unable to vacate Carnegie Hall for some time longer, perhaps years," said the developer. "We certainly do not wish to be part of any program which would disrupt the cultural contribution of this institution to the community. That would be a disservice to the public, and, as such, outrageous to our sense of civic interest. Accordingly, the Carnegie Hall deal has been taken out of our hands by circumstances beyond our reach."

By late summer 1958 all eyes were back on Simon. Now that Glickman had pulled out, what was to be the fate of the concert house? people demanded to know. Simon was noncommittal: "It is entirely conceivable that Carnegie Hall will remain standing," he said. "It could be a television studio, for instance. It is also conceivable that the building will be torn down." The latter seemed the most likely possibility after ground was broken for Lincoln Center, in May 1959, and arrangements were made to house the Philharmonic at Hunter College until its new uptown home was ready. Sure enough, early in January 1960 Simon sounded the death knell for Carnegie Hall. Demolition of the concert house, he said, would begin in the summer.

Isaac Stern, c. 1950.

The public and performers alike took Simon at his word. After the announcement, long-faced ticket holders filed into Carnegie Hall, never expecting to hear another note resound through the hallowed auditorium the next season. Visiting soloists and symphonies quickly reshuffled their programs to include at least one musical tribute to the doomed concert house, and the American National Theatre and Academy began lining up artists for a bang-up May 20 concert billed as "Farewell to Carnegie Hall."

But as painters sloshed giant white *X*s across Carnegie Hall's windows in preparation for the wrecking crews, Isaac Stern arrived on the scene, determined to rescue the sixty-nine-year-old music shrine from oblivion. To raze the hall for some anonymous skyscraper would be like "tearing down La Scala and putting up a garage," cried the violinist. "How dare we take away from them, the musicians and audiences of the future, one of the great music rooms of the world?" Fueling Stern's indignation were feelings of deep personal gratitude to the concert house on Fifty-seventh Street; it was there in 1943 that the then twenty-three-year-old virtuoso had been catapulted to musical fame.

Just a few days after Simon's announcement, on January 10, 1960, Stern called a meeting at his home, only hours before leaving on a two-month concert tour. Carnegie Hall, he feared, would be gone by the time he got back. There were but a few scant weeks to save the house; something had to be done, and quickly, he said. How to save the musical landmark from certain ruin was left to the infant Citizens Committee for Carnegie Hall, whose founding members included Raymond S. Rubinow, administrator of the J. M. Kaplan Fund; Jack deSimone, a veteran public relations man; and Vera Stern, the violinist's wife. Over the following weeks, while Stern was away on tour, the small group gathered every few days to plot out a rescue strategy, ever aware that their most formidable and immediate opponent was the clock. Initially, remembers Rubinow, they considered "finding an angel—someone like Andrew Carnegie himself," who would step in and buy the concert hall, but realizing that was a multimillion-dollar pipe dream, the committee consulted a fund raiser to see if the money to purchase the hall could be obtained some other way. It could, was the answer, but it would take a least six months, by which time Carnegie Hall would be reduced to a hill of bricks. Next, from Vera Stern, came the idea of forming a "musical cooperative" of musicians, singers, and orchestras to raise the $5 million necessary to buy the concert house. After some deliberation that scheme was also scratched because, as Rubinow recalls, it was thought that while many in the cooperative might love Carnegie Hall, "they might not all love each other."

With private financial channels closed to the committee and precious days ticking away, Rubinow suggested to his colleagues that they immediately pursue a "government rescue plan." Hoping for municipal assistance, they went first to Mayor Robert Wagner, but the mayor, while sympathetic to the cause, explained that he had his hands full trying to bail City Center out from its financial woes. A meeting with U.S. Senator Jacob K. Javits to determine if federal funds were available to save the concert house proved equally fruitless. Indeed, there was an active national historic preservation program, Javits informed them, but, with hundreds of buildings on the waiting list for financial help, Carnegie Hall's chances of receiving aid before the wrecker's ball began to swing were close to nil. That left Albany as the sole remaining source for funds, but, says Rubinow, the committee worried that the upstate farm community would object mightily to paying for a city slicker's concert hall, and the last thing committee members needed was a drawn-out debate in the legislature.

Their final plan, conceived in early February, offered an ingenious solution. With the aid of Colonel Harold Riegelman, an attorney; Mayor Wagner; and State Senator MacNeil Mitchell, whose district included Carnegie Hall, two bills were drafted and submitted to the State Legislature in March 1960. One proposed permitting all New York municipalities to acquire by purchase, lease, or condemnation any property having "special historical or aesthetic interest or value." The second bill proposed authorizing New York City to issue bonds for the renovation of the concert hall, and to form the Carnegie Hall Corporation, a nonprofit organization that would lease the building from the city, amortizing the bonds over a thirty-year period with rents and other revenues. Once the bonds were retired, the corporation would own Carnegie Hall. Thus, neither New Yorkers upstate nor downstate would be required to lay out a single tax dollar for the music hall.

As the bills were routed through the legislature, Isaac Stern was performing to packed houses across the United States and Canada but seizing every opportunity to mobilize friends and associates to join the battle to save Carnegie Hall. Thanks to Stern, the ranks of the Citizens Committee soon swelled to become a veritable Who's Who in Music; thanks also to Stern, the new recruits kept a steady stream of messages coming in support of the venerable concert house. Carnegie Hall "is a consecrated house," declared Jasha Heifetz, Dimitri

Mitropoulos, Pablo Casals, Eugene Normandy, George Szell, and a dozen other musical giants in a telegram to Mayor Wagner. "In the minds of civilized men and women everywhere, it is the gateway to musical America. To destroy it for 'practical reasons' is an act of irresponsibility damaging to the U.S. and our prestige in the entire civilized world." In another message of support, Leopold Stokowski cabled, "To destroy this monument would be eloquent testimony for the accusation leveled at Americans that we have little regard for the heritage that is rooted in cultural values."

On April 16, 1960, while conducting a children's concert at Carnegie Hall, it was Stokowski who had the pleasure of announcing from the podium that, moments earlier, both bills to save the house had been signed into law by Governor Nelson Rockefeller. Carnegie Hall would live on! Spontaneously, the young audience sent up a loud and lusty cheer.

During the summer of 1960, the Philharmonic moved out of Carnegie Hall and workmen moved in. The dingy mulberry-colored interior was repainted a glistening white and trimmed with gilt. Red velvet plush was stretched over two thousand seats, a mile of new carpet was unrolled, and sparking chandeliers were carefully hoisted to the lobby ceiling. At a preview reception in September 1960, Isaac Stern waved a proud hand over the refurbished concert house and with customary modesty said, "You see here the realization of a hope and a little bit of a miracle."

Uptown, at Sixty-fifth Street and Columbus Avenue, meanwhile, a large pit showed the beginnings of Philharmonic Hall (later renamed Avery Fisher Hall), New York's second concert house and the first of several buildings to go up at the city's new acropolis of music and drama, Lincoln Center for the Performing Arts. When the glass-and-marble building made its debut in 1962, skeptics predicted that New York could never support two music meccas. They were soon proved wrong. During the 1962–63 season, as placards slashed with bold diagonals proclaimed sold-out performances at Carnegie Hall, crowds of faithful Philharmonic fans wended their way around sand heaps and bulldozers to fill the new concert house at Lincoln Center.

Lincoln Center remained a vast construction zone for nearly a decade while the pieces of the cultural complex—the New York State Theater (1964), the Vivian Beaumont Theater (1965), the Metropolitan Opera House (1966), and the Juilliard School of Music (1968)—were set into place around a formal central plaza. Last to be developed, just south of the Metropolitan Opera House, was Damrosch Park (1969), a two-and-a-half-acre square reserved for free outdoor concerts. On summer evenings in the park, the sound of Sousa, Gershwin, and Verdi waft upward through the trees and into the sky, commemorating the Damrosches with the gift they gave New York—music, glorious music.

TRANSPORTATION

High on most New Yorkers' current list of urban gripes is the city's public transportation system. The gripe is not new. In fact, if one could ascribe a sound effect to New York City's transportation history, it would be one long, tired groan, uttered by several generations of straphangers who collectively have been plagued by overcrowded cars, crime, and erratic service for more than 150 years. In that time stagecoaches, omnibuses, trolleys, double-decker buses, aerial trams, elevated trains, subways, cable cars, and almost every other form of vehicle ever invented have been put to the test in New York City. Not one has proved to be the ideal method of moving the city's millions for very long. Over the years commuters have described the city's transit facilities as "disgracefully inadequate" (1858), "a free field for bullies and ruffians" (1882), and "an echo of hell" (1922). In 1984 an irate subway rider added "electric sewer" to this glossary.

Since at least the 1830s proposals to improve the commuter's lot have regularly been deposited on the mayor's desk. Many of the schemes anticipated the city's future needs, and many of them were feasible, but New York has typically put off implementing any plan unless faced with a crisis situation. Such was the case of the horse-drawn streetcar, invented in the early 1830s but not permitted to operate on the city's streets for another twenty years, until the crammed omnibuses, New Yorkers' principal means of getting about town, were ready to burst open with the strain of their load. It took grim statistics of death and injury caused by the hopeless snarl of horse-drawn vehicles in downtown streets for the city to move to build an elevated transit system in the late 1860s, although one had been proposed as early as 1844. And a subway, first suggested in 1864, did not open until 1904, by which time New York had grown to encompass five boroughs and over three million people. Given this record, today's commuters may have a long wait

Seats are at a premium in this 1867 satirical view of a New York omnibus interior.

ahead of them before the graffiti-smothered trains are cleaned up, the screeching wheels muffled, and city buses scheduled to arrive as single units, rather than in elephantlike processions.

But New York's transportation history does contain one bright chapter. Commuting life has periodically been made more palatable by such extras as the mohair seats and mirrored interiors featured on the Brooklyn Manhattan Transit line (BMT) in 1941; by the "Bicycle Train," which accommodated riders and their two-wheelers for an experimental period in 1897; and by the half-fare schedule that was offered on weekends and holidays by the Metropolitan Transportation Authority in the mid-1970s. The city can also boast having produced America's first streetcar, in 1832, as well as having experimented with the world's first automatic train, in the early 1960s. And, as transit officials today like to remind commuters, for all the derailments, crime, crowding, and delays, with 700 miles of main-line subway track and 1,011 miles of bus routes carrying an average total of 5.1 million riders per day, New York City still manages to run the most extensive and efficient—if not exactly the most beloved—transportation system in the country.

Fifth Avenue, looking north from the southeast corner of Twenty-seventh Street, c. 1865.

BELOW:
The busy intersection of Broadway and Park Row, south of City Hall Park, c. 1868.

New York emerged from the Civil War prosperous and vigorous. The city that only fifteen years earlier had been contained below Fourteenth Street was advancing north to Fifty-ninth Street, the southern perimeter of the newly created Central Park, and it showed no signs of stopping. It seemed that everywhere one looked, marveled the *New York Times,* homes, churches, stores, and hotels were springing up in "iron, marble and brownstone." George William Curtis, writing in *Harper's* magazine, wistfully recalled the city in the good old days of the 1840s, when "beyond 9th Street the city unraveled out into the fields. Union Park was an inclosure. Madison Square was out on the island. Where now the choicest fashion dwells, cows and donkeys browsed. Dear me, how changed everything is!"

What had not changed was the abominable state of public transportation in New York. To get uptown, downtown, or across town, New Yorkers had no alternative, save their own two feet, but to suffer a ride on a horse-drawn omnibus or on a street railway. A ride in an omnibus, the *New York Herald* stated, constituted nothing less than an act of "modern martyrdom":

> The discomforts, inconveniences and annoyances of a trip in one of these vehicles are almost intolerable . . . There are quarrels about getting out and quarrels about getting in . . . The driver swears at the passengers and the passengers harangue the driver . . . Ladies are disgusted, frightened and insulted. Children are alarmed and lift up their voices and weep. Thus, the omnibus rolls along, a perfect Bedlam on wheels.

Besides offering wretched service, the private livery stables that owned and operated the omnibuses had also successfully managed for twenty years to stave off a rival form of transportation, called the horsecar or street railway. This vehicle, a predecessor to the electric trolley, had made its debut in 1832 on a run between Prince Street and Fourteenth Street along the Bowery and lower Fourth Avenue, but it was not until the early 1850s that horsecar companies finally landed charters to line the city's av-

enues with tracks. By the mid-1860s the grinding of iron wheels and the rhythmic clomping of horses' hooves could be heard on Sixth, Seventh, Eighth, and Ninth avenues from Barclay Street to Fifty-ninth Street, and along Third Avenue all the way to Yorkville. The Second Avenue line, the longest of them all, extended to the outbacks of Harlem.

Given the choice between an omnibus and a horsecar, most New Yorkers took the horsecar. A horsecar ride was smoother, cheaper, and—at seven miles per hour in ideal circumstances—usually faster than a ride on an omnibus. But by all accounts, a horsecar trip was every bit as disagreeable as an omnibus trip. Cars were unheated in winter, sweltering in the summer, and bulging with passengers no matter what the season. A New York horsecar, if one could "stomach it," Mark Twain wrote, guaranteed a commute of at least forty-five minutes, no matter what the distance, and was so crowded that people clung to the exterior platforms of the cars by their "eyelashes and . . . toenails."

Packed with commuters, the omnibuses and horsecars were, in turn, packing the city's streets. By the mid-1860s twenty-nine omnibus lines, comprising 671 vehicles, and fourteen horsecar lines, operating nearly 300 cars, were in service, and most circulated in lower Manhattan. Adding to this vehicular crush were drays, carts, hackneys, and private carriages, not to mention the thousands of horses and mules that served as pulling power. By one estimate in 1866, nearly 18,000 vehicles per day traveled up and down lower Broadway. Although these figures were probably inflated—a year later one patient *New York Tribune* reporter counted some 13,000—other statistics indicated that the city's traffic glut was indeed cause for alarm. In the first six months of 1866 alone, twenty-five people were killed by omnibuses and horsecars, and approximately five hundred nonfatal accidents were attributed annually to the vehicles.

In 1863 London, the first city to build a subway, had demonstrated that an underground transit system was feasible, efficient, and safe. When Hugh B. Willson, a Michigan railroad man, proposed building a similar system in New York City in 1864,

A New York City horsecar, 1867.

he was laughed out of the State Legislature. Two years later, however, Albany buckled under public pressure and appointed a commission to investigate ways of bringing rapid transit to New York. In June 1866 the commission advertised for plans and suggestions from the public; by October more than thirty proposals had been submitted and almost all were designs for transit systems that avoided the congested surface of the city's streets. If New Yorkers wanted *rapid* transit, the proposals overwhelmingly indicated, they would have to travel above the city's traffic on elevated tracks or below it in underground trains.

Of all the underground proposals received by the commission, the most novel was the plan for the Arcade Railway, designed by a collaborative of engineers headed by Egbert Ludovicus Viele. No mere tunnel, this subway system incorporated four tracks, subterranean promenades, and a shopper's paradise fifteen feet beneath Broadway along an arcade that reached from the Battery to 219th Street. "Twenty minutes to Harlem!" promised Viele in a promotional leaflet that showed express trains powered by steam locomotives traveling on the inside tracks of the Arcade Railway at fifteen miles per hour. On the outside tracks, "way," or local, trains poked along at five miles per hour, stopping

at stations at the request of passengers. Edging the twelve-and-a-half-mile-long route were several hundred stores, created in what formerly had been "valueless cellars," and a continuous promenade for shoppers and strollers. In its beauty and utility, Viele envisioned the subterranean corridor as "surpassing any other street in the world."

Scientific American foresaw the Arcade Railway as becoming "an attraction to out of town visitors second only to that of the Great Central Park," a bittersweet accolade for Viele, whose 1856 design for the park was discarded in favor of Olmsted and Vaux's "Greensward" plan. In fact, the Arcade Railway was altogether an unusual venture for Viele, who by 1866 was better known for his work above ground. Born in upstate New York in 1825, Viele hailed from an established Dutch family that had hoped he would follow in the footsteps of his father, a former state senator, and study law. But Viele embarked instead on a military career. In the 1850s, with engineering skills acquired in the U.S. Army, he reentered civilian life and opened an engineering practice in New York City. By the 1860s he had prepared topographical surveys of Central Park and

Cross section of the proposed Arcade Railway. Egbert L. Viele, chief engineer, 1866. View is north, up Broadway, from the corner of Wall Street.

RIGHT:
Egbert Ludovicus Viele, c. 1865.

Prospect Park, and a geodetic survey of the state of New Jersey, and was at work on a study of the original topography of Manhattan Island. What prompted Viele to descend into the bowels of Manhattan he did not say.

As hungry as New Yorkers were for rapid transit in 1866, not all could accept the idea of the Arcade Railway. Some people believed that the trains' vibrations would topple the steeple of Trinity Church. The *New York Times* worried about passengers surviving the "unwholesome vapors" emitted by the steam locomotives, and with good cause, since the only provisions for ventilation in the scheme consisted of open gratings set into the sidewalks at intervals along Broadway. But the person most agitated by the plan for the Arcade Railway was the department store magnate Alexander T. Stewart, who owned two huge dry goods emporiums on Broadway—the wondrous "Marble Palace," America's first department store, still standing on the corner of Chambers and Reade streets—and an equally imposing structure at Ninth Street. Although Viele had taken great pains to explain that excavation and construction of the railway were to be carried out simultaneously at several points along its projected route, and would be covered with temporary bridges to minimize obstruction of traffic, it was apparently not enough to placate Stewart. The thought of months, maybe years, of noisy construction and a dearth of customers, only to end with a competitor right in his own basement, prompted Stewart to testify against the underground plan before the Senate Railroad Committee. In a statement one imagines was accompanied by some fist-pounding, Stewart said: "Why the loss to the business interest, gentlemen, would be millions of dollars. Millions of dollars!" Stewart allegedly ended up spending close to that to kill the plan.

But it wasn't Stewart who put an end to the subway scheme. In 1870, after passage in both the Assembly and the Senate, the bill authorizing construction of the Arcade Railway was vetoed by Governor John T. Hoffman. In his veto message, Hoffman acknowledged that New York was in dire need of rapid transit, but in his judgment the Arcade Railway was a "new and untried experiment . . . a visionary project," which if approved would, in the short run, interrupt business and travel on Broadway, and in the long run, set a dangerous precedent of giving city property to a private corporation.

Rapid transit advocates were disappointed by Hoffman's decision but hardly surprised. It was no secret that Hoffman, mayor of New York City from 1866 to 1868, had been helped to the governorship by William Marcy Tweed, the most powerful, corrupt, and slippery politician New York State had ever seen. It was also no secret that Tweed intended to build a viaduct railway of massive stone arches, forty feet high, running the length of Manhattan Island—a scheme that had unlimited potential for hefty kickbacks, bogus contracts, and shady deals,

all of which were Tweed's specialties. Predictably, after vetoing the Arcade plan, Hoffman affixed his signature to a bill authorizing the Viaduct Railway Company to begin construction.

In his long political career, Tweed had held many positions, sometimes several at once, including president of the Department of Public Works, state senator, and New York City school commissioner. His unofficial title was "Boss" Tweed, and his most lucrative job came as leader of a handful of highly placed city officials who together were known as "the Ring." The figures vary, but it has been estimated that between 1861 and 1871 Tweed and his cohorts quietly stuffed their pockets with anywhere from $30 million to $200 million, a large chunk of that coming from the construction of the County Courthouse in City Hall Park, which on paper cost $12 million to build but in reality tallied little more than $3 million. The Viaduct Railway was an open-ended opportunity for even greater Ring skullduggery. For starters, the act signed by Hoffman granted the company $5 million from the city treasury and exemption from all taxes and assessments. Moreover, the company was authorized to build the hulking elevated structure along any roads or avenues it saw fit, and was empowered to condemn and raze anything in its path. Tweed must have been delirious with greedy joy.

But Tweed never got a chance to pull off this swindle, because in October 1871, just six months after the Viaduct bill was signed into law, the Ring was toppled, and the Viaduct scheme disappeared. Variations on the Arcade plan, on the other hand, reappeared almost yearly throughout the 1870s and 1880s. After its initial failure, in 1870, however, Viele disengaged himself from the underground project and returned to more familiar territory. In 1874 he published the *Topographical Atlas of the City of New York,* which became an indispensable reference work for a new breed of builders—skyscraper architects—and in the early 1880s he served as city parks commissioner. Viele was probably not counting, but between 1864, the year Hugh B. Willson proposed the first underground railway for New York City, and 1902, the year Viele died, sixteen companies received charters to build a subway in

Cross section showing Egbert L. Viele's proposed method of construction for the Arcade Railway. Here work crews excavate below Broadway, near Saint Paul's Chapel, while traffic rolls unimpeded over temporary iron bridges.

Construction of the County Courthouse (sometimes called the Tweed Courthouse), as viewed from Chambers Street, 1871.

Manhattan. Only one system managed to transcend public opposition, political scams, and technological drawbacks: the Broadway IRT.

Most New Yorkers who pressed through the subway turnstiles in 1904 for their first underground ride had only an inkling of the IRT's protracted birth. Many were undoubtedly saying precisely what Viele had so optimistically prophesied for the Arcade Railway in the 1860s: "When it shall have been completed and thronged through all hours of the day and night, instead of being regarded as singular in conception and a wonder in execution, the only marvel will be why it was not done before."

In January 1867 the New York State Legislature granted the inventor Charles T. Harvey a charter to erect an experimental stretch of elevated railroad on Greenwich Street, between the Battery and Morris Street. Harvey lost no time getting to work; before the year's end, a quarter-mile section of the world's first elevated transit system was constructed and in operation. Initially, New Yorkers approached the "air-line" with trepidation. "This narrow road of five feet across runs along the tops of the pillars; and as you look up at it you protest it has a remarkable acrobatic, airy and perched-up appearance," said a New York Times *editorial in early 1868. "The truth is, a man is apt to feel cowardly on the first sight of that railway—or rather of its rudiments. But this weakness should be overcome. We don't see why this sort of traveling by post should be more deadly than the general run of railway travel."*

By the early 1870s the el reached all the way to Thirtieth Street via Greenwich Avenue and its extension, Ninth Avenue. Acquired from Harvey in 1871 by the New York Elevated Company, and converted from cable to steam power, the system sped commuters uptown or downtown over a two-mile-long route in a mere fifteen minutes, a time that by comparison made a ride in an omnibus or a horsecar over the same distance seem an eternity. In the 1870s, as subway proponents produced schemes for subterranean systems, another group of rapid transit advocates looked to the city's long avenues and imagined them straddled with miles of elevated tracks.

Manhattan seemed strangely quiet in October 1872. The usual ceaseless rumble of iron and wooden wheels rolling over the city's cobblestone streets had been reduced to an isolated clatter. Heavy hooves echoed grimly in the deserted streets, and the strident shouts of impatient omnibus drivers, normally lost in a larger cacophony, were eerily distinct: New York City, swept by distemper, was virtually horseless.

By Halloween the disease had passed "from stable to stable with a silent and mysterious rapidity," reported the *New York Times,* striking fifteen thousand of the animals and paralyzing the city of a million people that functioned almost solely on the strength of horsepower. Grocers, bakers, and butchers, unable to receive or deliver goods, closed up shop. Fire engines and ambulances were temporarily laid to rest, with prayers that their services would not be needed. One by one, omnibus and horsecar operators were forced to pull their weakened teams off the streets and sequester them in uptown stables, leaving thousands of workers no choice but to walk to work in the morning and wearily trudge back home at night. Companies that attempted to work an ill horse—and several did—were likely to be relinquished of their property by officers of the American Society for the Prevention of Cruelty to Animals, who stood posted at street

Charles T. Harvey makes a test run along a section of his elevated railroad as onlookers watch from the corner of Greenwich and Morris streets, c. 1867. When the line opened to the public, enclosed box cars replaced the experimental vehicle Harvey is seen operating here.

corners on the lookout for the telltale drooping head and deep cough of a stricken animal. Still, there being more street corners than officers, hundreds of ailing horses escaped the watchful eye of the ASPCA, only to collapse and die in the streets, where they lay decomposing until the wagons of the Rendering Company made their rounds.

By mid-November the disease had run its course. No official death tally was to be had, for the Rendering Company refused to open its books, but some estimated that more than two thousand horses, from thick-limbed nags to "high-bred teams of up-

town fashionables," had succumbed to the epidemic. Economically the four-week disease had added up to a "commercial calamity," declared the *World*. Indeed, in the aftermath of the epidemic, many New Yorkers were questioning the wisdom of running a metropolis on the uncertain element of horsepower when other forms of transportation were readily available and infinitely more dependable, the proof of that being the infant New York Elevated line. Throughout the month-long scourge, while horsecar and omnibus service disintegrated, the packed cars of the elevated, powered by steam locomotives, had faithfully rolled overhead between lower Manhattan and Thirtieth Street.

Pronouncing horse-drawn transportation as "antique," the *New York Times* was the first to renew the perennial cry for a comprehensive rapid

At the height of the distemper epidemic in 1871, Henry Bergh, founder of the American Society for the Prevention of Cruelty to Animals, instructs a horsecar driver to remove his ailing team from the streets.

transit system. "The recent distemper among horses, which threatened at one time to leave our citizens without any mode of conveyance to and from their places of business, has brought home to all the absolute necessity that something in the way of quick transit should be undertaken by someone and carried forward without delay," said an exasperated editorial. Of the dozen or so transit plans circulating in 1872, the only one the newspaper saw as holding any immediate promise was an elevated system designed by Dr. Rufus Gilbert, who had received authorization from the State Legislature in June 1872 to begin construction. Gilbert's scheme not only dispensed with horsepower, it went beyond the realm of steam power, proposing to whoosh riders uptown and downtown by the force of pneumatic air in circular cars, eight feet in diameter, through iron tubes. Hoping to make the system as attractive as it would be efficient, Gilbert encased

the tubes in a series of ornate Gothic arches that soared twenty-four feet above the street from cast-iron Corinthian columns. To reach the tubes, passengers had merely to step into one of the pneumatic elevators located at each station, spaced one-half mile apart.

The *Times* lauded Gilbert's scheme as "an ornament to the streets" and prophesied that it would surely become "the pride and boast of the people riding along the line," an endorsement that must have cheered Gilbert, because his friends and family were convinced he had gone crazy. Educated at the College of Physicians and Surgeons in New

Scheme for a pneumatically powered elevated system. Dr. Rufus Gilbert, 1872.

Dr. Rufus Gilbert, c. 1865.

York City, and decorated in the Civil War for performing the first surgical operation ever executed under fire, Gilbert had unexpectedly abandoned medicine in the mid-1860s at the peak of his career to experiment with transportation. But as it turned out, the doctor's sudden interest in the science of moving people was not unrelated to the science of healing people. Rapid transit, Gilbert believed, was potentially the most effective antidote to cholera, typhus, and smallpox, spawned in the crowded and befouled slums of lower Manhattan that the poor had no way of fleeing. Cheap, swift transportation, Gilbert reasoned, would enable thousands of people to take up residence in northern Manhattan, where sunshine, clean air, and pure water were all to be had in abundance.

Working through six alternative designs, Gilbert arrived at his fanciful Gothic scheme in the late

BELOW:
Sixth Avenue elevated station at West Fourteenth Street, c. 1879.

1860s and paired it with a pneumatic tube system, for which he secured a patent in 1870. In 1872, at the age of forty, Gilbert had no other ambition than to see his plan become a reality. But any chances the inventor might have had in finding capital for the project were dimmed by the financial panic of 1873 and by the depression that followed. Throughout 1874 and most of 1875, Gilbert was unable to find investors who would take a chance on his pneumatic transit system. Meanwhile, he watched enviously as the New York Elevated Company moved ahead with plans to build new tracks up Ninth Avenue from Thirtieth Street to Fifty-ninth Street.

Gilbert's elevated line was saved, albeit minus its Gothic splendor, by the Rapid Transit Commission, created in 1875 to establish future transit routes and fare schedules. In September 1875 the commission authorized the New York Elevated Company to build a new line along Third Avenue. To the only other existing chartered company, the Gilbert Elevated Railway, it parceled out Second

and Sixth avenues as routes—on the condition that the doctor give up his madcap notion of pneumatic tubes and Gothic arches for a more conventional design.

Gilbert's Gothic vision died then and there. After three disheartening years trying to sell a scheme no one was interested in, Gilbert was ready to design a plan, any plan, that investors would agree to finance. Thus, the tubes, the round cars, and the ornamental arches were traded in for stanchions, tracks, and box cars. Steam locomotives replaced the proposed pneumatic system, and stairs were built instead of elevators. But Gilbert did manage to sneak a little Gothicism into his plan. When the Sixth Avenue line opened in 1878, passengers alighted at cottage-like, Victorian Gothic stations, each of which was a small marvel of gables, decorative grillwork, and gingerbread, painted a delicate green. Gilbert's whimsical stamp remained imprinted on New York's cityscape until the late 1930s, when the Sixth Avenue elevated line and the stations were torn down.

About 1870, encouraged by his company's booming volume of local sales, Alfred Speer, a wealthy inventor and wine merchant from Passaic, New Jersey, established an office and a wine emporium on lower Broadway, near City Hall, to capture the New York market. For business there was no better place to be. Famed for its shops, fine hotels, art galleries, and amusement halls, Broadway was the city's busiest thoroughfare, and its great tide of humanity kept the small brass bell above Speer's door ringing all day long. But if the swirl of crowds, traffic, and noise outside his store spelled dollars to Speer the merchant, to Speer the inventor the unceasing chaos pointed to Broadway's most pressing need: rapid transit.

By the 1870s a number of transit schemes had been proposed for Broadway—and felled. In 1846 John Randel, Jr., (best remembered as the surveyor charged with laying out Manhattan's 1811 street plan) suggested building an elevated train system,

powered by cable, from the Battery to Fourteenth Street. The city fathers summarily rejected the project, arguing that it "would no doubt destroy the appearance of the street, as well as drive citizens entirely from it." In the 1850s horsecar companies were repeatedly frustrated in their attempts to obtain charters to lay iron rails along the celebrated thoroughfare. Eventually, over the objections of Broadway merchants, who were loath to see the city's premier shopping street scarred with tracks, and despite the vociferous protest of the omnibus operators who monopolized transportation on Broadway, one horsecar company was authorized to build a line north of Fourteenth Street. But that still left commuters with a traffic-choked, three-mile-long stretch between Fourteenth Street and the Battery to negotiate by omnibus. When Egbert L. Viele in 1866 proposed building a subway system that would burrow beneath the congested surface of Broadway, he won the support of the State Leg-

Design for an endless traveling train. Alfred Speer, 1873.

Alfred Speer, c. 1880.

omnibus), a conductor would set the small car in motion, and, quickly accelerating, bring it to the speed of twelve miles per hour to reach the inner, perpetually moving belt, where passengers would be deposited.

No more time lost stopping to talk to friends on the street! Once on the pleasant promenade of the endless moving loop, conversation could be conducted walking, standing, or sitting while traveling to one's destination. Wooden benches ringing the loop's perimeter were perfect spots for a chat and certainly the best seats in town for a bird's-eye view of Broadway's hustle and bustle. In the event of a sudden rainstorm or during cold weather, men could remove to the cozy confines of one of several Smoking Rooms located on the inner moving belt, and women to one of the Ladies' Drawing Rooms, all of which were to be outfitted with a "warming apparatus."

No more lungfuls of smoke or sudden earaches! This system, run by underground steam engines, was to be as quiet as it was clean. Not only did it dispense with thundering locomotives that gushed cinders and heavy black smoke, the tracks utilized by the transfer cars were to be bedded in rubber bearings, and the wheels covered with hide to keep noise to a minimum. The total cost of this superior system: $3,722,400.00.

Speer sold the State Legislature on the proposal, but not Governor John Dix, who vetoed the scheme in 1873 because the elevated protruded over Broadway's sidewalks. Speer shifted the loop several feet inward toward the center of the street, whereupon the legislature was ready to hand the inventor another charter. But Dix was not so easy to please. Even though Peter Cooper, founder of the Cooper Union and a widely respected businessman, offered $100,000 to build an experimental section of Speer's system, Dix vetoed the plan again in 1874, this time on the grounds that the huge oval crossed Broadway twice. Speer puzzled a little over that reasoning and then realized he was stuck: if it didn't cross Broadway twice it wasn't a loop; if it wasn't a loop the system wouldn't be endless; if it wasn't endless, then, as far as the inventor was concerned, it wasn't rapid transit.

islature, but not that of Governor John T. Hoffman, who later quashed the plan.

Speer undoubtedly knew of the unsuccessful attempts to provide improved transit on lower Broadway, but in 1873, undeterred, he boarded a train for Albany, prepared to "convert and convince the incredulous." He carried with him a working model, a sheaf of plans, and construction cost sheets figured to the last dollar for his "endless traveling train," patented in 1871. Here was "the solution, and the only true solution of rapid transit," Speer boasted. Imagine a giant elevated loop, propelled by cables, encircling lower Broadway nonstop from dawn until 1:00 A.M. No more insufferable trips in an omnibus! To get uptown or downtown, all one had to do was head for the nearest corner and climb the stairs to the elevated station, where exactly every fifty seconds a "transfer car" would pull up to take in passengers. After collecting the nickel fare (five cents less than it cost to ride in an

A stock certificate for Speer's proposed transit system.

Speer rolled up his plans and took them home to Passaic, obviously stung by the rejection of so splendid an invention. If New York didn't want his scheme, he would find another city that did. But where? In a surge of inspiration, Speer whisked out pen and paper and with a few quick strokes incorporated the New Jersey towns of Passaic, Paterson, and Newark, annexed Staten Island, and developed a port that made New York's seem inconsequential. Speer called this proud new city Metropolis; its transportation system, of course, was the endless traveling loop. While he was at it, Speer also created the American Rapid Transit Company to construct and operate the elevated, and even went so far as to print stock certificates of $100 shares, each illustrated with a miniature picture of the endless loop running on the New Jersey side of the Hudson River.

But Speer, never at a loss for new ideas, soon abandoned his scheme for Metropolis and the endless traveling loop, and turned to other projects.

By 1888 the inventor had secured patents for a piano with four keyboards, an outdoor electric clock, and a monorail that hurtled along a track at 120 miles per hour. For the growing mill town of Passaic, he installed electric street lamps, built sidewalks, and established a weekly newspaper. In what became an annual summer tradition until his death in 1910, Speer treated the children of Passaic to a carefree day of rides, cotton candy, and ocean breezes at Luna Park on Coney Island.

By 1885 on lower Broadway, meanwhile, rails for a horsecar line had been laid between the Battery and Fourteenth Street, and the reign of the omnibus had come to a close. Elsewhere in Manhattan, elevated lines were in operation along Second, Third, Sixth, and Ninth avenues, providing rapid transit from one end of the island to the other, and carrying a willing population north to live in areas that had formerly lain outside a convenient commute by omnibus or horsecar. The el, however, was a two-headed beast. While it stimulated the development of pleasant residential neighborhoods, it transformed the city's avenues into long, dark tunnels and created miles of slums along its path. In exchange for speed, New Yorkers had to contend with the constant clatter of wheels overhead and with snorting locomotives that spewed sparks, ashes, and grease into the air. (The elevated lines were not electrified until the early 1900s.) Most disillusioning of all, the el, that great shining hope of rapid transit, could not keep pace with the expansion it had helped to nurture. In 1880 sixty million passengers rode the 32½-mile system. By 1890 ridership had more than tripled to 186 million riders, but the elevated system had not grown an inch.

It would take the work of two rapid transit commissions, the perseverance of engineer William Barclay Parsons, and the capital of financier August Belmont before New York built its first subway. On March 24, 1900, to the wild cheers of thousands of onlookers, Mayor Robert Van Wyck stuck a Tiffany shovel into the ground near City Hall and dug up what the *New York Herald* proclaimed the "most important bit of earth removed from the surface of Manhattan Island since the turf was pierced for the foundations of the first civilized dwelling." With that, construction of the Interborough Rapid Transit system was begun.

When the Broadway IRT subway line opened on the evening of October 27, 1904, 125,000 curious New Yorkers stormed the stations to make their first subterranean trip. Most were wholly unprepared for the sensation of speeding underground at thirty-five miles per hour. Streaking by platforms, pillars, and station masters, passengers rubbed their eyes in bewilderment, trying to absorb the "mad dance of flying shadows past the car windows." Motormen, rushing the trains through a circus of colored signal lights, felt as if they were "jumping into the quick-opening jaws of some jeweled monster." More than a few riders worried they would suffocate from lack of air. But once they grew accustomed to underground travel, New Yorkers unanimously praised the new system as "one of the greatest public works of the city," and pronounced its service "excellent." An especially enthralled passenger swore he would "rather ride in the subway than eat home-made apple pie."

That was in 1904. Only six years later New Yorkers were grumbling about the system. One rider characterized conditions on the IRT as "vile and dangerous," and predicted that subway travel would soon be attempted by only "the most hardy" of commuters. Others criticized the system for its limited reach, even though by 1910 the IRT extended to the western part of the Bronx and to Brooklyn Heights. As Max E. Schmidt saw it, the

IRT's greatest flaw was its rigid north-south plan, which in Manhattan subjected commuters to either a long walk across town or to an extra fare on a bus or a trolley. Schmidt knew something about transportation, having designed the three-speed continuously moving platform that had been such a hit at Chicago's Columbian Exposition in 1893. While less adventuresome souls stuck to the gondolas that glided in and around the fair's inlets and canals, some three million visitors screwed up their courage and learned to step from one moving belt to the next, landing triumphantly in seats for a breezy ride along a pier that jutted out a half mile into Lake Michigan. In November 1893, just six months after the fair opened, the *Street Railway Review* proclaimed Schmidt's traveling platform an enormous success:

> The great crowds carried without a single incident have, with one acclaim, voted the moving sidewalk the most satisfactory enjoyment of the Exposition. The cheap fare and long ride, the comfortable seats, the safety, and the ease of mounting and dismounting, conspired to make it the Mecca of tired humanity at all hours of the day.

In 1910 Schmidt saw no reason why his invention could not be adapted for use in New York City—right under Thirty-fourth Street—and for that matter, eventually beneath all the major crosstown

The moving platform, designed by Max E. Schmidt, at the World's Columbian Exposition, Chicago, 1893.

streets. Schmidt undoubtedly settled on Thirty-fourth Street as the inaugural stretch for his projected moving platform network because the opening of Pennsylvania Station that year guaranteed a never-ending stream of crosstown customers. Then, too, there was a new generation of midtown department stores—R. H. Macy's, B. Altman's, and Best & Company—which in the early 1900s had moved from the Ladies' Mile shopping district to relocate in the Thirty-fourth Street area, on or near Fifth Avenue. What weary shopper laden with parcels wouldn't welcome a quiet, comfortable ride beneath Manhattan's long crosstown blocks?

Schmidt apparently had an inordinate faith in the logistics of his system and in the ability of New Yorkers to master it. Somehow he believed seventy thousand people per hour could descend into stations placed a block apart from river to river along Thirty-fourth Street, and without hesitating, stumbling, or bunching step from a rubber-topped platform that moved at three miles per hour to one that moved at six miles per hour, reach the wooden benches traveling at nine miles per hour, and casually sit down and open a book. To exit at one of the stations, passengers would simply reverse the process, ideally without bumping into riders just getting on.

The machinery to keep 140,000 legs in constant motion was to lie beneath the platform in a concrete trough, six feet deep, that ran the length of Thirty-fourth Street. Like the IRT, the elevateds, and many metropolitan railroad lines in 1910, Schmidt's scheme dispensed with old-fashioned steam power in favor of electricity, provided in this plan by ten-horse-power motors mounted every seventy-five feet on the floor of the platform bed. The motors, turning a series of transverse shafts, propelled thousands of driving wheels of various sizes that determined the speed of each moving platform. To keep the motion of the platform both smooth and silent, the wheels were to be cushioned in rubber.

In late January 1910 Schmidt presented his plans to the Public Service Commission; the two-and-a-half-mile-long moving platform did not leap to the top of the commission's list of priorities. The commission had more pressing tasks at hand—namely, planning and monitoring the extension of the city's infant subway system into Queens, Brooklyn, and the Bronx, a job that was complicated in 1911 when the Brooklyn Rapid Transit Company (BRT) suddenly jumped into the ring, ready to fight it out with the IRT for control of the proposed new routes. Schmidt's plan languished while the commission, the IRT, and the BRT (now the BMT) negotiated for a mutually satisfactory division of the coveted territory.

Approval in July 1911 of the Dual System, as the final IRT-BRT arrangement was called, ultimately spelled the end of Schmidt's scheme. In drawing up plans for the Thirty-fourth Street stop at Sixth Avenue, BRT engineers discovered that, as proposed, Schmidt's crosstown platform would intersect the station. Since both projects were designed to stay as close to the street's surface as possible, for the two systems to coexist either the BRT would have to sink its station four feet deeper—a hugely expensive alternative—or Schmidt would have to revise his scheme substantially to make the moving platform feasible at a grade far below street level. The BRT, firmly opposed to digging deeper, refused to move its station. Schmidt, also unwilling to go deeper, had no option but to withdraw his proposal. But transit officials had not seen the last of Schmidt; in 1922 he would be back.

Plan for an underground moving platform along Thirty-fourth Street. Max E. Schmidt, 1910.

The original Broadway IRT route, once aptly described as resembling "the crank of an old Ford," ran from City Hall up the East Side to Grand Central Terminal, where it veered west along Forty-second Street to Times Square and continued its way north under Broadway. When the first stretch of the Lexington IRT was added to the subway system in 1917, new stations were added north of Grand Central, and the Broadway route was extended south along Seventh Avenue, giving the city separate East Side and West Side subway lines. The former crosstown spur of the Broadway IRT became the Grand Central–Times Square shuttle.

Detail of a sterling silver tray engraved with the original route of the Broadway IRT subway system. The tray, now in the collection of the Museum of the City of New York, belonged to the financier August Belmont, whose capital enabled the construction of New York's first subway system.

The shuttle opened on August 1, 1918, to mass confusion. Passengers in search of a train swarmed the underground corridors trying to find their way through a maze of new entrances, exits, turns, and stairways with not a sign to guide them. Despite subway guards who barked out directions into the noisy crowd, hundreds of disoriented riders boarded the wrong train or made a full circle, ending up right where they had started from. Many finally gave up, reported the *New York Tribune,* "and returned to the street—when they could find their way out."

Two days later, the shuttle closed down for six weeks while directional signs were installed. But even when the system reopened, sporting new color-coded markers on the walls to make navigation of the underground labyrinth easier, the crosstown line did not get glowing reviews. For one thing,

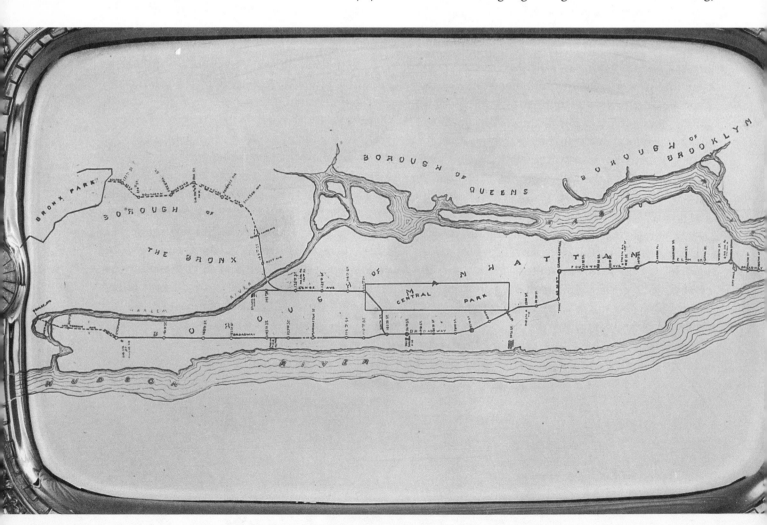

riders complained, the walk between the Lexington IRT line and the shuttle was ridiculously long. For another, once on the train for the half-mile trip, the crowded conditions were enough to make one envy "the sardine his commodious can."

In 1922 Max E. Schmidt reappeared, with just the remedy for the shuttle's ills—his continually moving platform. In place of the crowded shuttle cars, riders would find a procession of upholstered benches that traveled nonstop along a system of conveyor belts. There would never be a wait to get across town and everyone was guaranteed a seat. Or so Schmidt envisioned it. One New Yorker, who more realistically pictured a mad stampede for the benches, advised commuters to "take a half hour off, visit a department store somewhere and practice mounting and dismounting an escalator. Such training may help to beat the other fellow to the first seat on the moving platform." But no such training was necessary. Schmidt's proposed $10-million system was rejected by transit officials as too costly.

During the following decades, the shuttle became a favorite do-it-yourself project for fed-up commuters, who mentally redesigned the crosstown line on their way to and from work. One rider suggested running trains on only two of the three tracks and constructing a continually moving sidewalk between them. Another proposed doing away with the shuttle altogether and instituting a system of small cars drawn by electric locomotives that would operate in passageways beneath Forty-second Street. Several people recommended extending the line from river to river, an idea that made particular sense in the 1940s, after it was announced that the United Nations would be built on the East River at Forty-second Street. But by 1947 the only major physical improvement the shuttle had undergone since its inauguration in 1918 was the construction of a concrete walk at the Grand Central end of the station, which replaced an old wooden platform.

In 1951 the Goodyear Tire and Rubber Company came up with a plan that to many commuters seemed to be more the stuff of amusement parks than serious big-city transit. Under the Goodyear proposal, instead of sprinting for Track 1, 3, or 4 (the mysterious Track 2 has lain buried beneath the platform ever since 1918), riders would simply step onto a six-foot-wide traveling sidewalk that moved at one and a half miles per hour, slip into a transparent bubble-topped car that moved on a parallel conveyor belt, and be zipped across town at fifteen miles per hour in just two minutes. At the other end of the line, exiting passengers would hop out onto another moving sidewalk before the car turned around at the head of the loop-shaped system to take in new passengers and make the return trip.

Sidney H. Bingham, chairman of the city's Board of Transportation, was intrigued by the Goodyear scheme and promptly had several experts investigate its feasibility, a move that was applauded by the *New York Times*, which was a near neighbor to the Seventh Avenue end of the shuttle line. "We have put up with an atrocity in this shuttle for many years," said a *Times* editorial. "This time let's fix it right."

By 1953 it looked as if the $5-million shuttle would be built, bubble tops and all. After the Transit Authority (successor to the Board of Transportation) invited contract bids for the conveyor belts and 130 cars, officials announced that the two-year transformation would begin before 1954 was out. They even promised that riding this small slice of transit fun would not cost more than the existing fifteen-cent fare.

If shuttle veterans thought the plan sounded too good to be true, they were right. In September 1955 Charles Patterson, chairman of the Transit Authority, declared that he was not convinced the crosstown shuttle belt was economically feasible or even necessary. Some months later the Transit Authority announced it would modernize the system at a lesser cost.

And modernize it did. In the late 1950s a plan was unveiled to run the world's first fully automated passenger train on Track 4. The train was to be operated solely by a system of electrical relays that would start and stop the train, slow it down, accelerate it, and open and close all doors. Preparations for the new train began in May 1961.

ARCADE
WITH
MOVING · PLATFORM

Scheme for the Forty-second
Street shuttle. Max. E.
Schmidt, 1922.

RIGHT:
The loading area of the pro-
posed replacement for the
Forty-second Street shuttle.
Goodyear Tire and Rubber
Company, 1951.

Detail of the proposed shuttle car. Goodyear Tire and Rubber Company, 1951.

When it appeared that the Transit Authority was actually going to go ahead with the plan, Michael Quill, the fiery president of the Transport Workers Union, threatened to call a general strike of the city's thirty thousand transit employees and also of eight thousand private bus employees. A compromise was reached, whereby the "headless horseman," as Quill called the three-car train, would be attended by union motormen, albeit only symbolically.

The automatic shuttle train began service in 1962 under what was to be a six-month trial period. Two years later the train was still in operation, and it might still be running today had it not been destroyed by the worst fire in New York's subway history, which swept the Grand Central end of the shuttle on April 21, 1964. The train was never replaced.

In 1966 the shuttle line and end stations were repainted, retiled, and relit. Shuttling across town, however, was—and remains—hardly any different than in 1918. Despite the S signs posted here and there, strangers to the subway system still lose their way, and the walk from the Lexington IRT line to the shuttle has become no shorter. Nor has the shuttle scramble disappeared with the years. Racing through the station, dodging people and pillars, hauling briefcases or suitcases, most riders reach the crosstown line harried and breathless, only to find that the train is not going anywhere for another several minutes.

Although New York City was hooked up to a transcontinental railroad network and was ringed with a necklace of ship terminals, it was miserably unprepared for the age of aviation. In 1927, the year Charles Lindbergh electrified the world with his solo transatlantic flight, approximately one thousand airfields were scattered across the United States. New York City could claim one: Miller Field, a military airstrip on Staten Island.

In 1931 New York opened its first municipal airport, Floyd Bennett Field, in Brooklyn, named for the pilot who with Richard Byrd in 1926 made the first flight over the North Pole. The city might have limped along for years with only Miller Field and the Brooklyn airport, had it not been for Mayor Fiorello H. La Guardia, an early enthusiast of air travel, who saw to it that a second municipal airport was built in Queens. Shortly after its dedication, in October 1939, the airport was renamed in honor of La Guardia. Idlewild (later renamed John F. Kennedy International Airport) was also developed during La Guardia's administration. The first section of what would become a sprawling complex of 4,900 acres of landfill in Jamaica Bay, Queens, opened in 1942.

But long before the first planes taxied down the runways at La Guardia and Idlewild, and even before Bennett Field was laid out, a former automobile executive proposed building a most unusual airport right in the heart of Manhattan.

The contest to build the world's tallest building was serious—and sneaky—business. When John J. Raskob, vice-president of Empire State, Inc., announced his intent in August 1929 to put up an eighty-story, 1,000-foot tower on Thirty-fourth Street and Fifth Avenue, he snatched the tallest-skyscraper title from the Chrysler Building, slated to top out on Forty-second Street and Lexington Avenue at 925 feet. Still, despite the 75-foot lead, Raskob was edgy. "Raskob was worried Walter Chrysler would pull a trick—like hiding a rod in the spire and then sticking it up at the last minute," recalled Hamilton Weber, the rental manager for the Empire State Building. This is precisely what Chrysler did. In October 1929 a stainless steel lance that had been secretly constructed inside the tower was hoisted up and out, giving the Chrysler Building a total height of 1,046 feet and leaving Raskob clutching plans for the world's second-tallest building.

Not to be outdone, Raskob swiftly responded to this stunt by instructing his architects to immediately raise the Empire State Building to eighty-five stories. But that was small revenge, for at eighty-five stories the skyscraper would be only 4 feet higher than the Chrysler Building, hardly a figure that would fire the public's imagination. Then Raskob had the most extraordinary idea. He would plant a 200-foot mooring mast for dirigibles on top of the eighty-fifth floor, making the Empire State Building both a spectacular 1,250 feet high *and* an international airport. Now here was a building so unique that people would sit up and take notice.

Though Raskob would never have admitted it, dirigibles were not really what the mooring mast

John J. Raskob, 1928.

was about. With two million square feet of office space to rent and a $27-million loan to repay on the tail of the stock market crash, Raskob needed a marketing ploy. The mooring mast, used or unused, served that purpose perfectly. Fantastic? Maybe. But no one was going to argue with the man who had made sales history with another gimmick. In 1902, at the age of twenty-three, Raskob became secretary to Pierre S. Du Pont, president of an Ohio steel concern. Du Pont later joined the family gunpowder company, which due to World War I became such a profitable business that he was able to acquire a controlling interest in General Motors. Raskob moved with him, becoming General Motors' vice-president of finance, and there he devised the installment plan for buying cars, a plan that revolutionized the automobile industry and earned the young executive fame and fortune. Obviously, when it came to selling a product, Raskob knew what he was talking about.

The architecture firm that accommodated Raskob's fits of inspiration with almost mythical patience was Shreve, Lamb & Harmon. The design team, headed by William Lamb, labored through sixteen versions of the Empire State Building before settling on a plan with Raskob they thought was final. If the architects were daunted by the late addition of the mooring mast, they didn't let on. All that one member of the firm had to say about the unusual commission was it "presented a problem in design quite unprecedented." This was a bit of an understatement. Somehow Lamb and his partners were to come up with a plan for a mast that would withstand a horizontal pull of fifty tons, hold mooring equipment, and provide arrival and departure areas for dirigible passengers. Furthermore, the mast was to integrate visually with the eighty-five stories already designed and, in the event the idea of mooring dirigibles was abandoned, the interior layout was to be flexible enough to function purely as a sightseeing spot. Raskob, in other words, was covering all of his bases and, as it turned out, wisely so. The age of long-distance dirigible travel, which got off to a grand start in 1928 with the transatlantic flight of the *Graf Zeppelin,* soon lost ground to the airplane and terminated alto-

gether in 1937, when the *Hindenburg* exploded at Lakehurst, New Jersey, killing thirty-six of the ninety-seven people on board.

The *Hindenburg* tragedy was unforeseen, of course, when Shreve, Lamb & Harmon sat down to grapple with Raskob's list of design specifications, all of which they managed to fulfill. With the mooring facilities of the Saint Hubert Air Field in Montreal as a model, two hundred tons of extra steel were carried from bedrock to the eighty-fifth floor to strengthen the building against wind pressure and a "ship pull" of one hundred thousand pounds. The mast itself rose from the building's top in a slender tower of aluminum, steel, and glass, framed by decorative corner piers, a design that cleverly disguised the mast's true function. Inside, beneath a conical roof, the mast housed a retractable "mooring arm," winches, control machinery, an elevator shaft, stairs, a small circular room, and, near its base, a large glassed-in hall that was surrounded by a promenade lookout. Dirigibles drifting in at night would be greeted, and guided, by a blaze of white light pouring through the columns of windows that ran along the four sides of the mast and by floodlights hidden in the building's upper-floor setbacks. To cap off this breathtaking entry to Manhattan, eight portholes at the mast's tip would shoot out mile-long streamers of light, illuminating the downtown sky and announcing to the entire city that a dirigible had arrived.

Flying to the Empire State Building would definitely not have been recommended for the faint-of-heart. After floating across the Atlantic Ocean for five days—no doubt a harrowing enough experience in itself—passengers were expected to exit the belly of an airship, a quarter of a mile above the street, by way of a narrow gangplank that led to an open balcony on the 103rd floor. Having accomplished this feat, passengers would descend a short stairway to a small room on the 102nd floor, from which they would take an elevator to the large hall at the base of the mast, on the 86th floor. Here Shreve, Lamb & Harmon envisioned glamorous lounges, a ticket agency, customs offices, and baggage rooms to serve arriving and departing dirigible passengers.

Cross section of the mooring mast. Not all of the mooring mechanisms were installed.

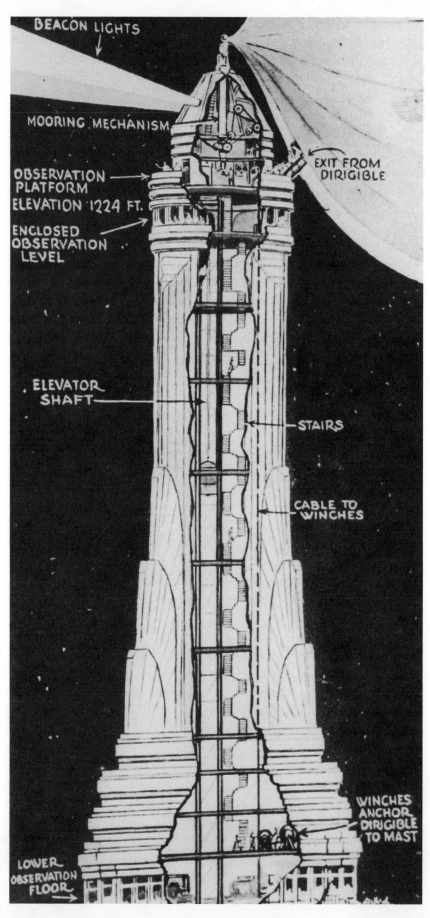

BEACON LIGHTS

MOORING MECHANISM

EXIT FROM DIRIGIBLE

OBSERVATION PLATFORM ELEVATION 1224 FT.

ENCLOSED OBSERVATION LEVEL

ELEVATOR SHAFT

STAIRS

CABLE TO WINCHES

WINCHES ANCHOR DIRIGIBLE TO MAST

LOWER OBSERVATION FLOOR

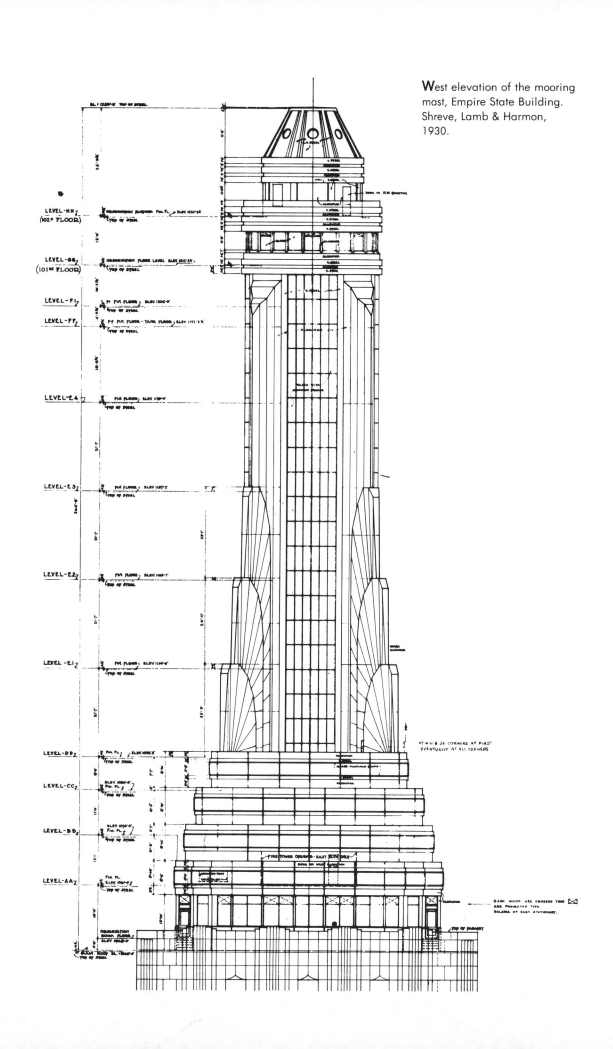

West elevation of the mooring mast, Empire State Building. Shreve, Lamb & Harmon, 1930.

The Empire State Building went up in record time. Excavation began in January 1930; ten months later the last piece of steel work for the mooring mast was mounted into place, and on May 1, 1931, the building was officially opened. At the opening ceremonies, Mayor Jimmy Walker extolled the city's sleek new skyscraper as "the most beautiful building in the world." Most people agreed with him, but some only up until the eighty-fifth floor. One critic scornfully dismissed the mooring mast as "a public comfort station for migratory birds"; someone else thought the two-hundred-foot tower was "stuck on the top as awkwardly as a thumb." Raskob couldn't have cared less what people thought about the mast, just so they talked about it. That, after all, was the point of this built-in advertisement. And it worked. People not only talked about the mast, they positively scrutinized it: from office windows, heading uptown in the el, out in the harbor, necks craned standing on street corners. The manmade tower even rivaled the heavenly bodies. "I do four or five times as much business in the daytime as I do at night," said a sidewalk astronomer, who charged a nickel a look. "People are much more curious about the mooring mast . . . than they are about the moon, and all the stars and planets."

But could the mast be used? Hugh Eckener, commander of the *Graf Zeppelin,* believed not. "Air over irregular ground is irregular," he said. "Over skyscrapers it is as rocky as can be, and particularly at the level of building tops . . . This is the worst possible air for airships. With any wind whatsoever, I should say it is almost impossibly dangerous." Nevertheless, on September 15, 1931, a Goodyear blimp, buffeted by forty-mile-per-hour winds, succeeded in tying up to the world's highest spire for three minutes. Two weeks later, in celebration of the *Evening Journal*'s thirty-fifth anniversary, another dirigible hovered near the mast long enough to lower a batch of newspapers to a man leaning out from the 103rd-floor balcony armed with a penknife to cut the delivery loose. When the same ship tried to moor a few days later, the pilot had all of midtown gaping and traffic snarled up for blocks while he maneuvered around the tip of the mast for an hour before giving up.

Throughout the autumn of 1931, virtually every blimp crew in the New York area headed the noses of their silver-skinned craft in the direction of Thirty-fourth Street and Fifth Avenue to attempt the ultimate mooring challenge. With the exception of one small ship, all failed to make contact. Eckener was right. At 1,250 feet, it was far too windy for that kind of aerial escapade. Following Raskob's alternative plans, the small room at the mast's tip was converted to the 102nd-floor observatory, and the large hall at the base of the mooring mast, never outfitted for dirigible travel, was turned over to souvenir shops and concession stands. Millions of tourists today know it as the 86th-floor observatory.

A Navy blimp nears the mooring mast, which, in this photograph, is still under construction.

BRIDGES

When the first proposals to span the Hudson and the East rivers were put forward in the early 1800s, New York City—then consisting of only Manhattan Island—could count exactly three humble bridges over its waters. Dyckman's Bridge and King's Bridge, small stone and wooden structures predating the American Revolution, crossed Spuyten Duyvil Creek at Manhattan's northern end, and a low timber draw-bridge spanned the Harlem River near what today is East 125th Street. All three bridges joined the island with the mainland, the Bronx, but they were of little service to most New Yorkers who resided, one hundred thousand strong, below Chambers Street, at Manhattan's southern tip, hemmed in on one side by the East River, on the other by the Hudson, and to the south by the bay. The only way to cross the triangular moat was by ferry. Flat-bottomed mackinaws, sloops, wherries, rafts, dinghies—in short, any vessel that wind or oar could move—served as the city's economic and social lifelines. Ice and fog frequently severed those lifelines, isolating Manhattan for days. Yet remarkably, ferries, later powered by steam, remained New York's principal link to the outside world until the opening, in 1883, of the Brooklyn Bridge, the first modern vehicular crossing to be built over New York City waters.

After the birth of Greater New York, in 1898, the city embarked on an era of frenetic bridge building that would have astounded even the ancient Romans. By 1910 arcs of steel and stone spanned the Dutch Kills, Newtown Creek, and the Gowanus Canal, and eight bridges over the Harlem River linked the shores of Manhattan and the Bronx. On the East River, the Brooklyn Bridge was joined by the Williamsburg Bridge, the Queensboro Bridge, and the Manhattan Bridge. However, the Hudson (or North River, as it was sometimes called) was not so easily conquered. Despite several attempts made between the early 1800s and the 1920s to build a bridge across the formidable barrier, six railroad tunnels and the city's first vehicular tube, the Holland Tunnel, were constructed before the George Washington Bridge was dedicated in 1931.

Bridges and tunnels eventually spelled the demise of ferry travel in New York. By 1955, after more than a hundred years of service, gone were the Christopher Street ferry to Hoboken; its elder East River cousin, the Fulton ferry; and the *Ellis Island,* which in its lifetime had carried twelve million future Americans to Manhattan's shores. In 1959 the Weehawken line was ended, and a few years later ferry service was discontinued between Staten Island and Brooklyn. The last to go were the

Jersey Central and Erie Lackawanna boats, which made their final runs across the Hudson in 1967.

Today more than seventy-five bridges span the waterways of New York City's archipelago. The youngest of these is the Verrazano-Narrows Bridge, which opened in 1964. Unless a proposal put forward by the city in 1987 to raze and replace the ailing Williamsburg Bridge is carried out, it is unlikely that a new bridge, interstate or interborough, will go up in New York. Bridges are costly to build and require large, open upland areas (increasingly scarce in the city) to accommodate approaches and connecting highways. Moreover, New York has rediscovered the ferry. In the mid-1980s, a half century after the last boat shuttled between Brooklyn and Manhattan, a small ferry began experimental runs between the South Street Seaport and Fulton Ferry Landing. The public's response was overwhelmingly enthusiastic. Since then, the fleet of boats on the Hudson and the East rivers has gradually expanded, servicing the growing number of commuters who would rather rest their elbows on a deck railing than suffer a subway ride or spend the rush-hour stuck behind a steering wheel. Of course, the pleasures of boat travel that scores of initiates are just beginning to discover have long been known to veteran passengers of New York's oldest surviving commuter line—the Staten Island ferry.

Bird's-eye view of Manhattan Island before major bridges linked it to neighboring shores, 1867.

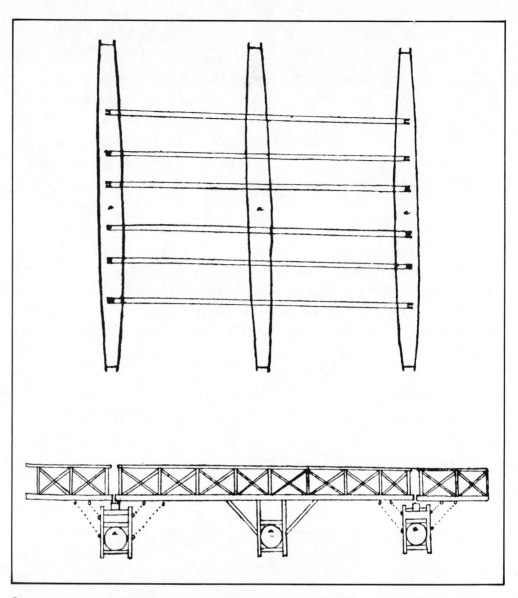

Scheme for a floating bridge, showing one of the 130 pontoon sections (top) and a detail of the stringers and anchors (bottom). John Stevens, 1805.

"It is very probable that at first view my project may appear to you as chimerical," Colonel John Stevens wrote a friend in 1805. "I confess it is with no small degree of hesitation I now venture to communicate it to you. From the prejudices which naturally arise against everything bearing the stamp of novelty, and from an aversion and indeed inability of most men to give their attention to subjects remote from their ordinary train of thinking, few indeed are to be found in the circle of my acquaintances to whose judgement I should venture to submit a proposal which, no doubt, will generally be considered as extravagant."

Extravagant was not the word most people in 1805 would have picked to describe Stevens's scheme. Dangerous, foolhardy, or just plain daft would have been closer to the mark, for the ink drawing enclosed with Stevens's letter sketched out a brazen plan to construct a bridge across the Hudson River. Not a soul yet had dared attempt such a project, and for good reason; in the early nineteenth century the science of bridge building was still far from the day when watery barriers as wide as the Hudson could be spanned by a strip of terra firma. But the fifty-six-year-old colonel believed he had found a way around the limitations of available technology: instead of building a bridge *over* the river, he would build one *in* the river. To wit, what he envisioned was a wooden pontoon bridge, forty-two feet wide, and more than a mile long, that would float in the water between the foot of his Hoboken, New Jersey, estate and West Eleventh Street in Manhattan.

This was no passing fancy, he assured his friend. He had the plan for the bridge all worked out, right down to the last "fastening pin." Here is how it would be built. A total of 130 pontoon sections, each consisting of three hollow wooden casks, braced with stringers, and connected to one another with massive iron chains, would be constructed on land and launched into the river. At the New York and the New Jersey ends of the bridge, and at intervals in between, cables and anchors would be attached to secure the structure to the shores and to weight it to the river's bottom. Last, wooden planking for the trans-Hudson roadway would be pounded into

place. It wasn't very complicated—risky, yes. But, after all, Stevens wrote his friend, "Without boldness and some degree of adventurous spirit, nothing great can be performed."

One imagines interstate commuters would have had to muster up some of their own adventurous spirit before they crossed the bobbing bridge. Not so, said Stevens, who had pages of mathematical equations to prove it. According to his calculations, which took into account the forces of buoyancy, tension, and tides, the floating giant would never sink, or pitch or yaw appreciably enough to send pedestrians, wagons, and livestock ricocheting between the timber guard rails—or worse, over the railings and into the Hudson. Even "a carriage heavily laden," the colonel claimed, "would make not the least impression thereon; and thus the bridge would, in fact, be as firm and steady as if it were permanently affixed." Moreover, navigation could continue uninterrupted. Two draw sections, rigged "to fly open and shut in an instant," would allow boats unimpeded passage up and down the Hudson

Colonel John Stevens, c. 1824.

View of Manhattan from the Hoboken ferry house, 1800.

during the day, Stevens explained; after sundown, they would be left to stand open, "with lamps constantly lit and so disposed as to direct vessels in their proper course through."

Although Stevens's plan for a Hudson River bridge is the earliest on record, there was nothing particularly innovative about the type of crossing he designed. Cyrus the Great had sent his Persian troops thundering over a pontoon roadway to capture Babylon in 538 B.C. Caligula, boasting that he could turn sea into land, had built a floating bridge three miles long in the Mediterranean purely on a whim. But because of their easily destructible nature, floating bridges were built as temporary spans that were either dismantled or left to drift downstream once they had outlived their usefulness. In fact, Stevens himself soon had second thoughts about the strength and flexibility of his bridge, and eventually came to the realization that the pontoon

scheme was an impossible one. Even if the money for the $40,000 project had been raised and the enormous job of constructing and launching 130 sections completed, the colonel conceded that the bridge would never have survived stormy waters or the ramming of the ice floes that clotted the Hudson River in winter. Both conditions would have exerted great strain on the iron chains of the colossal bridge, wrenching it apart; at best, they would have rearranged the pontoon sections into a series of serpentine curls.

Stevens's bridge scheme was just a footnote in a long and checkered career. After graduating from King's College (now Columbia University) in 1768, Stevens studied law, dabbled in politics, and went on to serve briefly as loan commissioner to the

— 120 —

Continental Army under George Washington. In 1776 he became state treasurer of New Jersey, rising to the rank of colonel, and a few years later was appointed surveyor-general for the eastern portion of New Jersey. Upon his marriage in the early 1780s to Rachel Cox, Stevens purchased several hundred acres of land in Hoboken and built his bride a dramatic villa on the bluffs overlooking the Hudson River. To any casual observer the colonel seemed to have settled into the leisurely role of a country gentleman. But it was in Hoboken, on the shores of the Hudson, that Stevens began patching together pumps, boilers, and pistons in his search for a steam engine that could be adapted to power boats. Though his first experimental vessel foundered in 1798 on the Passaic River, in 1804—three years before Robert Fulton sent his legendary invention, the *Clermont*, puffing up the Hudson to Albany—Stevens's rowboat-sized steamboat, the *Little Juliana*, sailed from Hoboken to the Battery in Manhattan and back without a hitch. Elated by her successful run, Stevens stepped up his experimentation on designs for larger steamboats, which he predicted would one day replace the sailboats and scows that provided such perilous passage over the Hudson and the East rivers.

Why then would John Stevens, champion of the steamboat, propose building a Hudson River bridge? Probably out of revenge. In 1800 Stevens had entered into a twenty-year agreement with his brother-in-law, the eminent statesman Robert R. Livingston, Jr., to develop a passenger steamboat. The match seemed to have been arranged by the gods, for Stevens possessed the engineering know-how and Livingston held an invaluable monopoly that gave him the exclusive right to operate steamboats in New York waters. But when Livingston enthusiastically introduced Robert Fulton to the partnership about 1804, Stevens, skeptical of the inventor's work, and reluctant to share his own, refused to join the men. The colonel had to down some bitter medicine in return: by withdrawing from the partnership, Stevens had forfeited his rights to test his experimental boats on the Hudson. It seems likely, then, that his plan for the floating bridge was conceived with the intention of under-

The *Phoenix,* in a painting attributed to Charles B. Lawrence, c. 1818.

mining Livingston's monopoly. Had the crossing been built, it would have presented stiff competition to the fleet of steam ferries Livingston and Fulton hoped to operate between New York and New Jersey.

After abandoning the scheme for the floating bridge, Stevens toyed briefly with the equally impossible idea of building a vehicular tunnel beneath the Hudson. But by 1806 he was back to steamboat construction, determined to take his rivals on in their own game. In June 1809 the inventor's one-hundred-foot craft, the *Phoenix,* was surreptitiously sailed from Hoboken to the Narrows, where it plunged into the open seas of the Atlantic and journeyed along the coast to Philadelphia, becoming the first steamboat to ply ocean waters. Two years later the colonel openly defied the restrictions imposed by the monopoly and set the *Juliana* afloat in the Hudson. For a few months in 1811 and 1812, until threats of expensive lawsuits by Livingston forced Stevens to remove her from the river, the trim vessel, crammed with enthralled passengers, shuttled sixteen times a day between Hoboken, New Jersey, and Vesey Street in Manhattan, providing the first regularly scheduled steam ferry service in America.

The Livingston monopoly was dissolved by order of the United States Supreme Court in 1824. By that time, Stevens's bridge scheme lay buried under a pile of plans for a Hudson River ferry line, a steam locomotive, and a railroad company, all of which the colonel had the satisfaction of realizing before his death, in 1838. Today, on the grounds of the inventor's former estate stands the Stevens Institute of Technology, founded by the colonel's son, Edwin, in 1870. From the school's campus one can catch the silver silhouette of the first (and only) Hudson River bridge to be built at New York City—the George Washington Bridge, which opened to traffic in 1931, more than 125 years after John Stevens had first set his vision to paper.

When Thomas Pope came to town in 1811, bragging about his "stupendous" bridge, there was hardly a New Yorker or a Brooklynite who hadn't at one time or another cursed the sprit sailboats and the oar barges that provided ferriage across the East River. Early nineteenth-century accounts of the half-mile trip in the crude vessels abound with tales of peril, disaster, and "vexatious delay." Several tell of narrow escapes in storms when towering green waves curled over the sides of the open boats, washing hapless passengers and their possessions into the roiling waters. Others recall how even on a perfectly glorious day the most experienced skippers could be outfoxed by shifting winds that left sailboats and their occupants marooned, sometimes only a maddening twenty feet from shore (which is probably why in 1789 the city passed an ordinance requiring all ferries to carry "four good Oars"). Not a thing, however, could help the poor ferryman whose restless boatload of livestock had suddenly rushed to the starboard side, capsizing the craft, and—to the despair of waiting butchers—met a watery doom.

Obviously, said Mr. Pope, whose calling card identified him as an "architect and landscape gardener," it was high time that the city of New York and the town of Brooklyn were linked by a bridge. And as it just so happened, he had one to sell. The sum of $144,000 would buy the neighbors a covered bridge or an open bridge—he had plans for both—and each came packaged in precut parts that could be neatly assembled over the water. What was more, said Pope, the design was "so wond'rous" it could be adapted to span the East River at any point and, with some adjustments, even the broad expanse of the Hudson.

Pope called his plan the Flying Pendant Lever Bridge, or, for short, the Rainbow, and on paper the effect was indeed wond'rous: without piers or any other visible means of support, the timber bridge soared from shore to shore in a single elegant arc, clearing even the lofty masts of clipper ships. The engineering secrets behind the miraculous structure were divulged in Pope's book, *A Treatise on Bridge Architecture,* which laid out fully illustrated, step-by-step directions for its design and construction. People who had no time to plow through a technical discussion of king-bents and joggles, or who had trouble understanding the accompanying diagrams, had merely to flip to the back of the leather-bound volume, where the inventor offered a handy synopsis of his plan in eight pages of heroic couplets. The abutments to support the bridge were to be built first, on both shores:

> The butments built of stone, where stone is found,
> For nought can last so long or keep so sound,
> But if the place should timber only grant,
> Then stone and iron the builder will not want.

As Pope saw it, the abutments sprouted domes, towers, and obelisks—although these extras were entirely optional, the inventor emphasized. But if the city fathers of New York and Brooklyn did wish to spend a little more and invest in an architectural flourish or two, it was best to select a style aesthetically compatible "to the requirements of the local situation," he advised. Not enough money for even the no-frills model? Consider this possibility, suggested Pope, who had his sales pitch down pat: lease the empty space inside the abutments as "warehouses, stores or dwelling houses . . . The rent they furnish pays the building's cost/Which in all [other] Bridges must be lost."

The bridge proper consisted of two bowed timber arms, each springing "like half a rainbow," 223 feet high, over the East River. As Pope described the construction process, two teams of carpenters working simultaneously on the Brooklyn and Manhattan sides would piece together the cantilevered arms, building out from the abutments on either shore, and inch their way slowly to mid-river, using the finished portions of the arms as scaffolding. Once completed, the two halves would be joined in midstream by a center section, approximately 50 feet long. Should an unusually tall ship come sailing up the river, this piece, Pope explained, could be quickly dismantled in just a few hours, and once the ship had passed, just as easily reassembled.

View from Brooklyn, across the East River to Manhattan, 1802.

Pope mocked the skeptics:

> Is hard for us (some say) to understand,
> How timber Bridges can fly off the land,
> Without a prop or scaffold from the strand,
> And meet to join in centre hand in hand,
> Is truly strange and marvellous to me,
> And, till I see it, never can it be!

"Persons of this description," Pope sniffed, are "under the influence of one of two things: namely, a total ignorance of the invention, or a contemptible opposition to its success." Certainly not the Shipwrights of New-York. After examining the plan for the Flying Pendant Lever Bridge, members of the guild pronounced the scheme "preferable to all others of timber theretofore invented, on account of [its] superior strength, durability and chaste preservation of navigation." That, however, was the only endorsement Pope got. According to a subscription list at the beginning of the *Treatise*, over four hundred people purchased a copy of the inventor's book, including Daniel D. Tompkins, governor of New York, and Robert Fulton, the

The proposed "Rainbow," or Flying Pendant
Lever Bridge. Thomas Pope, 1811.

An arm of the Flying Pendant Lever Bridge as it would look during construction. Warehouses occupy the anchorage of the bridge.

OPPOSITE:
A page from Thomas Pope's book, *A Treatise on Bridge Architecture*, showing some of the detail
drawings to be followed in constructing the "Rainbow" bridge.

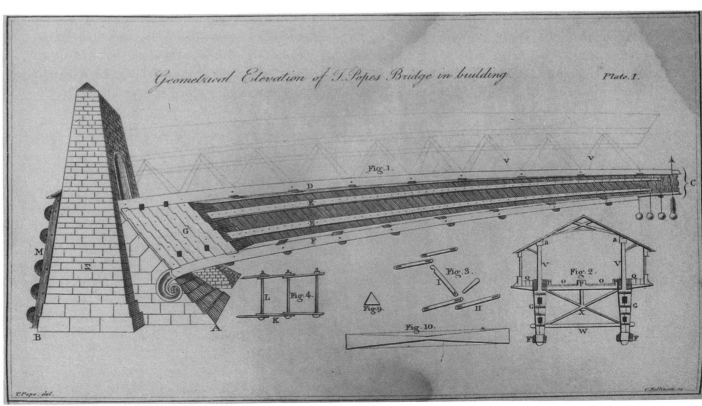

Geometrical Elevation of T. Popes Bridge in building.   Plate. 1.

steamboat pioneer. Evidently most of them failed to recognize the "golden properties" of the Rainbow bridge, because in 1812 Pope left New York to try his luck in Philadelphia.

The hopeful salesman was not the first to take plans for a bridge to the Quaker city. Since its days as the nation's capital, in the 1790s, Philadelphia had welcomed and encouraged America's most innovative engineers to come and spin their visions over the Schuylkill River. In this receptive climate Timothy Palmer had built a covered bridge that swept the water in three graceful arches at Market Street. Farther upstream, one of the Western world's first modern suspension bridges, designed by James Finley in 1809, hung from a series of iron chains, and nearby, in 1812, construction of the Colossus, a 340-foot single-span bridge, made of wood and wrought iron, was under way. Now it was Pope's turn.

Upon arriving in Philadelphia, Pope set up a model of the Flying Pendant Lever Bridge in his parlor on Library Street and placed an announcement in the *Aurora General Advertiser,* inviting the public to come and take a look for the admission price of fifty cents, and "discover the superior excellence of this invention." But apparently even Philadelphians weren't ready for the Rainbow, because they didn't buy many tickets, and they certainly didn't place an order for the bridge.

Discouraged and nearly penniless, Pope moved to Pittsburgh in 1814 to seek employment. He soon found a friend in the architect Benjamin Latrobe, who himself had proposed an East River bridge in 1804 and understood well the frustration of seeing an idea rejected by myopic critics. Although it is not known what Latrobe thought of the Rainbow bridge, in a letter to a captain of the United States Army he praised Pope as "a perfect master of the practice of building & surveying," and recommended him highly for the position of draftsman on the Allegheny Arsenal project.

Pope assisted on the project for only a year. Described by Latrobe as "crazy about his patent lever bridge," it may have been with this dream in mind that the inventor returned to Philadelphia in 1815. What happened to Pope and his curious invention after this date is unfortunately not known. Later listings for Thomas Pope, in the city directories of Pittsburgh, Philadelphia, and New York, indicate that he continued to lead an itinerant life; an 1850 New York directory lists Elizabeth Pope, residing at West Seventeenth Street, as "the widow of Thomas."

One of the few vignettes about Pope—probably legend—has it that as he and Robert Fulton were sailing up the East River one day after a spring rain, a magnificent rainbow appeared over the water. "Look, Pope," his companion exclaimed, "even the heavens favor you with good omens!" But clearly the timber arc could never have spanned the East River, much less the mighty Hudson. Nonetheless, in the history of bridge building, the two-armed rainbow has the distinction of having been the first cantilever bridge proposed in the United States.

On May 8, 1814, Robert Fulton's boat, the Nassau, *chugged between Fulton Street in Brooklyn and Peck Slip in Manhattan, becoming the first steam-powered vessel to provide ferry service on the East River. Less than thirty years later, steam ferries were commonplace. In the waters that encircled Manhattan Island, the* Hunchback, *the* Transit, *the* Relief, *and scores of other tubby sidewheelers mowed through the waves, shuttling foot passengers, cargo, coaches and saddle horses to neighboring shores that formerly had been reachable only by wind- and oar-powered craft.*

To New Yorkers, who could well recall the days when crossing the Hudson or the East River had been more "formidable than a voyage to Europe," the steamboats—warm, swift, and comfortable—came as a revolutionary improvement. They also made a bridge seem a perfectly superfluous proposition. "The idea of a bridge is as rare a conception

as 'a fifth wheel to a coach' and about as desirable," wrote a Brooklyn resident in 1845. "Steam-boats are constantly plying, so that the intervals of their departure (at least on the Fulton ferry) rarely exceed 3 minutes, and the passage is made in 3 to 5 minutes. Under these circumstances, who would think of crossing a bridge if one stood in the way?"

But, as ferry passengers found out the hard way, the steam-powered boats were not exempt from collisions, boiler explosions, and the whims of Mother Nature, who without warning whipped up tempests, blizzards, and banks of thick fog that delayed and often suspended ferry service altogether. Nor could the steamboats carry their landlubber cousin, the steam locomotive. By the 1860s engineers were back at the drawing board.

A steam ferry pushes off from Manhattan, bound for Brooklyn, 1845.

On the morning of January 23, 1867, residents of New York and Brooklyn awoke to a rare and awesome sight: the blizzards and bitter temperatures that had gripped the cities for almost a week had transformed the waters of the East River into a gigantic field of thick ice. "Ice bridge!" rang the cry, as thousands rushed to the river's edge to make the once-in-a-lifetime crossing by foot. For several

hours people gleefully slipped and slid their way between the two cities, tossing snowballs at neighbors and colliding good-naturedly with strangers. One daredevil stunned onlookers by galloping over the river by horse and sleigh, and even the Fulton Baseball Club took to the ice, where it managed to play a rousing game of almost nine innings before the tides swept the temporary diamond upstream.

Ice bridge on the East River, January 23, 1867.

But the ensuing week was not much fun for commuters who had to travel between Brooklyn and Manhattan. Ferry service was so sporadic that people who left for work in the morning could never be sure the steamboats would be running later to take them home at night. The rare ferry that did appear took an average of an hour and a half to make the crossing, every minute of which was terror-filled. Moaning ice floes swarmed in the water, like sea monsters seeking prey, ready to crush hulls or devour paddle wheels. What looked from afar like a clear path across the river often turned out to be an ice-clotted vein that trapped boats for hours in mid-stream until currents finally freed them. At the very least, disembarking passengers knew to brace themselves for the possibility of a slippery scramble over the spiles to get to shore, because on some days the wall of ice along the piers was so thick that ferry pilots couldn't dock.

After suffering this inconvenience for a week, and after two days of no ferry service at all, disgruntled citizens crowded the office of the Union Ferry Company to sign a petition demanding the immediate construction of an East River bridge. At the end of January, the *New York Times* reported

that so many people had affixed their signatures to the petition that yards of paper "hung in festoons from the ceiling and around the chandelier." Politicians in Albany took notice. Within months of the thaw, two companies were authorized by the State Legislature to build a bridge over the East River. Only one company would succeed. The New York Bridge Company, following plans drawn up by John and Washington Roebling, began work in 1869 on what would later be named the Brooklyn Bridge. Farther upstream, Dr. Thomas Rainey, director of the New York and Long Island Bridge Company, undertook to build a crossing between Manhattan and Queens, via Blackwell's (now Roosevelt) Island. Forty years later, he would bitterly call the twice-failed bridge "the ruin of my life."

A native of North Carolina, Rainey had amassed a small fortune by the late 1860s running a fleet of steamships out of New York City to South America. (His title of doctor seems to have been self-ascribed, for, as far as is known, Rainey completed neither a degree in medicine nor in any other field.) Upon assuming directorship of the New York and Long Island Bridge Company, the fifty-year-old entrepreneur plunked down $30,000, confident that his investment would net him a handsome return. A toll bridge from Manhattan to the "high, unoccupied and healthy lands" of Queens, he wrote in one of several promotional pamphlets, would shortly be filled by the "tens of thousands who greatly prefer the country life." If the bridge were equipped to carry trains, Rainey calculated, it would bring in a tidy income serving the Long Island Rail Road, which, for lack of any other way to clear the East River, had to shuttle its passengers between New York and Long Island City by boat. Undercut the ferries by a few cents, and Manhattan's funeral trade—which made several trips daily to some nineteen cemeteries on Long Island—would also cross the river by bridge instead of by boat. Rainey didn't see how he could lose.

Rainey's partners in this venture included William Steinway, founder of the renowned piano firm, Charles Pratt, co-owner of the Standard Oil Company, and Eliphalet Bliss, a successful press and die manufacturer. These men stood much to gain from a Blackwell's Island bridge, since all three owned factories on the Long Island side and were entirely dependent on ferries to transport raw materials, finished products, and employees across the river—a system that cut sharply into profits. The businessmen pinned few economic hopes on the Brooklyn Bridge, because the bridge was not designed to carry freight trains.

In 1877, after several years of considering various plans for the Blackwell's Island bridge, Rainey announced that the New York and Long Island Bridge Company had selected to build a scheme submitted by Thomas Clarke and Adolphus Bonzano, partners in the Philadelphia-based firm of Clarke, Reeves & Company. In the nascent science of railroad bridge and viaduct design, Bonzano's pioneering breakthroughs in iron construction and Clarke's expertise in masonry and foundation work had established the partners as two of the most respected civil engineers in the country. By the 1870s they had built dozens of railroad spans across the

The Brooklyn Bridge under construction, 1877.

rivers and ravines of North America, although in New York they were better known as the men who had erected the iron stanchions and trackbeds for the Ninth Avenue elevated line. Clarke would later go on to build in New York the Willis Avenue Bridge (1898) and the Third Avenue Bridge (1901), over the Harlem River, both of which are still in use today.

For the Blackwell's Island bridge, Bonzano and

— 129 —

Proposed bridge for Blackwell's (now Roosevelt) Island, East River, viewed from Manhattan near East Seventy-seventh Street. Adolphus Bonzano and Thomas Clarke, 1877.

Clarke proposed erecting a confection of lacy ironwork, only fifty-six feet wide, strung between eight slender towers, each tipped with a conical cap. To New Yorkers, whose definition of a bridge had been shaped by the massive steel and granite structure the Roeblings were building downstream, the engineers' bridge looked like it might have been more at home over the moat of a fairy-tale castle than over the East River. Actually, the public was informed, this was a "trussed chain suspension bridge," and the only one of its kind in the world. It would skip across the river in twin spans, one from East Seventy-seventh Street in Manhattan to Blackwell's Island, the other from the island to the vicinity of Thirty-fourth Avenue in Queens, and it would carry two railroad tracks, sidewalks, and a carriage way. In Manhattan the bridge would connect with Park Avenue and feed trains into the New York Central and Hudson River Railroad system.

Work began on the $5-million crossing in 1881, and within a few months a cofferdam had been sunk on the Queens side of the river in preparation for construction of the first bridge pier. But when the Brooklyn Bridge opened to a dazzling display of golden and emerald fireworks, on May 24, 1883, the upriver venture was at a standstill: the New York and Long Island Bridge Company had gone bankrupt. Steinway, who knew a sinking ship when he saw one, bailed out of the project. His exit was followed by the financial panic of 1893, which ruined hundreds of banks and institutions across the country and left Rainey despairing of ever being able to salvage the Blackwell's Island bridge.

Meanwhile, Austin Corbin, president of the Long Island Rail Road, was investigating ways to bring his company's trains over the East River to Manhattan. On the advice of Charles M. Jacobs, a British engineer who had come to work in New York at Corbin's invitation, it was decided that burrowing a tunnel beneath the river would be too risky an undertaking. Yet a bridge, they knew, while technologically feasible, would require a long journey through Albany's legislative labyrinth to secure a charter, which could hold up the project for years.

About 1894 Corbin approached Rainey and suggested that they join forces to build a bridge over the East River. Corbin was so eager to span the river that he offered not only to finance the crossing, he presented Rainey with a set of finished blueprints for the bridge. Designed by Jacobs, the plan called for a steel cantilever bridge that would cross the river from East Sixty-fourth Street in Manhattan to Long Island City at Fortieth Avenue in three main spans supported by solid granite piers. The bridge was to accommodate a double set of railway tracks, pedestrian walkways, and a carriage road, and was to connect with a railroad station on the Manhattan side, near East Sixty-fourth Street, between Second and Third avenues.

There wasn't much for Rainey to think over. His company held the charter for the East River crossing; Corbin's company offered money and a sound plan. The offer was accepted.

Scheme for Blackwell's Island bridge, East River. Charles M. Jacobs, c. 1894.

Excavation work began on Blackwell's Island in 1895, with expectations that the trains of the Long Island Rail Road could begin rolling over the bridge by 1897. But the bridge was destined to grow only by inches. The death, in 1896, of Corbin, who was thrown from his carriage in a hit-and-run accident, temporarily halted all work on the crossing. The Spanish-American War, in 1898, further delayed progress on the bridge. By the turn of the century, and thousands of dollars later, only two piers had been built on Blackwell's Island. The project met its final setback in 1901, when, in Rainey's words, "the Mayor of New York, one Van Wyck, came out with a flourish of trumpets and promised to build another bridge . . . only four blocks away." That bridge was the Queensboro Bridge (also called the Fifty-ninth Street Bridge), designed by Gustav Lindenthal, and the third of ten eventual crossings to be erected over the East River.

Shortly after the Queensboro Bridge opened, in 1909, Rainey, eighty-four years old and in poor health, shuffled across the new East River span to inspect Lindenthal's handiwork. Although he was still bitter that fate had not been kinder to his scheme, he had high praise for the frothy steel cantilever structure that leapt over Blackwell's Island. "It is a grand bridge," he said, "much grander than the one I had in mind. It will be of great service to thousands in the years to come, when Dr. Rainey and his bridge projects will long have been gathered into the archives of the past." Rainey died only a year later. He was never to know that, in 1912, in honor of his efforts, the city fathers set aside a small tract of land on the site of what would have been the Queens end of the bridge designed by Bonzano and Clarke. It is called Rainey Park.

By the 1880s the Pennsylvania Railroad was the second-largest passenger carrier in the United States and offered its long-distance riders steam-heated cars, plush dining rooms, game salons, and even small libraries "filled with popular books of fiction." But what the Pennsylvania Railroad could not offer, unfortunately, was direct service to New York. The company's line dead-ended at Exchange Place in Jersey City, at which point passengers had to make a cumbersome transfer from trains to one of the four ferry lines operated by the railroad and shuttle over the Hudson River by boat to Manhattan or Brooklyn. Once on the New York side, thirty minutes later (barring fog or storms), disembarking passengers found themselves on the tumultuous quays of the waterfront district, faced with the disagreeable prospect of having to haul limb and luggage into town.

Much to the Pennsylvania Railroad's unending chagrin, its greatest rival, the Vanderbilt-controlled New York Central and Hudson River Railroad, traversed the Hudson at Albany and entered the heart of Manhattan via a railroad crossing over the Harlem River at Mott Haven. Passengers who rode the line were conveniently deposited at the company's impressive brick station, Grand Central Depot, located on Park Avenue and East Forty-second Street, just steps away from hotels, shops, and the city's most fashionable neighborhoods. Given the choice, it was not surprising that savvy travelers booked a seat with the New York Central.

West Street in Manhattan, looking north from Hubert Street along the traffic-choked waterfront, 1898. The Pennsylvania Railroad's ferry terminal is at far left.

In the mid-1880s, prompted by this competition and by increasing complaints of the "antiquated manner" in which the Pennsylvania Railroad delivered passengers to New York City, the directors of the railroad took a deep breath and voted to extend the company's tracks to Manhattan. It was a monumental decision to make, because there were only two ways trains could cross the Hudson—by tunnel or by bridge—and both propositions posed engineering hurdles so formidable that no one yet had managed to build either one to New York City.

After deliberating between the two seemingly impossible options, the company soon decided that a tunnel was out of the question. For one thing, the efforts of Colonel DeWitt Haskin to construct a tunnel between Manhattan and Jersey City had all but proved that any similar undertaking would

be doomed to failure. Begun in 1874, the project had been riddled with bouts of bankruptcy, tragic accidents, and lawsuits; by the mid-1880s the sub-aqueous link had grown only a little over one thousand feet. But even if Haskin could show that construction of a tunnel was feasible, the directors of the Pennsylvania Railroad feared the sulfurous fumes that spewed from the steam locomotives would asphyxiate the passengers and the crew before the trains resurfaced from the depths of the Hudson.

So it was agreed: the company would build a bridge. Upon hearing the news, several smaller railroads, also eager to gain direct access to Manhattan from New Jersey, offered to aid the Pennsylvania Railroad in financing the crossing. They were gladly taken on board, and, with a toast to a brave new chapter in railroad history, the partners set out to give the Vanderbilts a run for their money.

In 1885 the bridge project was laid in the hands

Grand Central Depot, Park Avenue and East Forty-second Street, in early 1872, just a few months after it opened.

Gustav Lindenthal, c. 1885.

conquered the Hudson in a central span, 3,100 feet long, between West Twenty-third Street in Manhattan and Twelfth Street in Hoboken. The bridge was to carry trains on ten railroad tracks and to connect with a passenger station on the New York side, at Sixth Avenue near West Twenty-third Street. Including the approaches, the bridge measured more than a mile in length, and it came with a price as enormous as its size—$15 million. Acquisition of rights-of-way and construction of the station were expected to add another $25 million to that figure, bringing the project to a total cost of $40 million— almost exactly what it cost to run the city of New York in 1888. But the $40-million expenditure seemed justified to the Pennsylvania Railroad and its partners, who were coping with other, equally staggering figures. Between them, the railroads had nearly nine hundred trains a day arriving and departing on the New Jersey side of the Hudson, and each day they had to see that fifty thousand of their passengers were safely shuttled over the river. Projecting ahead ten years, railroad executives conservatively estimated that those numbers would at least double.

In 1888 the application to build Lindenthal's crossing was sent to Congress, which reviewed all plans for structures erected over federally controlled navigable waterways. While awaiting word from Washington, Lindenthal vigorously promoted the bridge in lectures, articles, and interviews. He fully realized that there were thousands of people who thought the scheme was preposterous, and that half of them, including some of his engineering colleagues, in fact, would sooner have swum across the Hudson than risked their lives traveling over the water on his railroad bridge. In a paper he delivered at a conference of the American Society of Civil Engineers, Lindenthal tried to assure disbelievers that his plan was sound:

> It is a popular assumption that suspension bridges cannot be well used for railroad purposes, or that at least they are not so well suited as truss bridges or cantilever bridges . . . A suspension bridge can have any degree of flexibility and looseness of construction, but as long as the cables and fastenings hold, the bridge cannot collapse.

of Gustav Lindenthal, a young engineer then working in Pittsburgh. Bridges were Lindenthal's specialty, and he built them with amazing speed and energy. Born in Austria-Hungary in 1850 and educated at the Polytechnic schools in Brünn and Vienna, Lindenthal had emigrated to the United States at the age of twenty-four. After working on the construction of the Centennial Exposition in Philadelphia for three years, and later in the engineering divisions of the Keystone Bridge Company and the Atlantic and Great Western Railroad, Lindenthal set up his own engineering firm in Pittsburgh in 1881. By 1885, the year he contracted to work for the Pennsylvania Railroad, Lindenthal had designed in Pittsburgh the Smithfield Bridge over the Monongahela River (the bridge is today a historic landmark), and the Seventh Street Bridge over the Allegheny.

Lindenthal undertook the Hudson River bridge scheme with equal fervor. By 1888 he had prepared a detailed set of plans for a gargantuan suspension bridge, unprecedented in scale and scope, which

Proposed Hudson River suspension bridge, viewed from Hoboken. Gustav Lindenthal, 1888. In the distance, the Brooklyn Bridge spans the East River.

At the time of Lindenthal's proposal there was only one railroad suspension bridge in the country, an 821-foot span over the Niagara River at Niagara Falls, New York, completed in 1855 by John Roebling, the future builder of the Brooklyn Bridge; in 1896, however, the structure was replaced by a steel arch bridge, precisely because its flexibility made it unsuitable for heavy railroad use. But Congress didn't foresee any such end for Lindenthal's work. After all, as planned, each anchorage of the bridge was half as large as the Capitol Building in Washington and contained 50 percent more masonry than the Khufu Pyramid in Egypt. At five hundred feet, the towers were almost twice as high as those of the Brooklyn Bridge, and there were 42,000 tons of iron and steel in the construct. It

didn't appear likely that the vibrations and weight of train traffic would topple this bridge. In 1890 Congress authorized the newly incorporated North River Bridge Company to begin construction of Lindenthal's bridge.

Just a few months after they received the go-ahead from Washington, the Pennsylvania Railroad and its partners were surprised to find they had a rival. The long-dormant New York and New Jersey Bridge Company, chartered in the 1860s, had submitted plans to erect a cantilever bridge that would carry trains over the Hudson River from West Seventieth Street in Manhattan to the township of Union, New Jersey. What was more, in its application to Congress the company had tried to sabotage the West Twenty-third Street project by smearing Lindenthal's suspension bridge as too dangerous for railroad traffic, wildly expensive, and certain to take years to build. To the relief of the North River Bridge Company, a board of engineers appointed by President Benjamin Harrison found the allegations to be groundless. The board further

— 137 —

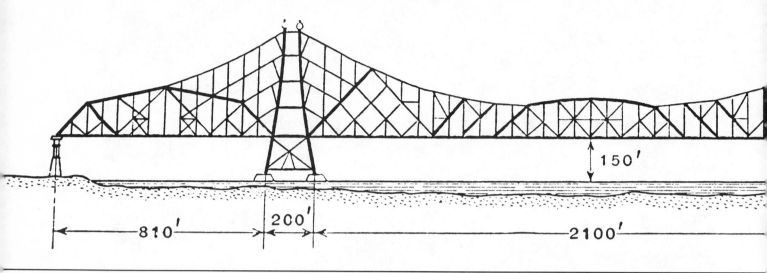

150'

810' 200' 2100'

Proposed West Seventieth
Street bridge, Hudson River.
New York–New Jersey Bridge
Company, 1890.

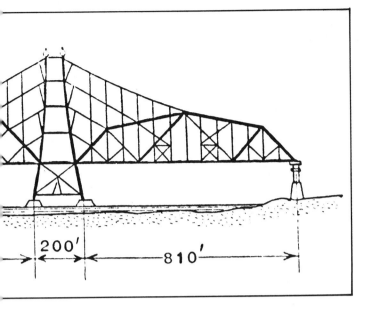

Elevation of West Seventieth Street bridge.

concluded that the New York and New Jersey Bridge Company's own plan was flawed. As designed, the proposed structure's two supporting piers, each located approximately eight hundred feet in the water from either shore, would impede river navigation, said the board, and therefore the plan for the cantilever bridge could not be approved.

With the Hudson all to itself, the North River Bridge Company began condemnation proceedings in Hoboken about 1892. Work on the crossing was held up by the financial panic of 1893, which bankrupted most of the smaller railroad companies that had pledged their dollars to the venture, but two years later, impatient to move ahead with the project, the directors of the Pennsylvania Railroad gave the signal to begin excavations for the foundation of the Hoboken anchorage. Ground was broken on the New Jersey side on June 8, 1895; in a small ceremony ten days later the cornerstone of the massive anchorage was laid in place.

The stirrings in Hoboken apparently rekindled the ambitions of the New York and New Jersey Bridge Company, because in July 1895 it was back, armed with a new scheme and eating its words about the dangers of suspension bridges. To meet with federal navigational guidelines, the company's stockholders had commissioned Charles MacDonald to draw up a plan for a suspension bridge that would cross the Hudson at West Fifty-ninth Street, Manhattan, in a single span, without troublesome, off-shore piers. The Canadian-born engineer was well equipped to meet that challenge, having designed the Poughkeepsie Bridge, farther up the Hudson in 1889, and in 1886 the mile-long steel railroad bridge over the Hawkesbury River near Sydney, Australia, which was the first bridge to be built abroad by an American company. However, he wasn't about to engage in any Lindenthalian bravura. The central span of the six-track suspension bridge MacDonald produced was stiffened with trusses to prevent gross fluctuations of the deck under the load of moving trains. The result was a cluttered-looking bridge, without any of the majesty of Lindenthal's design, but the extra stability provided by the trusses undoubtedly allowed stockholders of the New York and New Jersey Bridge Company to sleep more easily at night. Part two of MacDonald's plan called for an immense passenger station to be built on Eighth Avenue between West Forty-ninth and Fiftieth streets, which would connect with the bridge by way of a curved viaduct that snaked through several blocks of the West Side.

When the $60-million bridge and terminal plan was approved by the federal government in 1896, optimists predicted that by the turn of the century the Hudson would have not one but two bridges over its waters at New York City. Lindenthal's gigantic construct would sweep the river at West Twenty-third Street, and upstream, MacDonald's bridge would join Manhattan and New Jersey at West Fifty-ninth Street. Ultimately neither was built. In 1896, shortly after they received authorization from Congress to build MacDonald's bridge, stockholders of the New York and New Jersey Bridge Company fell to quarreling among themselves, each side claiming that the other had tried to seize control of the project. While they bickered, their charter for the crossing lapsed, and the company eventually became defunct.

In Hoboken, meanwhile, crews had readied the foundation for the huge New Jersey anchorage of the Twenty-third Street bridge. Work progressed in fits and starts as the directors of the Pennsylvania Railroad waited—in vain—for their former partners to rejoin them. The company might have gone ahead and built the bridge alone had it not been for new developments made in tunnel construction and locomotive power. In 1902 the railroad watched closely as William McAdoo, an enterprising Georgia lawyer, and Charles M. Jacobs, the British engineer, set out to complete the subaqueous route Colonel Haskin had started to build in the 1870s,

Proposed Hudson River bridge at West Fifty-ninth Street and a railroad station. Charles MacDonald, 1895.

The cornerstone and the remains of the Hoboken anchorage belonging to the abandoned West Twenty-third Street bridge project were narrowly saved from the nose of a jackhammer by Gustav Lindenthal's grandson in 1984. In storage at the Stevens Institute of Technology since then, they seek a permanent resting place.

between Fifteenth Street in Jersey City and Morton Street in Manhattan. McAdoo and Jacobs not only finished Haskin's tube, they built another one next to it, as well as a pair of tunnels between Cortlandt Street in Manhattan and Exchange Place in Jersey City. (Today all four tunnels belong to the Port Authority Trans-Hudson, or PATH, system.) Almost in tandem with the resurrection of the interstate tunnel project came the advent of electrical traction, clearing the way, and the smoke, for safe passenger travel through train tunnels. Needing no further incentives, the Pennsylvania Railroad abandoned Lindenthal's bridge plan and in 1903 began construction of a tunnel system beneath the Hud-

son and another beneath the East River, the latter to carry the trains of the company's new acquisition, the Long Island Rail Road. By 1910 the subaqueous tunnels and Pennsylvania Station, a marble masterpiece occupying two city blocks on Seventh Avenue, were in full operation.

Lindenthal was crushed by this turn of events, but never for a moment did he consider surrendering the idea of bridging the Hudson. After dinner, summer or winter, remembers Lindenthal's niece, her uncle would pace the long porch that fronted the engineer's Metuchen, New Jersey, farmhouse before retiring to his study to fill notebooks with pages of long equations. The calculations may have been the theoretical framework to Lindenthal's designs for the Queensboro Bridge (1909), the Manhattan Bridge (1909), or the Hell Gate Bridge (1917)—or the tidy string of numbers might have been the mathematical prelude to the engineer's grand swan song, which he would unveil in 1921. Lindenthal had not given up.

People were incredulous. Yes, it was true that on Sundays or holidays mile-long ribbons of automobiles were stretched on the New Jersey side of the Hudson waiting for ferries. And the figures for trans-Hudson traffic were indeed staggering. In 1921 two hundred million people crossed the river by ferry or train tunnel, and freight shipped across the river that year tallied twenty-one million tons. But build a two-lane pontoon drawbridge between Yonkers, New York, and Alpine, New Jersey? It was a "fillip to the most jaded imagination," snorted the *New York Times*. Residents of Westchester and Bergen counties didn't want to hear a word about it; neither did operators of excursion lines, ferry companies, and freight carriers, all of whom were prepared to fight the pontoon scheme in court. It wasn't that anyone disputed the need for a bridge between New York and New Jersey; in fact it was a wonder the states had managed without one for so long. It just seemed to most people that by the 1920s—the age of skyscrapers, atomic physics, and jazz—surely someone could come up with a less primitive way of getting cars, people, and goods across a mile of water.

Someone had, the public was soon informed. The floating roadway would span the Hudson only temporarily, until such time as the "big bridge" could be built.

The man behind both bridges was Gustav Lindenthal, who in 1921 had hatched a peculiar scheme to see his thirty-year dream for a Hudson River crossing come true. If, for just a few months, commuters could experience the convenience of an interstate bridge, even one that bobbed in the water a few miles north of New York City, Lindenthal reasoned, they would be sure to send up a clamor demanding the construction of a permanent bridge. When officials on either side of the river began scrambling to find an engineer to build that bridge, he would be there to offer them a finished set of plans for the mightiest structure the Hudson had ever seen.

The scheme flopped. Not only was there little public support to span the Hudson with a pontoon roadway, neither New York nor New Jersey expressed any interest in examining the design for the so-called big bridge.

Disappointed, but not defeated, the seventy-one-year-old engineer decided to seek private capital to finance the great bridge. What the bridge would look like and how much the project would cost were first revealed in the April 1921 issue of *Scientific American*. More than a few jaws must have dropped at the sight of the astounding scheme. Spread across the pages of the magazine was a design for a $100-million, double-decked titan that swept the Hudson River from West Fifty-seventh Street in Manhattan to Fiftieth Street in Weehawken in three grand spans. The enormous construct boasted two steel and granite towers, each higher than the Woolworth Building, and two land anchorages, each wider than the New York Public Library at Forty-second Street is long. The central span of the suspension bridge, measuring 3,240 feet, would have easily accommodated three of the world's largest ocean liners of the day, and City Hall could have rested between the guard rails of the bridge's top deck with room to spare. From New York to Weehawken, the behemoth measured 7,460 feet in length, and was envisioned as carrying trolleys, buses, sixteen lanes of automobiles, and pedestrian walks through three arched openings on an upper deck, and twelve railroad tracks in six tunnels on a lower deck. Above the Manhattan anchorage rose a twenty-eight-story office building.

Publishing the scheme did not bring Lindenthal the investors he needed, but the plan did elicit high praise from critics who agreed that a bridge, big and bold, was the Hudson River's only salvation. The plan shows "an undeniable touch of genius"; the immense structure "could easily take care of the whole traffic which surges to and fro between Manhattan Island and the mainland," wrote *Scientific American*. It would be "the world's greatest bridge," declared one New Yorker. If built, exclaimed another, "miseries in transportation now suffered will be ended; fetters that now bind will be cut; growth and development now hindered will

Proposed pontoon bridge, Hudson River. Gustav Linden-thal, 1921.

be set free." One of the few who urged Lindenthal to scale down the proportions of his colossus was Othmar H. Ammann, who had worked as the engineer's assistant on the Hell Gate crossing in 1917. But evidently Lindenthal didn't care for any advice, particularly from young upstarts. Lindenthal reacted to this suggestion, said Ammann, by rebuking "me severely for my 'timidity' and 'shortsighted-

ness' in not looking far ahead enough. He stated that he was looking ahead for one thousand years."

But it was Ammann's plan, not Lindenthal's, that the Port of New York Authority ultimately chose to build across the Hudson River. The agency, created in 1921 to coordinate and develop the myriad activities—freight transfer, railroad service, terminal operation, and cargo distribution—that functioned independently with little rhyme or reason in one of the world's busiest harbors, announced in 1923 that, as part of its master plan for the port, it fa-

Othmar H. Ammann, 1931.

OVERLEAF:
Proposed Hudson River bridge at West Fifty-seventh Street. Gustav Lindenthal, 1921.

A tower of Gustav Lindenthal's West Fifty-seventh Street bridge (840 feet high) compared with the Woolworth Building (792 feet high).

vored "the construction at the earliest possible moment of additional vehicular tunnels or bridges" between New York and New Jersey. Subsequent studies made a bridge the priority. At this news, Ammann was quick to approach the Port Authority with cost sheets, projected revenue estimates, and drawings for a $60-million steel suspension bridge. Lindenthal, on the other hand, announced with characteristic stubbornness that he would consider collaborating with the Port of New York Authority only if it agreed to build the bridge at Fifty-seventh Street exactly as he had designed it. When Port Authority officials pointed out that the gargantuan bridge would cost $40 million more to build than Ammann's and that, even more objectionable, the traffic load generated by the bridge would paralyze circulation in the streets of mid-Manhattan, Lindenthal rolled up his plan and blithely informed them that he would build the West Fifty-seventh Street crossing alone.

Ammann's design for what would later be named the George Washington Bridge was formally adopted by the Port of New York Authority in 1925. It was decided to build the crossing between Fort Lee, New Jersey, and West 178th Street in Manhattan, a location that was removed from the congested midtown area yet close to the axes of New Jersey–New England–Westchester County travel. On October 21, 1927, as bands blared and thousands of spectators watched from both shores, officials on the New York and the New Jersey sides of the river simultaneously dug silver spades into the ground and turned over clumps of earth for the bridge that at long last would close the gap of the vast interstate divide. Just three weeks later, huge crowds again assembled near the water's edge, this time to participate in the ribbon-snipping festivities for the Holland Tunnel, the first vehicular tunnel to be built across the Hudson.

The import of the historic, back-to-back ceremonies was not lost on Lindenthal, but the engineer was too busy seeking financial backers for the Fifty-seventh Street bridge crossing to pay much attention to all the hoopla surrounding the events. His perseverance paid off. In 1929, as the webbed towers of the George Washington Bridge grew taller,

Lindenthal's search ended in a handshake with the president of the Baltimore & Ohio Railroad, who was as eager to bring trains to Manhattan from the company's New Jersey terminals as Lindenthal was determined to see his vision for a Hudson River bridge become a three-dimensional reality.

Early in May 1929, despite the loud protestations of the Port Authority, Lindenthal sent off the plan for the Fifty-seventh Street bridge to the War Department, which had jurisdiction over bridges in tidal waters. Three weeks later, to his astonishment, he received word that his scheme had been rejected. Ironically, the roadway of the enormous bridge was found to be just twenty-five feet short of the two-hundred-foot government specification for clear height.

The George Washington Bridge was dedicated on October 25, 1931, almost four years to the day after ground had been broken for the crossing, and eight months ahead of schedule. Some time was saved on the project by the decision to abandon details of the original plan, which called for the towers to be sheathed in granite after designs drawn up by Cass Gilbert, the architect of the Woolworth Building. In the onset of the Depression, however, the stone facing was struck from the plan, and the towers were left to stand with all their underpinnings showing. Many people seemed to prefer the naked steelwork. At the dedication, Governor Franklin D. Roosevelt was moved to call the bridge "almost superhuman in perfection." The Swiss architect Le Corbusier would later say of the towers, "Their structure is so pure, so resolute, so regular that here, finally, steel architecture seems to laugh." As for Lindenthal, he thought the bridge, with or without the granite facing, was "skimpy," recalls his niece.

Lindenthal and Ammann arrived together at the dedication ceremony in an open car. As they rode across the central span of the new bridge, five thousand guests seated in grandstands burst into "the greatest and most spontaneous" applause accorded anyone that day, reported the *New York Times*. But if, as the men rode by, some spectators reflected that they might be witnessing a changing of the guard, they were right. The George Washington

Bridge was Ammann's springboard to a stellar career that would match Lindenthal's in breadth and virtuosity. After completing the crossing at West 178th Street, the Swiss-born engineer, twenty-nine years Lindenthal's junior, went on to build (among others) the Triborough (1936), the Bronx-Whitestone (1939), the Throgs Neck (1961), and the Verrazano-Narrows (1964) bridges. Lindenthal, whose name by 1931 was linked with the design of three mighty bridges over the East River, and with the construction of bridges in Pennsylvania, Ohio, and Oregon, would spend the remaining years of his life locked in a tenacious battle with Washington and the Port of New York Authority for authorization to span the Hudson with a bridge at West Fifty-seventh Street. Until the day of his death, in 1935, Lindenthal fervently believed that his titan would someday be built.

By 1939 Robert Moses, as chairman of the Triborough Bridge Authority, had built the Triborough Bridge, finished the Henry Hudson Memorial Bridge, and opened the Bronx-Whitestone Bridge. Now he stood poised and ready to command his newest vision for New York—a bridge from the Battery to Brooklyn. A bridge was not exactly what the city had planned for the Upper Bay. In fact, it had intentions to build a tunnel there, a plan Moses not only knew about but, as chairman of Triborough, had helped to make financially feasible. In 1938 Mayor Fiorello H. La Guardia and Moses had pooled their resources and struck a deal. In exchange for the mayor's promise to build the Belt Parkway, one of the missing links in Moses' dream for a circumferential highway that would ring the five boroughs, Moses had agreed to supplement the city's $55-million loan from Washington with $33 million in Triborough money to construct a Brooklyn-Battery tunnel and connecting highways.

In a surprise turnabout early in 1939, however, Moses informed the mayor that he would not part with a penny of Triborough's funds unless the tunnel were traded in for a bridge. Think of it this way, Moses wrote La Guardia. A bridge would cost $41 million, about half of what it would cost to build a tunnel. Moreover, a bridge could be built faster, would be cheaper than a tunnel to operate

and maintain, and would carry more traffic. Now what was there to argue?

La Guardia was floored by Moses' reversal—and after he discovered there were no legal measures he could take to force Moses to hand over Triborough's revenue, he realized he was trapped. The city couldn't hope to construct a Brooklyn-Battery tube, estimated to cost close to $80 million, with its $55-million loan from Washington. Thus, if he turned Moses down there would be no Brooklyn-Battery crossing at all, and that certainly was no alternative. All anyone had to do to see why New Yorkers were lobbying for another link between Manhattan and Brooklyn was to take the elevator to the top floor of the Municipal Building and watch the bumper-to-bumper traffic creep across the East River bridges. Reluctantly, La Guardia gave in to the man who held the purse strings.

The bridge Moses had in mind entailed stretching 6,500 feet of steel over the Upper Bay and Buttermilk Channel between Battery Park in Manhattan and Hamilton Avenue in Brooklyn. Designed by Othmar H. Ammann, Triborough's chief engineer, the six-lane crossing was actually two suspension bridges, each the size of the Brooklyn Bridge, placed end to end, and sharing a common anchorage pier off Governor's Island. In conjunction with the bridge, Moses also planned major land construction. In Manhattan the West Side Highway would be extended south from its terminus at Duane Street, linking up with a double-decked, elevated roadway at Rector Street, and an elevated approach would go up in the northern

The tower design of the George Washington Bridge as originally conceived by the architect Cass Gilbert.

section of Battery Park, and along its eastern edge. In Brooklyn, Hamilton Avenue would be widened by several lanes, a toll plaza built, and a connecting highway added.

New Yorkers couldn't believe what they were hearing. All this "to enable a few million jaloppies to scurry to and from Brooklyn on inconsequential errands?" protested a Staten Island man, whose own borough was accessible to Manhattan and Brooklyn only by ferry. And all this for $41 million? asked Ole Singstad, chief engineer of the Queens-Midtown Tunnel, which in 1939 was a year away from completion. According to Singstad's figures, extending the West Side Highway would alone cost $11 million. Others opposed to the plan thought it was highly imprudent in the middle of a world war to build what amounted to a sitting duck for bombs, and Manhattan Borough president Stanley Isaacs, who at the outset was opposed to a Brooklyn-Battery crossing of any kind, was aghast to hear Moses boast that the six-lane bridge would have the capacity to daily bring several thousand more vehicles than a tunnel into lower Manhattan. But what really gnawed at New Yorkers' hearts was the image of concrete stanchions marching through Battery Park, destroying forever the three-hundred-year-old oasis and obliterating irrevocably the skyline spectacle "of the most surprising architectural phantasy man has ever built."

Balderdash, said Moses, who had answers for all of his opponents. He tacked another $3 million onto his $41-million figure and called that sum adequate for the project. The connecting highways to the bridge would absorb the traffic loads in lower Manhattan, he informed Isaacs, and to people who protested that the bridge would become an enemy target, he responded that a bomb could just as easily hit a tunnel as a bridge. As to fears that the Manhattan approach to the bridge would ruin the skyline view, that was plain "ridiculous," Moses snapped. If critics had bothered to take a close look

Bird's-eye view of the proposed Brooklyn-Battery bridge. Triborough Bridge Authority, 1939.

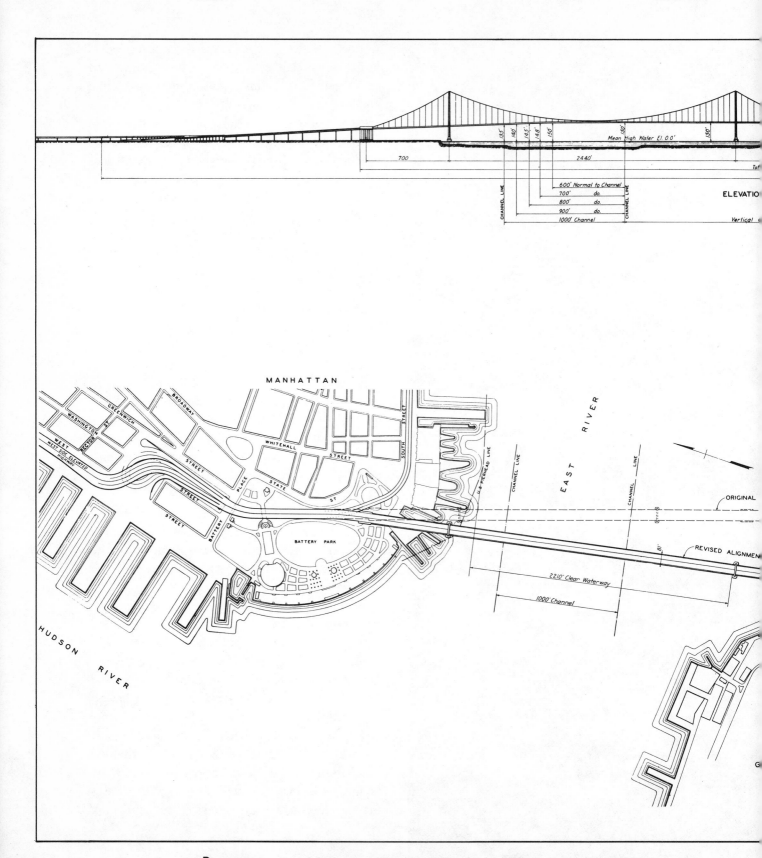

Plan and elevation of the proposed Brooklyn-Battery bridge. Othmar H. Ammann, 1939.

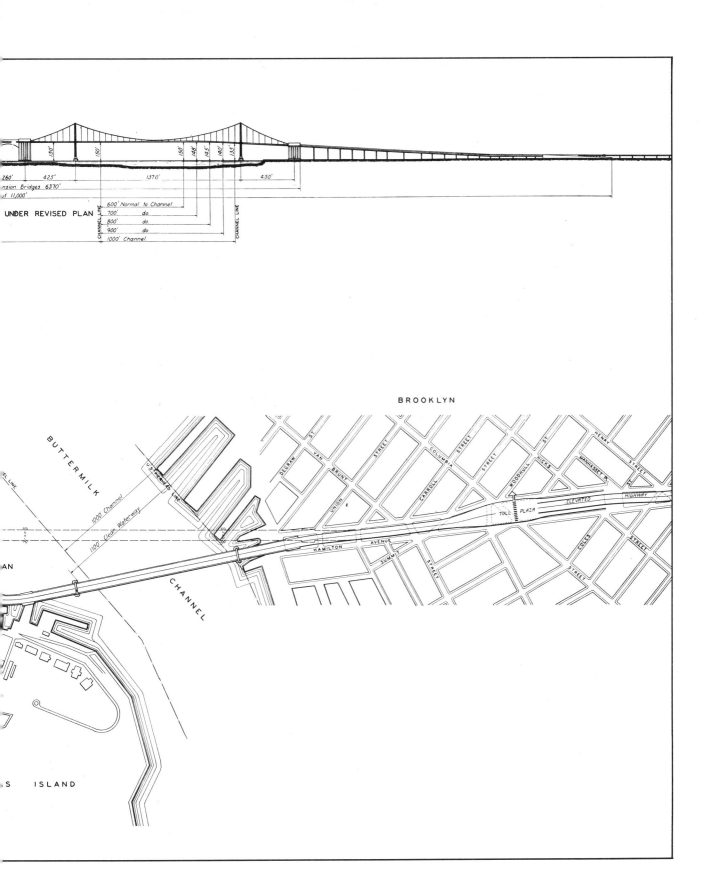

260' 425' 1370' 450'

150' 150' 150' 148' 145' 140' 135'

UNDER REVISED PLAN

nsion Bridges 6370'
ut 11,000'

600' Normal to Channel
700' do.
800' do.
900' do.
1000' Channel

CHANNEL LINE

CHANNEL LINE

BROOKLYN

BUTTERMILK

DEGRAW ST
VAN
BRUNT STREET
COLUMBIA STREET
STREET
HENRY
ST
STREET
HICKS
MANHASSET PL
WOODHULL
UNION
CARROLL
STREET
ELEVATED HIGHWAY
TOLL PLAZA
COLES STREET
HAMILTON AVENUE
SUMMIT STREET
STREET

EL LINE
U.S. PIERHEAD LINE
1000' Channel
1100' Clear Waterway

AN

CHANNEL

S ISLAND

Rendering of the proposed elevated highway and approach to the Brooklyn-Battery bridge, Manhattan. Triborough Bridge Authority, 1939.

at the plans for the bridge, they would have learned that the approach was "conceived as a most attractive type, consisting of light, graceful arches on masonry piers." Furthermore, added Ammann, the ten-story anchorage in Battery Park that everyone was so up in arms about "will hardly be noticeable in the general landscape."

"Light, graceful arches"? A ten-story anchorage sitting in Battery Park "hardly noticeable"? When the opposition sketched out its version of the plan, the half-mile approach that tore from Rector Street to the bay, grazing the Custom House and decimating Battery Park en route, looked more like the Great Wall of China. An unending stream of trucks and automobiles roared across the sky. Shadows and exhaust fumes blanketed the park. Battery Park, that reassuring constant in lower Manhattan's ever-growing forest of skyscrapers, had become an immense traffic island.

None of this was even hinted at in the photomontages prepared by the Triborough Bridge Authority, which depicted the approach and connecting elevated roads as mere ribbons floating sixty feet above the street. The bridge itself looked no more onerous on the face of the Upper Bay than a length of metallic rope flung across the water. Clever, said opponents to the scheme. And so the bridge might appear from fifteen thousand feet up in the air, "but what proportion of the population will ever see the bridge from an airplane?" By the same token, retorted Moses, how many would see it prone, from the ground? "Someone must have gotten down on his belly" to obtain the perspective used in the opposition's drawings, he scoffed.

The battle of the bridge moved to City Hall in March 1939. In a public hearing that lasted for several hours, representatives of the Architectural League, the Real Estate Board, the Municipal Art

Photomontage prepared by Ole Singstad to show the disastrous effect the Manhattan approach of the Brooklyn-Battery bridge would have on Battery Park and the downtown skyline, 1939.

The elevated approach to the Brooklyn-Battery bridge, as viewed from Battery Park, in a perspective study made by Hugh Ferriss and Chester Price, opponents to the bridge project, 1939. *A* indicates the U.S. Custom House; *B* points to the Battery Park Building (since demolished).

Society, the Broadway Association, and fourteen other civic and business groups stood up and condemned the project as bad planning from *any* perspective. Aside from destroying Battery Park and the view of the downtown skyline, which were reasons enough to reject the scheme, they said, the bridge would cause traffic mayhem in the narrow streets of lower Manhattan, reduce real estate values, and pose a war hazard.

But those arguments were not what members of the City Planning Commission heard when it came time to vote. What rang loudest in their ears was Moses shouting into the packed room: "This is a showdown on this project. Either you want it or you don't want it, and either you want it now or you don't get it at all." Faced with East River bridges that were clogged with traffic and with municipal coffers that couldn't buy a tunnel, the City Planning Commission yielded to Moses' bullying and approved the bridge.

But Moses was in for a rude shock. In July 1939, Secretary of War Harold Woodring summarily rejected the application for the Brooklyn-Battery bridge on the grounds that the crossing, if destroyed in time of war, "might block access from the sea" to the United States Navy Yard in Brooklyn.

Only one man was empowered to reverse Woodring's decision. In late October 1939 Mayor La Guardia headed straight for the White House and appealed personally to President Franklin D. Roosevelt to rescind the War Department's decision. While Roosevelt allowed that he was "very sympathetic with the desire of the people of New York to improve its traffic facilities," a Brooklyn-Battery bridge, he flatly declared, "would not be in the best interests of national defense."

But as Robert Caro recounts in his book *The Power Broker,* Roosevelt had other motives for felling the project. Moses and FDR had been feuding since the 1920s, when Moses, in his capacity as president of the New York State Council of Parks, had repeatedly used his friendship with Governor Al Smith as leverage to divert the council's funds out of the reach of Roosevelt, then chairman of the Taconic State Park Commission, and into his own park projects on Long Island. Sealing the men's

mutual animosity were Moses' vicious and unforgivable remarks about the disabled politician and his wife, Eleanor. In 1934, hoping to even the score, Roosevelt had tried to unseat Moses from his powerful position as chairman of the Triborough Bridge Authority. "Isn't the President of the United States entitled to one personal grudge?" FDR was overheard to grumble at the time. But now, in the Brooklyn-Battery bridge controversy, Roosevelt had seized the chance to finally strike down his old foe. Not only did Roosevelt reject the scheme for the bridge, he further saw to it that the city's $55-million federal loan was fattened by several million dollars to ensure the construction of a Brooklyn-Battery tube. And when ground for the tunnel was broken at Hamilton Avenue in Brooklyn on October 29, 1940, it was Roosevelt who dug up the first shovelful of dirt.

Moses had never been known as a gracious loser, but in the wake of the first major defeat of his career, he outdid even himself. As administrator of New York's scrap metal program, Moses recalled the 28,000 tons of cast iron that were to line the cylinders of the Brooklyn-Battery Tunnel, delaying work on the project for several years. He pestered La Guardia unceasingly until finally, in 1945, the mayor submitted and gave Moses something that he had wanted even more than a Brooklyn-Battery bridge—the New York City Tunnel Authority. As chairman of the new Triborough Bridge and Tunnel Authority, Moses then fired Ole Singstad from his position as chief engineer of the Brooklyn-Battery Tunnel. And so, when the Brooklyn-Battery Tunnel opened to traffic in 1950, it was all Moses' show.

Moses, however, never did quite get over his disappointment at having lost the bridge. Years later, in his book *Working for the People,* Moses still maintained that a Brooklyn-Battery bridge would have carried "twice the amount of traffic, cost half as much as a tunnel and could have been built in half the time." And he still insisted that a bridge would not "have defaced the area or spoiled the view from the bay." But, he added, "in this game you take what you can get and make the best of it."

PARKS

The commissioners appointed in 1807 to draw up a street plan for Manhattan were a little defensive when they unveiled their scheme four years later. "It may, to many, be a matter of surprise, that so few vacant spaces have been left, and those so small, for the benefit of fresh air, and consequent preservation of health," they said. "Certainly, if the City of New-York were destined to stand on the side of a small stream, such as the Seine or the Thames, a great number of ample places might be needful." But given the fortuitous fact that Manhattan was surrounded on all sides by "large arms of the sea," the commissioners explained, they had decided after mapping out a grid of streets and avenues that nine squares sprinkled here and there, totaling some five hundred acres, would be quite adequate for New Yorkers' "health and pleasure."

Unfortunately, the commissioners had neglected to factor a margin of greed into their calculations. Before long the waterfront of those "large arms of the sea" was seized for shipping and commerce, and broad swaths of three of the nine plots were shaved off and sold to developers, leaving New Yorkers mere paddocks of grass and trees. Such was the fate of Union Square, reduced from ten acres to its present size in 1832; the Market Place, which was trimmed away until only Tompkins Square remained; and the Parade, a seventy-three-acre tract intended for military drills that was whittled down to six acres, and renamed Madison Square, in the early 1840s. Harlem Square, Bloomingdale Square, Hamilton Square, the Harlem Marsh, and Observatory Place never made it off paper in any form. One by one the would-be parks were struck off the map and sliced into a grid of streets and avenues. By the late 1860s the only tract whose perimeters remained exactly as they had been drawn up by the commissioners was Manhattan Square, today the site of the American Museum of Natural History.

In the late 1850s the city compensated for the commissioners' stingy allotment of open space by roping off 840 acres in the middle of Manhattan Island for Central Park. The rectangular tract, transformed by Frederick Law Olmsted and Calvert Vaux from a melancholy wasteland into a verdant *rus in urbe,* was New York's—indeed America's—first large public preserve, and its beauty and popular acclaim soon inspired the creation of large landscaped public parks across the nation. By the turn of the century New York could boast Riverside Park, Prospect Park, Van Cortlandt Park, Pelham Bay Park, and a dozen others. Few of these urban oases were the brainchild of City Hall, however. Most were

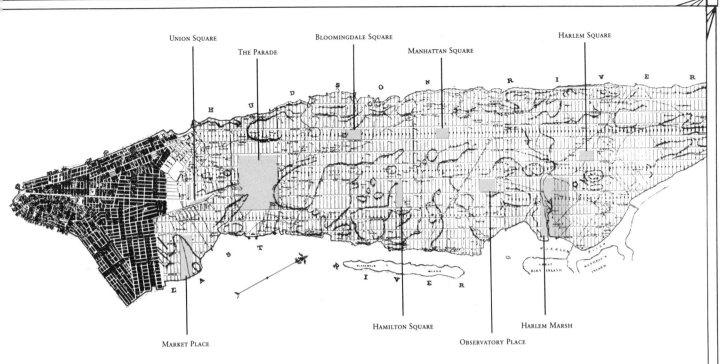

UNION SQUARE   THE PARADE   BLOOMINGDALE SQUARE   MANHATTAN SQUARE   HARLEM SQUARE

MARKET PLACE   HAMILTON SQUARE   OBSERVATORY PLACE   HARLEM MARSH

The open space allotted for Manhattan Island in the commissioners' plan of 1811.

set aside for posterity through the efforts of farsighted citizens whose reams of petitions and campaigns of many years were instrumental in persuading the city to purchase parcels of open land before they became forever buried beneath bricks and mortar. The city fathers were not necessarily against acquiring park space. What kept them all too often from racing speculators to the nearest For Sale sign was the high price of property, a harsh fact of New York real estate life that even the commissioners of 1811 had ruefully acknowledged.

But securing park space for New York City has taken more than an outlay of money and some monumental sleights of the landscaper's hand. To preserve the city's precious acres of green, New Yorkers have had to stand on constant guard to defend their parks against a host of unwelcome intrusions. Thanks to vigilant citizens Battery Park was not sawed in half for a canal in 1805, nor did Flushing Meadows–Corona Park become the home of a Grand Prix racing track in the mid-1980s. Central Park, which has inspired more dreadful plans than any other park in the city, was rescued in 1919 from having an airfield plopped in its center, and in 1964 from becoming the site of a housing project. What future generations will propose for New York's park system can only be surmised. Let us hope that they will seize every opportunity to create new public groves and meadows—or, at the very least, leave the picnic grounds as they found them.

New Brighton, Staten Island, 1836. This view appeared in a prospectus that advertised New Brighton's "beauty of location" and "salubrity of climate." The proposed development of villas and country homes pictured on the hill was never built.

On a scorching summer day in July 1844, William Cullen Bryant, the editor of the *Evening Post*, watched New Yorkers' annual mass exodus to places where the thermometer never climbed above a comfortable seventy-five degrees. The rich packed their steamer trunks and sailed off to European spas; others departed for a month in the mountains. People of lesser means beat the blistering heat by taking a day's excursion to the Elysian Fields in Hoboken or to the beaches of New Brighton on Staten Island. Still, that left most of Manhattan's 400,000 residents living between the Battery and Fourteenth Street to find a shady patch of grass in one of the dozen undersized, overused plots of green the city offered as park space.

It was for these people especially that Bryant put to paper an idea he had been ruminating about for several years. In an indignant editorial that appeared on the eve of the Fourth of July, Bryant wrote, "If the public authorities, who expend so much of our money in laying out the city, would do what is in their power, they might give our vast population an extensive pleasure ground for shade and recreation in these sultry afternoons, which we might reach without going out of town." If these same public authorities wondered where this great pleasure ground might be created, Bryant added, they had only to consult him. He had scouted the rural fringes of New York on horseback, and, in his opinion, for location, views, and beauty, there was no "finer situation for the public garden of a great city" than Jones' Wood, a thick virgin forest that stood between the East River and Third Avenue, from Sixty-sixth to Seventy-sixth streets. Readers of the *Evening Post*, sweltering in the oppressive July heat, must have been tantalized by Bryant's description of the site:

> The surface is varied in a very striking and picturesque manner, with craggy eminences, and hollows, and a little stream runs through the midst. The swift tides of the East River sweep its rocky shores, and the fresh breeze of the bay comes in, on every warm summer afternoon, over the restless waters. The trees are of almost every species that grows in our woods:—the different varieties of oak, the birch, the beech, the linden, the mulberry, the tulip tree, and others:

the azalea, the kalmia, and other flowering shrubs are in bloom here at their season, and the ground in spring is gay with flowers.

But if the forest were to become a park, New York had to act quickly, said Bryant. "Commerce is devouring inch by inch the coast of the island, and if we would rescue any part of it for health and recreation it must be done now."

The city fathers sat on Bryant's proposal for several years, while under their noses Manhattan's sixty-five acres of meager parkland were being worn thin by a population that had pushed north past Twenty-third Street and was fast approaching the half-million mark. Had it not been for the resolve of Mayor Ambrose Kingsland, an additional 300,000 New Yorkers would have shared the same sixty-five acres a decade later. Addressing the Common Council in May 1851, the new mayor all but commanded the city's aldermen to rouse themselves into "prompt action" before real estate prices rose any higher, and to secure for New Yorkers a

William Cullen Bryant, c. 1830.

large public park "of wood, lawn and water" that "would be at once the pride and ornament of the city." Think not only of our own teeming thousands, rich and poor, who would delight in the sylvan pleasures of a vast preserve, Kingsland urged his colleagues to consider—think to the future, to the "thousands yet unborn" who would be ever grateful for our "wisdom, sagacity and forethought" in procuring for them "the blessings of pure air, and the opportunity for innocent, healthful enjoyment."

The mayor's message took quick effect. Not four weeks later the Committee on Lands and Places, set up to select a park site, recommended taking Jones' Wood as a public park. Without so much

View looking north on the East River, from East Sixtieth Street to Jones' Wood, c. 1865.

as a few words of acknowledgment to William Cullen Bryant, the author of the idea, the committee reported, "The spot is easy of access from the city, it is abundantly shaded with trees of various descriptions, has a large waterfront, and could, by the exercise of proper care and a cultivated taste, be made equal in attractions to any park in this or the old countries of Europe." Moreover, reported the committee, Messrs. Jones and Schermerhorn, who owned most of the property within the contemplated park site, were prepared to negotiate a

Andrew Jackson Downing, c. 1850.

"definite proposal for its sale and purchase." The asking price was $700,000.

On July 11, 1851, almost seven years to the day after Bryant had suggested cordoning off Jones' Wood as a park, the city was authorized by the State Legislature to acquire the 160-acre forest with public funds and lay out a public preserve for the free use of all the citizens of New York.

Surprisingly, not everyone was thrilled by the prospect of a spacious pleasure ground. Parsimonious New Yorkers carped about the hike in taxes that the expense of the new park was sure to bring. Shipping interests opposed appropriating valuable waterfront property for such frivolous purposes. Another contingent of nay-sayers thought 160 acres was extravagantly large for New Yorkers' recreational needs. Too *large?* "Short-sighted economists!" scoffed Andrew Jackson Downing. Why, compared to London's 6,000 acres of parkland, which "would swallow up most of the 'unimproved' part of New York City," Jones' Wood was "only a child's playground," said Downing. "*Five*

hundred acres is the smallest area that should be reserved for the future wants of the city, *now,* while it may be obtained," he insisted.

People were inclined to listen to Mr. Downing, America's leading authority on horticulture and landscape gardening. Self-taught, Downing had rocketed to national fame in 1841 after the publication of his best-seller, *A Treatise on the Theory and Practice of Landscape Gardening,* which offered country dwellers a practical guide to laying out gardens and walks, erecting attractive fences, and planting ornamental trees, all with an eye to rendering "domestic life more delightful." The appearance the following year of *Cottage Residences,* a prettily illustrated volume suggesting ten designs for rural homes, cemented Downing's popular appeal. "Nobody, whether he be rich or poor, builds a house or lays out a garden without consulting Downing's works," commented a Swedish visitor to the United States in 1848.

Fame and fortune enabled the young author to sell the family nursery in Newburgh, New York, where he had garnered much of his horticultural experience, and devote his time, through writing and consultation, to shaping the American ideal of the rural home and garden. But, like William Cullen Bryant, Downing was also an early advocate of a large public park for New York City. A spacious *rus in urbe* of green fields, limpid lakes, and leafy drives would enable New Yorkers to "forget, for a time, the rattle of pavements and the glare of brick walls," Downing wrote in 1851. Add to the landscape monuments, music pavilions, and winter gardens, and citizens would come away imbued with an appreciation "of the beautiful in nature and art." Throw open the park to all classes—to the laborer, the clerk, and the millionaire—and they would "grow into social freedom by the very influence of easy intercourse, space, and beauty that surround them." But do not think for a minute that this urban Eden could be wrested from the small plot known as Jones' Wood, said Downing.

Fortunately, the city heeded his advice. In August 1851 the aldermen Daniel Dodge and Joseph Britton were charged with determining whether there was an alternative, affordable site to Jones' Wood,

A design for a rural cottage, from *Cottage Residences* by Andrew Jackson Downing, 1842.

of the size Downing had recommended, that could be taken as a public park.

Indeed there was, reported the aldermen in January 1852. Between Fifty-ninth Street and 106th Street, from Fifth Avenue to Eighth Avenue, lay 760 acres of "uneven and rocky surface," veined with natural streams and abounding in hill and dale—features that made the tract "almost entirely useless for building purposes" but eminently suitable for the most picturesque of pleasure grounds. The only significant structures within the boundaries of the forty-six-block parcel were the State Arsenal, located at Sixty-fourth Street and Fifth Avenue; Mount Saint Vincent's Convent, which stood near 105th Street and Sixth Avenue; and the Croton Reservoir, whose rectangular tank occupied 33 acres in the middle of the tract. These could be incorporated into the design of the future park, suggested the aldermen, thereby saving the expense of acquiring 57 acres of land. Since another 327 acres of the site were already city-owned, that left only 376 acres of private property to purchase, which could be had for $1,407,325—or about $600 less per acre than it would cost to buy Jones' Wood.

But however one wished to calculate it, said the aldermen, $1,407,325 was "a comparatively tri-

fling sum" to pay for a reach of land that, though at present far from attractive, was endowed with great potential for "tasteful embellishments." Surveying the expanse from atop a craggy hill near 105th Street and Eighth Avenue they had imagined a park "intersected by beautiful artificial lakes of various sizes; by small streams, crossed by numerous marble or rustic bridges; by beautiful groves of every variety, indigenous and exotic; by serpentine roads winding through velvet lawns decorated with sparkling fountains, and the whole surrounded by architectural works of every order and variety." This would be a park that all New Yorkers—present and future—could, "with honest pride, favorably compare with the most celebrated public grounds of the chief cities of Europe." This, in short, was the magnificent preserve Downing himself had envisioned for New York. For "the sake of convenience," said the aldermen, they had named the 760-acre tract "Central Park."

The city fathers scratched their heads and pondered the idea for over a year. Not the public. New Yorkers immediately began circulating petitions, asking any and all who had an opinion on the matter to state their preference: did they favor Central Park or Jones' Wood? Ten thousand citizens scrawled their signatures beneath the heading Jones' Park (as it came to be called), about an equal number opted for Central Park, and nearly seven hundred people dismissed either pleasure ground as a "mere luxury."

Horticulturists were divided on the issue. Some argued that, with a minimum of pruning and seeding, Jones' Wood could become an attractive public preserve virtually overnight. Other horticulturists thought the varied terrain of the Central Park site offered more creative landscaping possibilities, even though it was true that it would be principally later generations who would get to enjoy the fruits of their labor. Health experts were also of two minds. One faction maintained that, as "the lungs of the city," the park should be as large as possible and as close to "the greatest number of inhabitants for the purposes of air and exercise." Of the two sites, clearly Central Park best met those requirements. Those who favored taking Jones' Wood, where

Bird's-eye view of the Central Park site, 1854. The large building perched on a hill to the far left is Mount Saint Vincent's Convent; the Croton (later Yorkville) Reservoir is in the middle of the tract; and the State Arsenal (look for the eight towers) is located on the right.

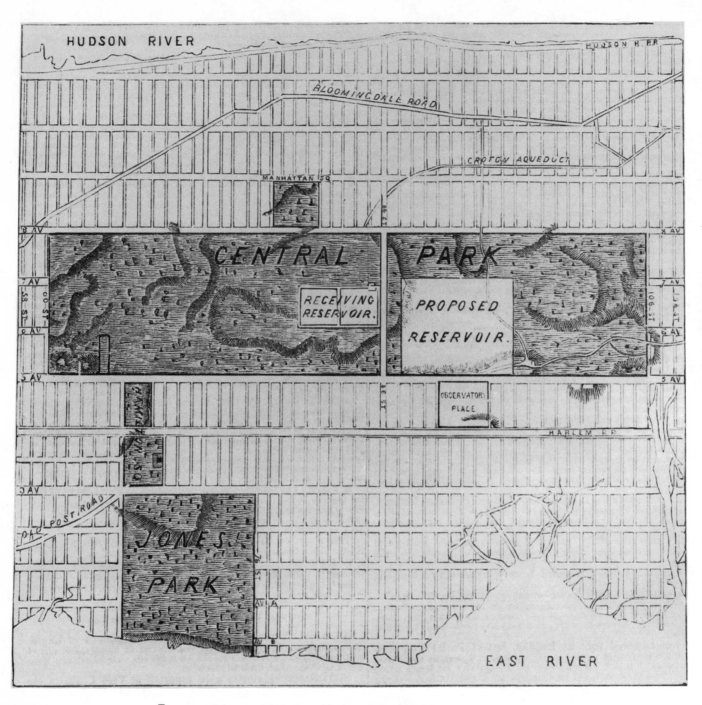

The great debate in 1853: Jones' Park or Central Park?

"health and pure air wafted in from the breezy river," pointed to the fetid swamps at the southern end of Central Park and warned of the risks of yellow fever.

As far as William Cullen Bryant was concerned, the way out of the quandary was simple: take both tracts. "There is now ample room and verge enough upon the island for two parks," he wrote in the *Evening Post*, "whereas if the matter is delayed for a few years, there will hardly be space left for one."

To New Yorkers' amazement, they did get both. On July 21, 1853, the State Legislature authorized the city to acquire the land between Fifty-ninth and 106th streets, giving Manhattan Island—on paper—a total of 920 acres of new park land. It was a staggering figure for New Yorkers to behold: nearly a thousand acres for a city that only the day before had claimed as its largest park the Battery, a paltry eleven acres of trees and graveled walks. But visions of New York blanketed in miles of umbrageous groves and emerald meadows were soon dispelled. A year later, the 1851 act to take Jones' Wood as

a public preserve was repealed, for one large park was considered ample for the city.

Andrew Jackson Downing, the guiding spirit behind Central Park, did not live to see the birth of the great green rectangle. Bound for Washington, D.C., on July 28, 1852, to supervise work on the design of the capital's Mall, Downing drowned in the Hudson River as he tried to rescue a fellow passenger from the fiery explosion of the steamboat *Henry Clay*. But the horticulturist, not yet thirty-seven years old, had unwittingly bequeathed to Central Park an invaluable fortune. Two years before his death, Downing had journeyed to London in search of an architect who could assist him in designing the Gothic-style villas illustrated in his books. He returned to Newburgh with a young Englishman named Calvert Vaux. It was at Downing's home in Newburgh, Vaux later recalled, that he first met Frederick Law Olmsted, a gentleman farmer from Staten Island. Little did either man imagine that they would meet again several years later to collaborate on the design of Central Park.

In May 1856, it seemed to Mayor Fernando Wood and street commissioner Joseph Taylor, the two men who made up the newly named Board of Commissioners of the Central Park, that their logical order of business was to first obtain a topographical survey of the tract between Fifty-ninth and 106th streets and then worry about a design. Certainly anyone who knew the site didn't expect miracles by morning. The park-to-be, a desolate expanse of stagnant swamps, rocks, and barren hillocks, was home to five thousand squatters living in rude hovels among a roaming population of geese, dogs, swine, and goats. Market gardeners had fenced off a portion of the tract to grow crops; milkmen and others had claimed the few grassy areas as pastureland for their cows. Bone-boiling works, pigsties, and slaughterhouses fouled the air. It was hard to imagine that this wretched scene would ever be transformed into a magnificent pleasure ground. What mortal could be equal to the task?

Egbert L. Viele thought he was. Not only had he at his own initiative begun a topographical survey of the park tract shortly after the city had been authorized to take the land in 1853, he had also drawn up a plan for the park's design. In June 1856 he deposited both, and an accompanying descriptive report, with commissioners Taylor and Wood.

That Viele, a civil engineer, had prepared a plan for Central Park did not strike the commissioners as odd. At the time America could claim no important practitioners of landscape design, and engineers were often called upon to lay out ponds, plantings, and walkways for large properties. (The engineer David Bates Douglass, for example, had designed the attractive, parklike grounds of Brooklyn's Greenwood Cemetery in the late 1830s.) Yet Viele must have felt a little apprehensive in undertaking a project so monumental. There were no large American public parks to which he could look for inspiration or guidance, and beyond the writ-

Central Park site, c. 1858, looking southwest from the craggy hill where Belvedere Castle was later built.

ings of Andrew Jackson Downing, little theory had been formulated regarding the kind of "people's park" a democratic society should strive to create. Viele only knew what Central Park should *not* be. To model it on the "smiling gardens" built in Europe by kings and despots, he wrote, would be "a [poor] reflection of our national taste."

In effect, Viele let the park design itself. Where mud holes and bogs dotted the 760-acre tract, the engineer envisioned small crystal lakes. Craggy rock masses were to be planted and left to stand as "charming hills," hollows were to become "alpine valleys," and large level expanses he reserved as recreational areas "for the encouragement of athletic and manly sports." Encircling "the ever-changing scenery" of the park was to be a broad carriage road called the Circuit.

Not only did the commissioners sign Viele on, in June 1856, to execute his design, they appointed him chief engineer of Central Park, with the understanding that he would also finish the topographical survey he had begun. Viele began work immediately. Before the first winter's snow in 1856 the engineer could report that a "minute deliberation of the topography" was under way, and that drainage studies and botanical profiles had been completed. If all went according to schedule, he hoped that work crews could begin clearing land by spring for construction of the Circuit.

The *New York Times* lauded the commissioners for adopting Viele's plan and placing the park under his supervision. "We have no doubt that the best talent will be employed hereafter in the various departments necessary to the improvement of this magnificent Park," said an editorial. *Harper's Weekly* published an illustration of Viele's design and confidently predicted that in five years "New Yorkers may boast of having the finest Park in the world. The time is long, one whole fourteenth of a human life," it sighed, "but such works as this can not be done in a day."

In the opinion of the architect Calvert Vaux, who proclaimed himself "thoroughly disgusted with the manifest defects of Viele's design," such works were best left to expire on paper. A hill here, a lake there, with a cricket ground somewhere in between, did not constitute a great public park. That was the very least he had learned from his late partner and mentor, Andrew Jackson Downing, America's "rural Socrates," whose definition of a park had called for the judicious melding of nature and art. If Viele's scheme was carried out, it "would be a disgrace to the City and to the memory of Mr. Downing," Vaux declared.

Unfortunately for Viele, the architect wielded enough clout to see that the plan was axed. Vaux was well acquainted with Charles Elliott, an iron manufacturer who had studied horticulture under Downing, and with John Gray, a director of the Bank of New York, for whom the architect had designed a home on Fifth Avenue and a bank on Wall Street. Both men served on the newly appointed, eleven-member Board of Commissioners of the Central Park, an august body comprised of lawyers and businessmen, and it wasn't long before Vaux showed up at their offices to convince them "and any other interested person who would listen" to discard Viele's scheme for the park and consider sponsoring a design competition.

He emerged triumphant.

In October 1857 a small notice appeared in the city's newspapers inviting the public to submit plans for the improvement of Central Park. The competition guidelines set by the Board of Commissioners stipulated that all designs include a parade ground; a public hall to be used for exhibitions or concerts; a large flower garden; three playgrounds; a fountain and a prospect tower; a place for winter skating; and at least four east-west roads. Plans for the park, each to be "accompanied by a well-digested written description," were due April 1, 1858. From the entries, three runners-up and one winner would be selected, sharing between them over four thousand dollars in prize money.

While hopeful contestants labored over their plans for Central Park, work on the two-and-a-half-mile-long rectangle continued. Egbert Viele, who had managed to hang on to his title of chief engineer even after his design for the park had been jettisoned, divided his days between finishing the topographical survey and directing the operations of ridding the 760-acre tract of squatters' dwellings, old stone fences, and dense underbrush. He had also a new superintendent to train, Frederick Law Olmsted, who had been hired by the board of commissioners to attend to the force of five hundred workmen employed in the park. From their first meeting, Viele had taken an instant dislike to his assistant. He had wanted a "practical man"—someone accustomed to rough outdoor work and savvy about the ways of the park's slothful laborers, who were often likely to be found buried behind a newspaper or dozing beneath a tree. The nearest experience Olmsted could claim in this capacity was his brief tenure as a gentleman farmer, which in Viele's opinion hardly qualified him for the job of superintendent.

But Olmsted soon proved himself to be immensely competent. He explored every acre of the park by foot and on horseback, recording his observations of soil conditions, geological formations, plant life, and water courses. Within weeks of his appointment as superintendent, Olmsted had prepared a comprehensive plan for the drainage of the park site as well as a report outlining his recommendations for the purchase of several varieties of trees and shrubs. He took charge of the park's work force, which in a few months was expanded to one thousand men. And, to Viele's irritation, he won high praise from the commissioners, who in early 1858 increased Olmsted's annual salary from $1,500 to $2,000.

It was in part Olmsted's familiarity with the to-

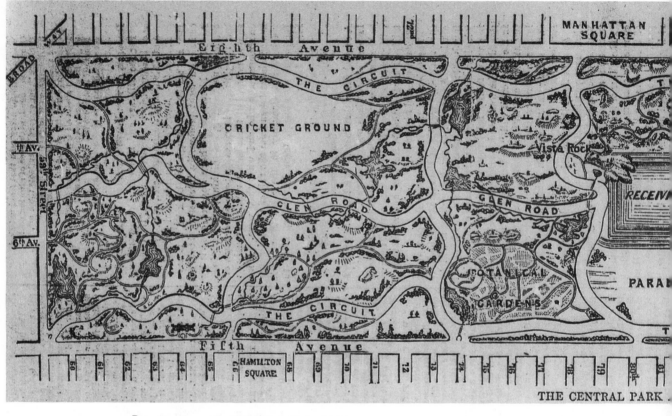

Plan for Central Park. Egbert L. Viele, 1856.

Topographical survey of the Central Park site made by Egbert L. Viele, 1856–57, showing out-croppings, existing hills, bogs, and streams. Construction of the park's second reservoir (later named Manhattan Lake), located between Eighty-sixth and Ninety-sixth streets, was not begun until 1858.

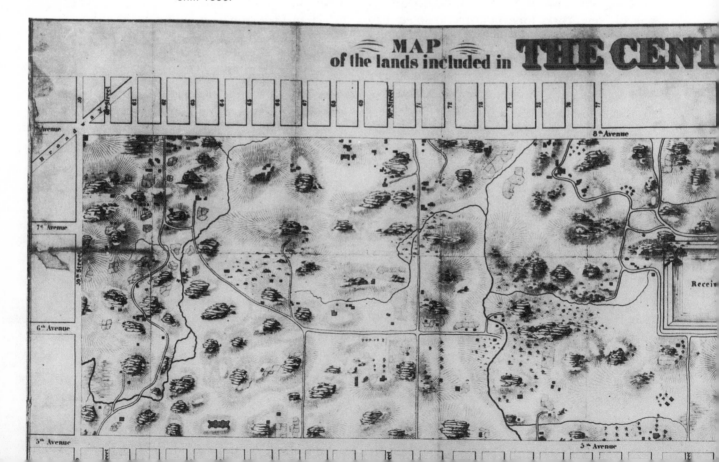

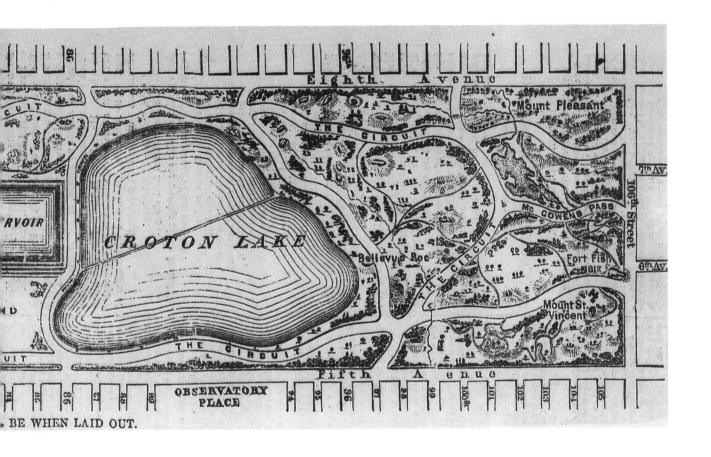

CIRCUIT
RESERVOIR
CROTON LAKE
Eighth Avenue
THE CIRCUIT
Mount Pleasant
7th Av
106th Street
McGOWENS PASS
Bellevue Roc
THE CIRCUIT
Fort Fish
1812
6th Av
Mount St.
Vincent
THE CIRCUIT
Fifth Avenue
OBSERVATORY
PLACE
BE WHEN LAID OUT.

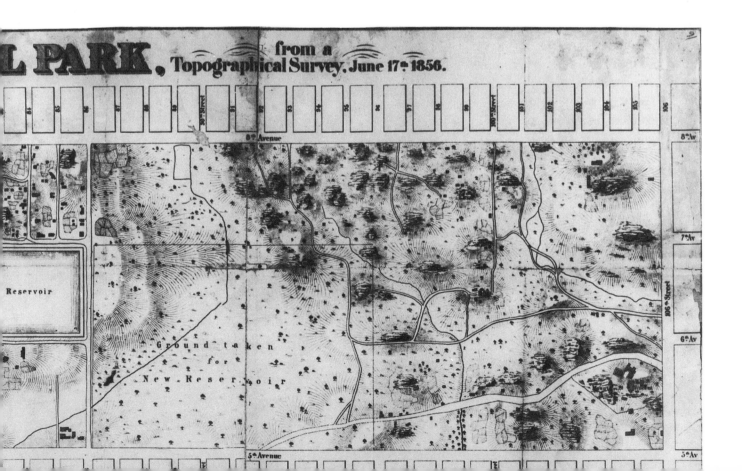

L PARK, *from a* Topographical Survey, June 17th 1856.

8th Avenue

8th Av

7th Av

106th Street

Reservoir

6th Av

Ground taken
for
New Reservoir

5th Avenue

5th Av

pography of Central Park, Vaux would later write, that prompted him to invite the new superintendent to join him in preparing a plan for the design competition. Initially, Olmsted was reluctant to collaborate with the architect because he knew that Viele also intended to enter the competition, and he did not wish to further sour a relationship already fraught with animosity. But when Viele brusquely declared that he didn't care one way or the other what his assistant did, Olmsted decided to accept Vaux's invitation—not out of a great desire to design America's first public park, it seems, but rather with the hopes of extracting himself from his pecuniary woes. His various past ventures as a sailor, a farmer, a writer, and a publisher, all underwritten by his indulgent father, a well-to-do Hartford, Connecticut, merchant, and all financial failures, had thrust Olmsted into deep debt at the age of thirty-five. The possibility of winning several hundred dollars in prize money was too tempting to pass up. "It is certainly worth while for me to go into the competition, the reward of success being so large," Olmsted candidly wrote his father early in 1858.

With the exception of the winning scheme and two drawings submitted by competitor No. 25, the plans entered for competition seem not to have survived. However, some idea of what awaited the commissioners when they assembled on April 2, 1858, to judge the plans can be gleaned from the descriptive reports that accompanied the proposed designs, since bound in a thick catalog and placed with the New-York Historical Society.

For the most part, the thirty-three entrants envisioned Central Park as a naturalistic landscape of thick groves, gurgling streams, and winding paths, dotted here and there with the architectural and recreational features required by the competition guidelines. But to this formula was added a great variety of "extras." Competitor No. 9 pictured the perimeter of the park edged with several small lodges for police and wardens, "each one of a different style. Thus we would have the Italian lodge, the Chinese lodge, the Norwegian lodge, the Japanese lodge . . . &c., &c." Competitor No. 5, J. Lauchaume of Yonkers, New York (one of the few

Calvert Vaux, c. 1860.

Frederick Law Olmsted, c. 1860.

Central Park competition entry. Roswell Graves (competitor No. 25), 1858. "Before" and "after" views, showing proposed improvement of park area north of Fifty-ninth Street.

competitors who did not submit his plan anonymously), suggested letting oxen, sheep, and goats roam the northern end of the park "to give it the country-like air of which we citizens of this great metropolis are so fond, and most of the time deprived." Since the commissioners were intent on ridding the park of just such animals, it is unlikely that the idea met with any enthusiasm. Competitor No. 28 needn't have bothered submitting his plan anonymously. From the descriptive report alone it is instantly recognizable as Egbert Viele's design of 1856, to which the engineer merely added a skating ground, a public hall, and a grotto. Other plans entered in the competition featured Greek temples; windmills figured in at least two designs; and one competitor suggested providing the park with an artillery range, 1,700 feet long, for cannon, musket, and pistol practice.

On April 28, 1858, not four weeks after the competition deadline, the Board of Commissioners announced the winners. The fourth prize, of $500, went to Howard Daniels, a New York architect and landscaper; Lachlan H. McIntosh, the property clerk of Central Park, and Michael Miller, the park's paymaster, shared the third prize, of $750; and Samuel Gustin, the park's superintendent of planting, came in second, for $1,000. The coveted first prize, of $2,000, was awarded to Calvert Vaux and Frederick Law Olmsted for their plan, which was entitled "Greensward."

While it would seem that the contestants in the employ of Central Park had an inside advantage in the competition, it will never be known conclusively what factors led to the selection of the four winning schemes, because nowhere in the official records of the Board of Central Park, or elsewhere, did the commissioners explain why they believed plans Nos. 26, 27, 30, and 33 to be the best of the schemes submitted. Howard Daniels (No. 26), who proposed for Central Park a hybrid of a pastoral and a formal landscape embellished with temples, kiosks, and summerhouses "more or less sylvan," may have impressed the commissioners with his scholarly essay on the principles of landscape gardening, which filled several pages of his descriptive report. McIntosh and Miller's cursory report, on

the other hand, merely itemized the architectural and landscape features they envisioned for the park, any of which—with the exception of a large saltwater lake—were to be found in a dozen other schemes submitted for the competition. (It is, of course, conceivable that McIntosh and Miller were more adept at rendering than at writing, and that the prize-winning qualities of plan No. 27 would be apparent were there a drawing to consult.)

Samuel Gustin (No. 30) probably leapt to second place because of his splendid "before" and "after" plaster models of the park, each twenty-two feet long, which no doubt the commissioners found very useful in visualizing the nurseryman's intended design. The elaborate plan, which borrowed several features from the Bois de Bologne in Paris, included a dairy, a grand cascade, a deer park, and several lakes, the largest of which was to contain an island with a "Swiss cottage for the sale of lemonade, ice-cream and other refreshments." Gustin thought there was also a place in Central Park for an amphitheater flanked by restaurants, a Greek temple, and a statue of George Washington "pouring out two streams of water from inverted urns."

In regard to the winning scheme, No. 33, it is not hard to see why the commissioners awarded it first prize. From their descriptive report alone, Olmsted and Vaux's plan stands out as one of the very few competition entries that envisioned Central Park as a tranquil, picturesque retreat for city-weary souls, rather than as some giant pedestal for the display of man's handiwork. "Buildings are scarcely a necessary part of a park; neither are flower-gardens, architectural terraces or fountains," declared the partners in their report. "They should, therefore, be constructed after dry walks and drives, greensward and shade, with other essentials, have been secured." Elaborating on this theme in the second half of their report, Olmsted and Vaux offered a schedule for drainage, soil improvement, and walkway construction, as well as a comprehensive list of the trees, shrubs, and other plantings that might be suitable for the park—subjects that, surprisingly, most of the other competitors did not bother to address. But what surely

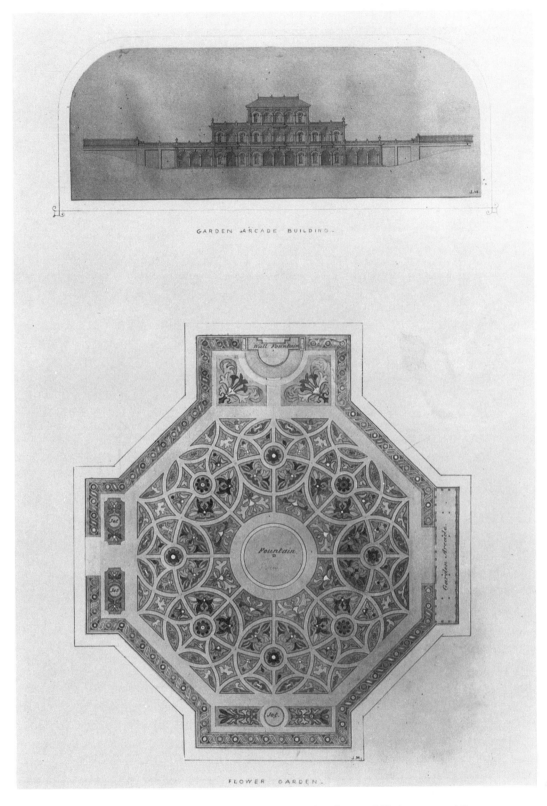

GARDEN ARCADE BUILDING.

FLOWER GARDEN.

Elevation and plan of a flower garden proposed for Central Park near Fifth Avenue and Seventy-fourth Street. Olmsted and Vaux, 1858. At the behest of the Board of Commissioners of the Central Park, Olmsted and Vaux revised their scheme for the site, and replaced the proposed flower garden with the Conservatory Pond.

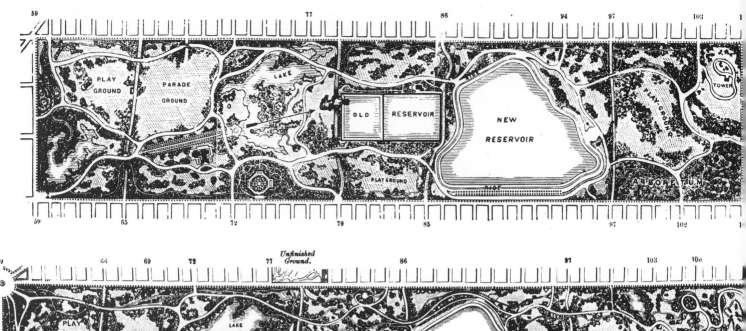

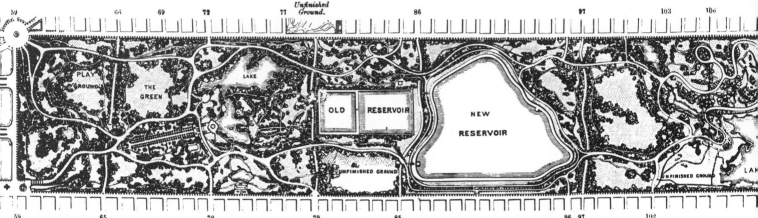

clinched the first prize for plan No. 33 was its ingenious proposal to sink the east-west roads several feet below the surface of the park as a way to both conceal crosstown traffic and give those riding or strolling in the park unbroken vistas of the surrounding landscape.

Olmsted came away from the competition not only a thousand dollars richer but with the title of architect-in-chief of Central Park, and the handsome annual salary of $2,500. Vaux was put on the payroll as a lowly "assistant" at five dollars a day, although he was eventually promoted to the position of consulting architect. Egbert Viele was fired. Outraged, the engineer promptly sued the city for several thousand dollars, claiming that he had never been paid for the design he had drawn up for the park in 1856, nor for the topographical survey. To the dismay of Olmsted and Vaux he also accused the partners of having copied his scheme.

Top: The Greensward plan, the winning entry in the design competition for Central Park. Olmsted and Vaux, 1858. Bottom: Revised plan for Central Park. Olmsted and Vaux, 1859. Olmsted and Vaux amended the original Greensward scheme, designing new ground for the area between 106th and 110th streets, which was added to the park in 1859.

Although the authorship of plan No. 33 was not directly challenged in Viele's lawsuit, it was called into question when the case came to trial in 1864. Viele contended that general features of the Greensward plan, such as the location of the flower garden, recreational areas, and the carriage drive, closely approached those in his design. Vaux testified that while he and Olmsted had indeed studied the engineer's scheme and discussed where it was "capable of improvement," the Greensward plan "was entirely original." Olmsted pointed out that similarities between all of the plans were inevitable, because the competition guidelines had required "certain common features, and the topography of the ground was such as to admit of no choice in the location of some of these." One might have been inclined to side with Viele in the controversy had he not made other, wholly preposterous, allegations regarding the competition. During the trial the engineer accused half of the contestants of having copied his scheme, and claimed moreover that he, with Lachlan McIntosh, had designed the plan that received third prize. There is no evidence to support this.

Viele was awarded nine thousand dollars in damages in 1864; two years later (perhaps with some of this windfall), the engineer launched the plan for the Arcade Railway.* Central Park, meanwhile, had been enlarged to include the area between 106th and 110th streets, and work on the 840-acre tract was well under way. To create a rural landscape, tunnels and roads were dynamited out of rock, hills were moved from one end of the park to the other, bogs were filled in with topsoil, and gardeners, armed with hoes and shovels, fanned out across the park to dig in tulip bulbs, wind flowers, rose bushes, and sapling trees. In the early 1870s, one amazed visitor to Central Park couldn't help but remark: "Looking around now upon the beautiful landscape, with its exquisite lawns and shrubbery, its picturesque hills, and romantic walks and drives, its sparkling lakes, cascades and fountains, it is hard to realize that so much loveliness was preceded by such hideousness."

By the 1880s gentlemen who enjoyed the popular nineteenth-century sport known as trotting were hard-pressed to find a long, straight, smooth—and above all—empty stretch of road in Manhattan for horse racing. Until the late 1850s a favorite track had been rural Third Avenue, from Murray Hill to Yorkville, "the exercise and trial ground of all fast trotters and pacers," according to John Jacob Astor's grandson. But the row of new buildings that continued a steady march north, and the meddlesome iron rails of the Third Avenue horsecar line, laid down mile by mile in the 1850s, eventually sent the sportsmen in their light, big-wheeled buggies to seek out new turf, far from the encroachments of city life, on Harlem Lane (today Saint Nicholas Avenue). By the time of the Civil War, the dirt country road was "the sight of sights," marveled a clergyman:

Fast old men, and fast young men, leaders of the bulls and bears on exchange, stock speculators, millionaires, railroad kings, bankers, book-men, and merchants, the bloods of the city, and all who can command a two-forty horse, appear on the drive. All is exhilaration; the road is full of dust; teams crowd the thoroughfare; horses tear up and down, to the horror of nervous and timid people; fast teams race with each other, and frequently interlock and smash up, while the tearing teams hold on their course, carrying terror and dismay along the whole road.

And then, in the 1880s, along came the bicycle craze and ruined it all. Flocks of happy pedalers weaving along Harlem Lane made it nigh impossible to race "thoroughbreds without having to pull up every moment on account of a wheelman cutting in," groused one man. You couldn't tell him about the racetracks out on Long Island or the Jerome Speedway in the Bronx—that was organized sport. What he and every other trotter yearned for was a long, empty road in Manhattan where turfmen could meet on afternoons for an impromptu "brush" without the formalities of gates and starting bells. Plenty of crack trotters would have welcomed the chance to tear around the bridle paths of Central Park, but alas, park rules forbade any horse and rig to travel faster than ten miles an hour.

Enter in 1890 Peter "Brains" Sweeny, who thought he had found the perfect site to build a

*See pages 86–90 for a description of Egbert L. Viele's Arcade Railway.

racetrack: Riverside Park. He could see it all—the whirling wheels, the cheering crowds, fine-blooded stock streaking along the Hudson River against the "broad, open views of captivating scenery." How splendid! At last there would be a place on Manhattan Island where a man could "speed his horse and get the enjoyment he was entitled to without being chased by a policeman," Sweeny crowed.

What the unctious former politician didn't say was why he had hatched the plan for the racetrack. The truth of the matter was that Sweeny, who had earned the nickname Brains—and a fortune through bribery and graft—as Boss Tweed's right-hand man, had bought up several choice lots along Riverside Drive in the 1870s. To his unending frustration, predictions that the drive was destined to become the address of "mansions that would splendidly eclipse anything and everything on Fifth Avenue" had not yet come to pass. In 1890, nearly twenty years after he had purchased the property, and a decade after the drive had been paved and landscaped, the winding boulevard was lined with a

Trotters on Harlem Lane, 1870.

motley assortment of leftover colonial manors, overgrown lots, squatters' shacks, and a sprinkling of stately new residences—the only encouraging sign of better days to come. But Sweeny, sixty-five years old and impatient to realize a profit on his investment, was tired of waiting for the market to pick up. A racetrack in Riverside Park, he reasoned, would lure the likes of the Vanderbilts, the Belmonts, and other wealthy trotting enthusiasts over to the West Side—if not to live, at least to play—and in the process do wonders for the drive's real estate value. So would the speedway's design, Sweeny believed, which was cleverly conceived to eliminate some of the flaws that were decidedly keeping the drive and its companion, Riverside Park, from realizing their potential as Fifth Avenue's magnificent rival.

Tar-papered shanty at Riverside Drive and West Eightieth Street, c. 1890.

At the time of Sweeny's proposal, work on the first stretch of Riverside Park, between Seventy-second and Seventy-ninth streets, was nearing completion. Designed by Frederick Law Olmsted in the mid-1870s, the park was essentially little more than a narrow strip of green cut with meandering footpaths that overlooked the open tracks of the New York Central and Hudson River Railroad, which ran along the water's edge. The riverfront was nothing short of an eyesore. Clam sloops and rotting canal boats littered the shore, and brick factories and ramshackle piers obstructed views onto the Hudson River from the drive. Since the racetrack would be built at the river's edge, thereby sweeping away this sorry sight, Sweeny figured he thus held three aces in his hand: the trotters were desperate for a place to race; home owners along

Peter "Brains" Sweeny, as portrayed in a cartoon by Thomas Nast in *Harper's Weekly*, November 1871, a month after "Boss" Tweed's corrupt ring was toppled.

Riverside Park and Riverside Drive, looking north from West Seventy-fourth Street, c. 1900. When the Henry Hudson Parkway was built in the late 1930s, the park was extended westward on landfill over the railroad tracks.

RIGHT:
Proposed Riverside Park racetrack, looking north. Leopold Eidlitz, engineer, 1890.

the drive were eager to improve their view; and New Yorkers with even an ounce of civic pride were sure to support a plan that beautified the waterfront.

As the *New York Herald* pointed out:

Tourists who approach New York by the bay exclaim, "Oh, what a beautiful city!" They change their minds when they have to continue their sail up the Hudson or East River. Successions of mud banks and dump docks do not lend much picturesqueness to uptown New York from the water.

Sweeny's proposed "Pleasure Ground for Lovers of the Horse" was to extend uninterruptedly from Seventy-second to Ninety-eighth Street on an elevated terrace created by fifty acres of landfill. Speed demons were to get an eighty-foot-wide course, divided into uptown and downtown lanes, allowing trotters to race their buggies in either direction as fast as their horses would carry them without fear of head-on collisions. To the east of the speedway, shielded from the tracks of the New York Central by a high stone wall, were planned a shaded promenade for leisurely riding and standing room

SECTION OF ROADWAY.

for spectators, who would reach the race course from the park by way of two bridges spanning the railroad tracks, at Seventy-second and Ninety-eighth streets. Directly on the Hudson, and several feet below the speedway, Sweeny suggested building a road reserved for "commercial and general purposes," which was clearly designed for no other purpose than to keep milk wagons, ash carts, omnibuses, and all other inelegant vehicles off the drive.

The trotting set thought the speedway was a capital idea. "It's grand! It's glorious! I've wanted for years to see such a scheme carried out," said Lawson Fuller, a wealthy boarding house proprietor who owned a stableful of thoroughbreds. When Russell Sage, another avid racer, was asked by the *New York Herald* what he thought of the proposed Riverside track, the millionaire responded: "In favor of a driveway there? Of course I am . . . Why what greater pleasure could a man have than driving a spirited horse, full of fire and go, over a fine drive such as that can be made?" Besides, he added, the speedway would be a "public benefit." An afternoon race in the park "would be a daily show, free to everyone, and without any bad surroundings

either," said Sage. "It would really be much more sensible to go see it than pay four dollars for a stall at the Metropolitan Opera House to hear the foreign squealers."

Sweeny submitted his plan to the Board of Estimate for review in September 1890, and attached to it a list that read like the Social Register. William Vanderbilt was all for the speedway; so were Chauncey Depew, James Gordon Bennett, William Rockefeller, and Charles Dana. But, unfortunately for Sweeny and his sportsmen friends, as much as residents of Riverside Drive wished to improve their view of the Hudson River, they had no intention of allowing a racetrack to be built in their front yard. The following year, as the *New York Times* noted, Sweeny's $4-million scheme "disappeared from public notice," and was never heard of again.

Much to their alarm, in March 1892, however, New Yorkers found out that trotting fanatics had quietly managed to push through a bill authorizing the construction of a seventy-foot-wide race course in Central Park, which was to extend from Fifty-ninth Street along the western edge of the park "to such northerly point" as deemed desirable by the

THE SPEEDWAY. NEW YORK.

COPR. DETROIT PUBLISHING CO.

A postcard view of the Harlem River Speedway, c. 1908.

commissioners of the Department of Public Parks. The plan was so vehemently protested by thousands of outraged citizens that the bill was repealed less than a month later. But the trotters persisted in their search. There had to be some corner of the city where a man could "get a little speed out of his nag." Why not just fill in the Harlem River with earth, build a speedway, and be done with it, suggested a Mr. Simon Stevens, who didn't seem to be the least bit troubled that his scheme would turn Manhattan Island into a peninsula.

As it happened, the Harlem River was filled in for a race course, though not quite as Mr. Stevens had proposed. In 1894 the first wagonfuls of stone and dirt were dumped along the western bank of the river to build a one-hundred-foot-wide horseman's paradise from 155th Street to 208th Street. No detail was overlooked. Engineers chiseled out subterranean passageways beneath the track to keep the course free of cross-traffic. Work crews fussed and sweated over the slightest suggestion of a bump on the surface of the roadbed. Gardeners were summoned to plant flower gardens and grass terraces along the two-and-a-half-mile stretch. On a July afternoon, four years and $3 million later, Lawson Fuller snapped the reins on the backs of Fleetwood and Fleetwing and thundered past the Jumel Mansion, through one of the massive arches of High Bridge, under the Washington Bridge, and with a triumphant cry pulled up minutes later at 208th Street. With that, the Harlem River Speedway was officially opened.

The extravagant playground remained a favorite in-town haunt of the equestrian set for nearly twenty years. As late as 1915, remembered a veteran road racer, there was "an average of ten brushes a day, and some days fourteen, with from two to eight horses contesting in each brush." But the modern age eventually caught up with the speedway. In 1916, despite loud protestations from the uptown racing clubs, the course was turned over to the "horseless carriage." These days, New Yorkers know the route of the former track as the Harlem River Drive.

The financier Frederick Richmond had looked out the window of his Sutton Place apartment a thousand times and hardly a day passed when he didn't contemplate the potential of Welfare Island, a 147-acre strip of land as cheerless as its name that lay stretched out in the middle of the East River between Forty-eighth and Eighty-sixth streets. Here was a two-mile length of city-owned property, stunningly situated with breathtaking views, and what was on it? An ugly hospital at one end, an ugly hospital at the other end, and nothing but a ghost town of abandoned buildings in between— grim reminders of the island's past as a repository for convicts, paupers, and the insane. If it were left to him, the financier thought, he would turn the island into a vibrant residential community, a New York Île de la Cité, that would be within easy reach of midtown and not an impossible commute from Wall Street. In place of the junk heaps, overgrown lots, and crumbling ruins there would be gleaming towers, parks, shops, *life*. If it were in his hands . . .

One day in 1961 Richmond stopped dreaming about his East River vision and put in a call to the architect and city planner Victor Gruen. "Right," said Gruen as he reached for a map of Welfare Island and a giant eraser. After rubbing out everything but the Bird S. Coler Hospital, located at the northern end of the island, the architect proceeded to deck over most of the island with a twenty-two-foot high, two-level concrete platform, stashing beneath it schools, shops, pedestrian concourses, a trash and freight handling system, and an internal transportation system run on conveyor belts (private automobiles were to be banned from the island). Above the platform rose a staggered line of fifty-story towers, loosely stitched together by an undulating wall of apartment buildings, ranging in height from eight to thirty stories. The remaining acreage of the island Gruen set aside as "richly landscaped" open space, containing swimming pools, tennis courts, fountains, and playing fields.

In the spring of 1961, the plan for the new town (estimated future population, 70,000) was baptized

with the more appealing name East Island and sent off to City Hall.

"It is imaginative and daring," said Mayor Robert Wagner, who promptly asked J. Clarence Davies, Jr., chairman of the Housing and Redevelopment Board, to investigate the feasibility of the proposal. It is horrendous, cried opponents to the scheme. How could officials seriously consider a plan that forced children "out of the sun to get their schooling—with adults similarly banished like moles, into the ground, to shop and work"? But more to the point, they argued, why close off city land for private housing? Why not open the island to *all* New Yorkers by developing it as a public park? "This is the last and single opportunity for the center of our city to be further beautified since the creation of Central Park," declared August Heckscher, Lewis Mumford, and half a dozen other civic leaders in a public statement. "Let nothing interfere with this glittering chance."

"We join the plea to keep the island a place of wood and fields," said the *New York Times* in an editorial. "No city can ever have enough parks," added the *New York Herald Tribune*. "So let's forget about the apartment houses."

Gruen spent a long summer defending the housing plan. "The East Island concept is a tool to counteract the flight of middle-income families to sprawling suburban areas," he explained in one of several letters to the editor in the *Herald Tribune*. "A park on Welfare Island may be a rather nice thing to have. But it would not stop the draining of lifeblood from the city core. It would not bolster the languishing retail trade and amusement industry. It would not enliven the theater, music or art."

Before the debate boiled over, Davies reported that after studying the Richmond-Gruen proposal, he had come to the conclusion that it was "not only unwise but impossible" to consider any kind of high-density development for Welfare Island until someone had figured out how to get large numbers of people on and off the finger of land. Clearly, neither the lift bridge that connected the island to

Aerial view of Welfare (now Roosevelt) Island, looking south, showing existing buildings, Queensboro Bridge, and drawbridge, 1961.

BELOW:
Proposed redevelopment plan for Welfare Island. Victor Gruen, 1961.

Queens nor the passenger elevators that operated between the Fifty-ninth Street Bridge and the island (since discontinued) could adequately serve the proposed community of 70,000 residents, said Davies. He recommended "an immediate study of the transportation problem."

It would be another four years before the study was completed and approved. In 1965 the Transit Authority released a $28-million plan to build a subway link under the East River from East Sixty-third Street in Manhattan to Long Island City in Queens, with a station on Welfare Island. Completion of the project was targeted for the early 1970s.

The promise of a subway suddenly sparked a welter of plans for the moribund strip of land. The island could become a college campus, someone proposed, or the home of a domed stadium, suggested sports fans. Con Edison put in a bid to acquire the southern end of the island as a possible site for a nuclear power plant. Richmond and Gruen reemerged with their housing scheme, and park advocates regrouped to voice their support for a 147-acre oasis of trees and grass.

The landscape architects and site planners Robert Zion and Harold Breen, the designers of Paley Park on East Fifty-third Street, and long the champions of other "vest-pocket" parks for New York, envisioned Welfare Island as more than trees and grass. Shoving Gruen's residential community over to Astoria's waterfront, Zion and Breen carpeted the island, end to end, with a sprawling pleasure ground, modeled after Tivoli Gardens, Copenhagen's famous in-town amusement and cultural park. The island would not be a garish, noisy reef of honky-tonk, the partners explained; rather, what they pictured was "an attractive informal country-like setting" that offered restaurants (in all price ranges), an open-air theater, a marina, "gentle rides" for children, such as a carousel, and a swimming pool that could be converted for use as an ice-skating rink in the winter.

Early in 1968 Zion and Breen's proposal, along with the other schemes suggested for the East River tract, was deposited with the Welfare Island Planning and Development Committee, a twenty-two-member group composed of city officials and private citizens who had been appointed by Mayor John V. Lindsay to determine the best possible use for the city-owned strip of land. As the committee began its study of the island's seemingly endless options, outraged New Yorkers were focused on another area of the city. The Metropolitan Museum of Art, they had learned, intended to build a new wing in Central Park, simply to give its American collection and its recent acquisition, the ancient Egyptian Temple of Dendur, a spacious new home. What gave the Met the right to encroach upon precious green? protested park protectionists. Was this the inch before the mile? Surely the museum's overflow could be exhibited elsewhere and still draw crowds. A case in point was the Met's medieval collection, displayed several miles away from Fifth Avenue and Eighty-second Street, at the Cloisters, a location that didn't seem to deter several thousand people a year from making the trek uptown.

During the uproar, the Welfare Island Planning and Development Committee received a new scheme to consider. As a postscript to their design for a Tivoli park, Zion and Breen proposed placing the Temple of Dendur at the southern tip of Welfare Island and constructing a museum for the Met's Egyptian collection behind it. The plan came with the enthusiastic endorsement of people who objected to the museum's expansion into Central Park. "The Temple of Dendur may be one of the gems of Egyptian civilization, but Central Park is one of the gems of our civilization," declared Assemblyman S. William Green. Displaying the temple on Welfare Island would allow the city to "have the one without damaging the other," he noted. And if the East River wasn't exactly the Nile, added the attorney Robert Makla, it would provide "a superlative water setting" for the ancient temple that the Met could never hope to duplicate indoors. Security? The temple would be enclosed in a vandal-proof (and pollution-free) transparent casing, entered by way of the adjacent museum, explained Zion and Breen. The frescoes, mummies, and golden treasures inside the museum building would also be safe, because the walls of the elongated, pyramid-

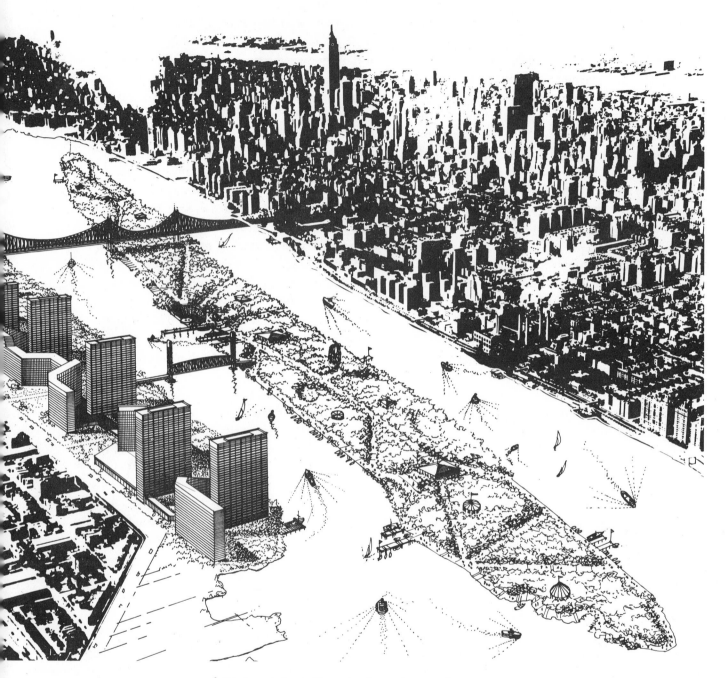

A Tivoli park for Welfare Island; new housing for Astoria. Zion & Breen Associates, 1965.

OPPOSITE, TOP:
Proposed marina and adjacent dock for water buses, Welfare Island. Zion & Breen Associates, 1965.

BOTTOM:
The Temple of Dendur re-created on the southern tip of Welfare Island and a proposed museum for Egyptian art. Zion & Breen Associates, 1968. Rendering by Brian Burr.

like structure were to be as thick as a pharaoh's tomb. Burglars would need dynamite to break in and enter.

The Welfare Island Planning and Development Committee did not consider the temple scheme to be a realistic proposition, nor did it support locating a stadium, a nuclear power plant, a large-scale housing project, or a university center in the middle of the East River. In its report, issued in 1969, the committee acknowledged that the city lacked both housing and park land, but believed that neither need could "be satisfied to any significant degree by Welfare Island." Therefore it recommended that the 147-acre strip be set aside for a mixed-use development, which would comprise the two existing hospitals, low-rise apartment buildings for about sixteen thousand people, and eighty acres of recreational space—with the possibility left open for a condensed, Tivoli-like park. It further recommended restoring several of the island's historic buildings, such as the Octagon Tower, a remnant of the former Lunatic Asylum built in the 1830s, and the Blackwell Farm House, the former home of the Blackwell family, which had sold the island to the city in 1828 for $32,500.

"Welfare Island is now on a firm course toward a new life," Mayor Lindsay pronounced in February 1969, after receiving the committee's report. And indeed, from there things happened very quickly for the erstwhile forgotten island. In May 1969, at the request of the mayor, the New York State Urban Development Corporation (UDC) was asked to carry out the recommendations made by the Welfare Island planning committee. The UDC in turn commissioned a design team, headed by Philip Johnson and John Burgee, to draw up a master plan. In October 1969 the plan for the new island community was unveiled at the Metropolitan Museum of Art. "This kind of speed would be magical anywhere," marveled the *New York Times*, "but in New York it qualifies as a supernatural happening."

Robert Zion and Harold Breen were retained as consulting landscape architects for the master plan. When they joined the design team, Zion recalls, the broad strokes of the master plan had already been painted. Projected were five thousand apartment units divided into two "towns," shops, offices, schools, a hotel, five parks of varying size, and a "Motorgate," where all private automobiles—banned from circulating on the island—were to be left. The Bird S. Coler and Goldwater Memorial hospitals were to be integrated into the new community, as were a number of the island's historic buildings. In short, the plan closely incorporated the recommendations made by the Welfare Island Planning and Development Committee—with the notable exception of a Tivoli-like park, which the UDC deemed too frivolous a project for the island in face of the city's great need for housing.

These days the East River island—renamed Roosevelt Island in the early 1970s—shows Manhattan a considerably sunnier face than the one Frederick Richmond saw from his window in 1961. Clusters of new apartment buildings have replaced the melancholy ruins. The once dilapidated Blackwell Farm House sits proudly in the middle of the island, restored and in use as the setting for exhibitions, parties, and other special events. Acres of tangled brush and crumbling lots have been reclaimed for parks and playing fields, and a pair of scenic promenades, designed by Zion and Breen, edge the east and west sides of the island's waterfront. Do Roosevelt Island residents care that construction of the promised subway, begun in 1970, creeps on, inch by troubled inch? Most would answer not a bit; they've got something better. They've got an aerial tram that swings them like urban Tarzans over the East River between home and Manhattan in four minutes flat.

MONUMENTS

If Cleopatra's Needle (1500 B.C.) is included in the count, New York City's collection of monuments spans more than three thousand years. Triumphal arches, equestrian statues, fountains, and memorial rotundas dot the city at almost every turn, commemorating explorers, presidents, men and women of the arts and letters, engineering milestones, and distant tragedies. But ask New Yorkers to identify the monument standing five feet away, and they will probably respond with a shrug.

It wasn't always so. During the golden age of the monument, a period that lasted roughly from the late 1850s to the First World War and that produced, among other works, the statue of Henry Ward Beecher in downtown Brooklyn, the Pulitzer Fountain near the Plaza Hotel, and Grant's Tomb, New Yorkers could not only name the city's monuments, they paused to admire them, tended to their upkeep, and decorated them on holidays with bunting, wreaths, and flowers. This show of civic pride was motivated by a rather simple reason. With the exception of works donated by foreign governments or by philanthropists, the monuments erected across the five boroughs went up through the concerted efforts of their own citizens. War veterans, ethnic clubs, and civic groups, all wishing to honor their own hero or special day in history, scraped together contributions, commissioned a sculptor or sponsored a design competition, sometimes quarreled about the results, but later always turned out in force for the unveiling.

Plans for statuary and memorials were sketched out for New York long before the golden age of the monument, of course, and have continued to come off the drawing board ever since. But as the city's stack of plans of unbuilt monuments reveals, a design on paper holds only a partial promise of becoming a three-dimensional reality. Many schemes for monuments were felled by poorly managed fund-raising campaigns. Sometimes disagreements arose between the artist and the sponsoring organization, resulting in the abandonment of the proposed monument. Other schemes were so ill-conceived that they were doomed almost from the moment they were set to paper. Such was the fate, for example, of the proposed veterans' memorial (1962), which called for an eighteen-story black granite building to rise in Union Square Park.

Since 1898 schemes for public monuments have had to clear another hurdle before reaching three-dimensional reality, the Art Commission of the City of New York, whose review and approval are required before plans for monuments and other works of art intended for city property

In September 1881, after its long voyage from Egypt, Cleopatra's Needle is unloaded from the bow of the *Dessoug* at West 96th Street and the Hudson River. The obelisk was transported across town to its resting place in Central Park on a temporary railway.

can be implemented. Although not entirely infallible in its judgment, the commission has spared New York from a number of disastrous monuments over the years, such as the gigantic Torah scroll envisioned for Riverside Park or the stainless steel obelisk proposed for upper Park Avenue, a work whose detractors argued was sure to cause temporary blindness in motorists when sunlight struck its reflective surface.

Beyond functioning as the city's aesthetic watchdog, the commission is also responsible for the maintenance of New York's vast art collection. In 1980 a comprehensive survey was conducted to inventory every sculpture in the city and to establish its condition. The survey confirmed what the commission already knew; it was alarming nonetheless: dozens of monuments, long exposed to air pollution, acid rain, and vandalism, were in urgent need of repair or restoration. Because it lacked the fiscal resources to rescue the monuments from slow but certain ruin (restoration of a single statue can cost several thousand dollars), the commission turned to the private sector for assistance, launching in March 1987 the Adopt-a-Monument program. Within a few months, sponsors had stepped forward with pledges to fund the restoration of fourteen works, including the statue of Joan of Arc, which stands on Riverside Drive at Ninety-third Street; the Columbus Monument at Columbus Circle; and the Lafayette Memorial in Prospect Park. Undoubtedly, as other monuments are claimed for restoration and brought back to their original luster, New Yorkers will regard these works with new, appreciative eyes. Perhaps they will even be moved to learn the names of some of the monuments that grace the cityscape.

The Manhattan Company's reservoir on Chambers Street, between Broadway and Centre Street, 1825.

"A want of good water is at present a great inconvenience to the citizens, there being few wells in the city," wrote an English visitor to New York in 1795. "Most of the people are supplied every day with fresh water, conveyed to their doors in casks, from a pump near the head of Pearl-street, which receives it from a spring almost a mile from the center of the city . . . Several proposals have been made by individuals to supply citizens by pipes, but none have yet been accepted."

Five years after this report, Aaron Burr's Manhattan Company was pumping water through six miles of wooden pipes to four hundred households from a reservoir located on Chambers Street. Subscribers to the system paid the stiff fee of five dollars per year, which later jumped to ten dollars, despite increasing complaints of poor service. "The Manhattan Water Works, which was originally intended as one of the greatest advantages of the city, has now become one of its greatest vexations," fumed an angry customer in 1809. "It is a general complaint, at the lower part of the town at least, that they can get no water, and indeed not without cause, for, as for myself, I have applied almost daily four months past, without being rewarded with a single drop. The company's clerk, however, is punctual in calling for their fees." Company officials had a hundred excuses for the dry spells: in winter they pleaded frozen pipes; in summer, poplar roots clogging the ducts were blamed. At any time of the year, the interruption of service was explained away by the repair or installation of new pumping machinery at the Chambers Street reservoir.

By 1823 the Manhattan Company had laid only twenty-three miles of pipe, hardly enough to supply a city whose population had more than doubled, to 125,000 inhabitants, since the utility's first days in 1800. Nor could the few New Yorkers who did benefit from the system—when it worked—pronounce themselves satisfied with the quality of the water. As a special committee of the Board of Aldermen put it, the company's water was simply "unfit for the use of man."

Only after a cholera epidemic, transmitted by the city's contaminated water supply, had claimed the lives of 3,500 New Yorkers in 1832 did politicians finally move to investigate ways of bringing to New York City "the great desideratum, so long delayed, so indispensable to the public health—a copious supply of good water." By 1835 a plan was sketched out to divert water from the Croton River in Westchester County by way of an aqueduct that would follow a path, some forty miles long, along the Hudson and over the Harlem River, and empty into a receiving reservoir between Seventy-ninth and Eighty-sixth streets in the middle of the island, in what would later become Central Park. From there the water was to be piped to a distributing reservoir at Fifth Avenue and Forty-second Street, on the present site of the New York Public Library. When the proposed system was put on the ballot in the mayoral election of 1835, 17,330 New Yorkers gave it their vote of confidence. They also reelected Mayor Cornelius Lawrence for a second term.

As the Croton Aqueduct Committee began its surveys to prepare for the construction of the system, Robert Fleming Gourlay, a Scotsman "detained at New York, 1834 and 1835, month after month, without object," whiled away the hours redesigning portions of Manhattan "which might have been better planned." In a letter to Mayor Lawrence dated July 15, 1835, Gourlay took it upon himself "to throw out a hint as to a species of improvement" for City Hall Park and enclosed a woodcut print for illustration. The plan was simple but fitting. To celebrate the municipal marvel of Croton water, Gourlay proposed cutting off the southern end of the park and erecting a fountain "with a Jet d'eau in the centre, and bason [sic] for the reception of the falling water, engroved with shrubbery and a few weeping willows." During New York's sweltering summers, Gourlay wrote, "the view of this would be delightfully refreshing, and the air around would be actually cooled by the projected stream. Indeed, were citizens accustomed to such luxuries, they would desire to have fountains throughout, in every place adapted for them;—such as the Bowling green, Franklin square, Chatham square, &c., &c."

"I had to fix my thoughts on something," Gour-

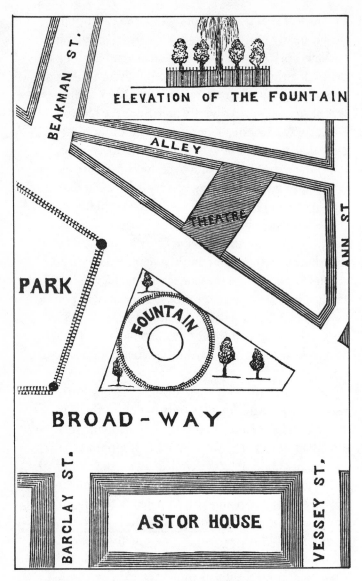

ELEVATION OF THE FOUNTAIN

BEAKMAN ST.

ALLEY

THEATRE

ANN ST.

PARK

FOUNTAIN

BROAD-WAY

BARCLAY ST.

ASTOR HOUSE

VESSEY ST.

Design for a fountain in City Hall Park. Robert Fleming Gourlay, 1835. Gourlay apologized for the poor quality of the woodcut but was confident the public would "have no difficulty in conjuring up something better."

Robert Fleming Gourlay, c. 1863.

lay later wrote of his long stay in New York, "and it was at least innocent to contemplate improvements of the city." Luckily, that was all he did. Gourlay, born near Edinburgh in 1778, had a reputation as a bit of a rabble-rouser, having campaigned as a young man in Scotland for the transfer of property to the working poor and, upon his emigration to Canada in 1817, for land reform in Ontario. He was apt to lash out at his adversaries with invectives or, as it had suited him on one occasion, with a riding crop. In 1819 he was banished from Canada. Ten years later, drifting between Great Britain and the United States, the Scotsman turned his attention to urban planning and, under the rousing motto "Go to, let us build us a City," freely dispensed his opinions on municipal improvement to anyone who would listen. Buffalo's main street, he informed its citizens, was far "too wide," and the city of Quebec was a shambles of "miserable planning." As for the "green and yellow melancholy" of the Boston Common, he

The fountain in City Hall Park, c. 1850.

sniffed, nothing could save it but a "Pagoda . . . with a Flower Garden."

Gourlay's well-intended suggestions, including his fountain plan for New York, fell upon deaf ears, although the Scotsman's crude 1835 woodcut may have sown the seeds for the city's decision seven years later to, in fact, build a fountain, and to build it on the very spot Gourlay had selected. In September 1842, three months after "the healthful streams of the Croton" began flowing through New York spigots, the Board of Aldermen appropriated $2,500 for the construction of a fountain at the southern end of City Hall Park, leaving its design and mechanics to the engineer Horatio Allen, who was second in command on the Croton aqueduct project.

The fountain was dedicated on October 14, 1842, in a day-long public celebration that began at dawn to the thunder of a hundred cannon and the joyous pealing of every church bell on Manhattan Island. Not a soul among the thousands who converged upon City Hall Park that day to view the new fountain went home disappointed, reported the *New York Herald*. Before the eyes of rapt New Yorkers a central jet, ringed by twenty-four subordinate sprays, soared toward the sky, undergoing in mid-air three magical transformations, the first "a close column fifty feet high, called 'Maid of the Mist'; the second, with centre and sides called the 'Croton Plume'; and the third, in an expanded shape, termed 'The Fan.' "

Robert Gourlay did not attend the celebration. Failing health, so he claimed, had sent him to partake of spa waters in upstate New York, but a month later he was back in town for a look at Horatio Allen's waterworks. In a terse critique mingled with disdain and jealousy, Gourlay wrote, "In my humble opinion, a simple jet would be in far better taste than the fantastic forms in which

City Hall Park in the 1920s, looking south over the roof of City Hall to the Post Office building. Frederick Mac-Monnies's fountain *Civic Virtue* stands in the center of the park.

the water is now made to play." Apparently forgetting that he had proposed placing his design of 1835 on the very same spot, the Scotsman added, "The fountain, where it is now, produces little effect; and, in fact, adds to the huddle of the ugly gate and loathsome corner." New Yorkers couldn't have disagreed more. No one tired of the aquatic displays in City Hall Park, and the marble-trimmed oasis, far from being a "loathsome corner," offered a refreshing respite from the churning dust and noise of Broadway, the city's busiest thoroughfare.

The symbol of New York City's first municipal water system splashed away for more than twenty years. In 1867, after it was learned that a post office was to be constructed at the southern end of City Hall Park, popular affection for the fountain prompted citizens to propose moving it to Madison Square Park. Efforts to save the Croton monument failed, however, and it was demolished in 1869.

But the park did not remain without a fountain for long. While the post office was under construction in 1871, the architect Jacob Wrey Mould, fresh from collaborating with Calvert Vaux on the decorative details of the Bethesda Terrace in Central Park, designed a second fountain, a somber-looking object of dark stone that stood in front of City Hall until it was transplanted to Crotona Park in 1921. It was replaced in 1922 by the sculptor Frederick MacMonnies's fountain entitled *Civic Virtue*, which featured at its center a muscular youth triumphantly towering over two ensnared maidens at his feet. Much to the satisfaction of outraged women who objected to the female personification of "civic vice," this fountain too was whisked away when, to the satisfaction of a great many others, the hulking post office was torn down in the late 1930s. *Civic Virtue* now stands in front of Queens Borough Hall.

The limestone and granite fountain currently situated at the southern end of the park was donated by the philanthropist George T. Delacorte and was designed by the landscape architect M. Paul Friedberg in the late 1970s. Were he alive today, Gourlay would surely give a nod of approval to the simple basin, faintly pink in color, that sends up a frothy circle of *jet d'eaux* to bobble at its center.

In 1843 the Washington Monument Association of New York City was founded to erect a memorial to America's first president. It was reprehensible, declared the association's trustees, that in the forty-four years since Washington's death, "the commercial metropolis of a country, which he so signally aided to place . . . has not raised a stone, or inscribed a marble to the memory of the 'Father of his Country.' " And surprising. Washington, after all, had been inaugurated in 1789 right on the second-floor balcony of old City Hall on Wall Street, and for a year the young republic's first capital had been proudly seated in the city of 33,000 people. Washington had lived among them, first at 3 Cherry Street, and later in more spacious quarters, at 39 Broadway. He was often seen at the theater, which he loved, or on his daily strolls through Battery Park. Some New Yorkers in 1843 could even claim having had the honor of meeting the president and his wife at the Washingtons' open house on New Year's Day, 1790.

The trustees of the Washington Monument Association were given three years by the State Legislature to raise fifty thousand dollars for the memorial. By late summer 1843, the association was well on the way to meeting its goal, aided by the modest contributions of pennies and dimes sent by clubs, schools, and churches, and by the largesse of a few wealthy citizens who handed the trustees gifts of five and ten thousand dollars, even though they hadn't the slightest idea of what the monument would look like or where it would be built.

On August 17, 1843, they found out. Illustrated on the front page of the *New York Daily Tribune* was an enormous pentagonal building, made of granite, rising in the center of Union Square Park. Designed by a self-taught architect named Calvin Pollard, the monument reached the dizzying height of 425 feet, nearly twice that of Trinity Church, still under construction in 1843, and soon to be the tallest building on the New York skyline. In fact, at first glance readers may have thought Trinity's spire had been hacked to the ground, for what Pollard envisioned for the Washington monument was a Gothic tower, laden on the exterior with a frenzied display of pinnacles, crockets, fretted stonework, and stained glass windows.

The interior was no less ambitious. On the ground floor, a large hall opened onto five projecting wings, which were to house a library of 400,000 volumes, memorabilia of the American Revolution, and an art gallery. The second story was given over to the "Monumental Rotunda," a space one hundred feet high, punctuated at its center with a statue of George

The inauguration of President George Washington, April 30, 1789. For the momentous occasion, City Hall, completed in 1703 at the corner of Wall and Nassau streets, was remodeled by the French architect Pierre L'Enfant and renamed Federal Hall. The Federal Hall National Memorial, built between 1842 and 1862, now occupies the site.

Washington. Figures of "the thirteen Major Generals . . . all to be finished in the full military costume of their day" stood guard in Gothic niches that ringed the rotunda, while a stone eagle, suspended from the middle of the ceiling, hovered above this picture of patriotism. The third floor of the memorial was set aside as studio space "for the use and encouragement of young men of genius in the study of Fine Arts," and the spire, reached by a wrought-iron spiral staircase, Pollard grandly reserved as nothing less than a "National Observatory."

New Yorkers were thunderstruck—not so much by the beehive of activity Pollard was suggesting, nor even by the building's unprecedented height. What they objected to the most was the flamboyant application of Gothic architecture to commemorate America's first president. "Gothic ornaments are well enough for the bishop, the antiquarian, the poet—but Washington in Gothic! The bare thought calls up at once a smile and a frown," said one dismayed citizen. "Washington's monument should have been pure Grecian, the republican style," chimed in *Scientific American*. Others took the Gothic idiom more lightly. The image of Washington's troops, outfitted in uniforms of 1776 and posed against a background of medieval architecture, had one man howling. "Do waltzing nuns and champagne drinking dervishes beat this?" he roared. "What on earth are these men meant for?"

The association couldn't answer that question, but one embarrassing fact was becoming clear. After having seen Pollard's design, New Yorkers weren't digging very deeply into their pockets for contributions to the monument, if at all. By 1846, the end of the three-year period allotted to the association to raise fifty thousand dollars, it was still several thousand dollars short of its goal.

In 1847 the association's function was extended an additional five years by the State Legislature. The trustees, hoping to find a plan that would win New Yorkers' approval—and their dollars—opened a design competition for the monument. By July 1847 seven entries had been submitted. Four were of "the Gothic order," the *New York Daily Tribune* reported, including one by Pollard, whose only

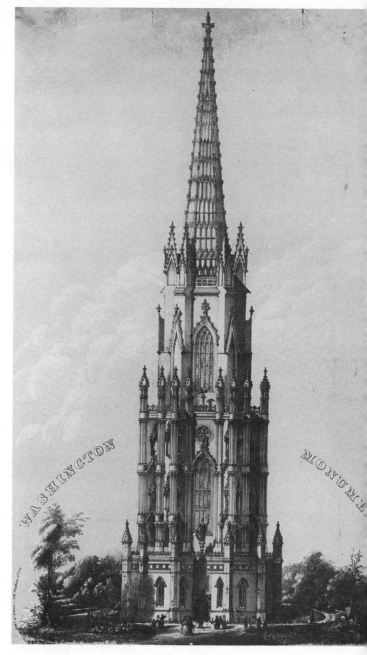

Design for a monument to George Washington. Calvin Pollard, 1843.

concession to the public was to make his original design a little less florid by shaving down the building's pinnacles—alterations that only served to give the tower an odd, blunted appearance. The other three proposals were described by the newspaper as "a Corinthian column surmounted by an enclosed statue," "an Egyptian obelisk," and one, without further explanation, as a "Fascia."

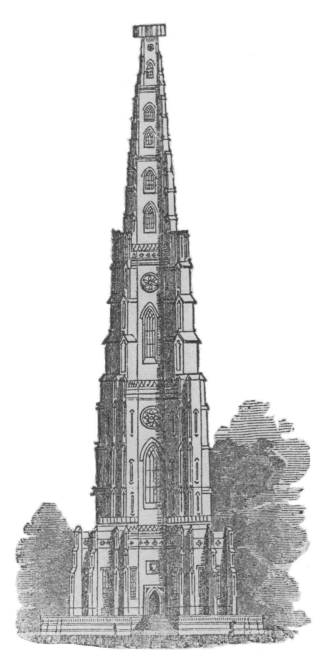

George Washington monument competition entry. Calvin Pollard, 1847.

The obelisk plan was submitted by Minard Lafever, one of New York's most renowned church architects, whose work, still standing, includes the Church of the Holy Apostles (1848) on West Twenty-eighth Street in Manhattan and the Church of the Saviour (1844) in Brooklyn Heights. For his ecclesiastical structures, Lafever preferred the Gothic and Greek Revival styles, but monuments, he ex-

plained, were most appropriately expressed through Egyptian architecture because it best conveyed "ideas of massiveness, strength and permanence." Lafever's obelisk, richly ornamented with broad bands of carved lotus buds, took form in a five-hundred-foot-high granite needle, rising from a two-story stepped pedestal. The base of the obelisk was to house a grand rotunda, where the architect proposed placing a statue of Washington and figures of "the heroes, orators and statesmen who have been instrumental in achieving our independence." Small rooms stacked all the way up to the twenty-seven-story shaft were to serve as repositories for relics, trophies, and manuscripts relating to the Revolution. All in all, Lafever believed, the monument would live on as a fitting symbol to "the illustrious Washington," as well as "a hallowed and instructive spot for every American."

For reasons best known to the association's trustees, Pollard's revised design for the Gothic tower was chosen as the winning scheme from the seven designs entered in the competition. Soon after, it was announced that the cornerstone of the monument would be dedicated on October 19, 1847, on the occasion of the sixty-sixth anniversary of Cornwallis's surrender to Washington at Yorktown. At the same time it was decided to move Pollard's controversial tower from its projected site at Union Square Park to Hamilton Square, an eighteen-acre tract that lay nearly three miles to the north, bounded by East Sixty-sixth Street, Fifth Avenue, East Sixty-eighth Street, and Third Avenue. Cordoned off in 1811 as future park space, Hamilton Square and the surrounding area were considered the backwoods of Manhattan, since most New Yorkers in 1847 lived below Fourteenth Street. But the purported advantage of the far-flung site was its lofty elevation, which, it was claimed, would enable even mariners fifty miles out in the Atlantic to see the new monument.

On October 19, 1847, New Yorkers turned out in force to watch what one account unintentionally punned as a most "georgeous" procession. Dignitaries in top hats and tailcoats, a sea of uniformed troops, brass bands, light cavalry, and members of various political and professional clubs swept up

George Washington monument competition entry. Minard Lafever, 1847.

Broadway and Third Avenue to the enthusiastic applause of spectators who lined the route from City Hall to Hamilton Square. As the parade neared the square, a few wizened veterans of 1776 fired a salute and the waiting throng edged expectantly closer for a better look at the massive cornerstone that hung suspended from a timber-framed tower. Buried inside the four-foot-thick slab was a leaden box containing Washington's autograph, the Washington Monument Association's bylaws, newspapers of the day, and other souvenirs of 1847.

The cornerstone was dedicated with due ceremony. George Washington Parke Custis, Washington's adopted grandson, delivered the address, and the chorus of the Musical Institute performed an ode especially composed for the occasion by George W. Morris, a popular poet of the day. After the blessing and another gun salute, Governor John Young lowered the marble cornerstone into the ground, whereupon the crowd immediately surged forward, reported the *New York Herald,* and threw autumn flowers and "coins of every kind—gold, silver and copper"—into the deep hole.

Several days after the dedication, former New York mayor Philip Hone recorded in his famous diary: "I hope I may be mistaken, but I cannot help predicting that the *corner stone* will be the only one laid of the Edifice." He was right. Opposition to Pollard's plan, which mounted steadily in the weeks before the ceremonies at Hamilton Square, had reached a high pitch by the time the cornerstone was laid. Walt Whitman, writing in the Brooklyn *Daily Eagle,* pronounced the plan for the monument "a mixture without uniformity, without apparent design and certainly without appropriateness." In an anonymous letter to the editor of the *Evening Post,* another critic said: "Any Gothicism would be bad, but Mr. Pollard's is very bad Gothic."

In December 1847, only two months after the dedication of the cornerstone, the association's trustees sponsored another competition. By early 1848 they had received several schemes. Lafever, ever hopeful, reentered his obelisk plan, and Pollard, apparently inured to public opinion by this time, resubmitted his plan for the Gothic tower.

Laying the cornerstone to the George Washington monument at Hamilton Square in Manhattan on October 19, 1847. The cornerstone can be made out faintly at the bottom of the frame tower. In the foreground, beneath the canopy of the Liberty float, thirteen young girls waving star-tipped wands surround a marble bust of Washington.

Among the new designs for the monument was the poet William Ross Wallace's scheme, awesome in its size, which piled a massive pedestal, a circle of columns, and a vast golden globe on a stepped pyramidal platform. On top of the globe Wallace planted a colossal statue of Washington. From the sculptor John Frazee came a proposal for a white marble temple ringed with thirteen columns and crowned by a dome inlaid with thirteen star-shaped windows, standing on a thirteen-sided terrace. In an accompanying description to the plan (Frazee's drawings for the monument appear to be lost), the

sculptor proudly proclaimed the invention of a new order of column, which combined figures of native Indians and sheaves of corn. Frazee called his new column type the "American order," but emphasized that the overall plan for the monument was designed according to the "purest principles of Grecian taste, order and style."

Late in 1848, unable to come to an agreement on any one of the plans, the association's trustees asked citizens who had contributed donations to the monument fund to cast votes for their preferred design. When the ballots were counted, Lafever's plan for the granite needle emerged the winner, with 367 votes; Frazee's plan came in second, with 222 votes; and the remaining entries shared 140 votes among them. Pollard's heart "was broken" by the outcome of the public vote, wrote his daughter many years later, but perhaps before the ar-

chitect died, in 1850, he found some solace in the fact that insufficient funds prevented Lafever's plan from materializing.

Having to start all over again, the trustees of the Washington Monument Association agreed to commission a more modest and hence less expensive memorial to the former president. In 1851 the association approached the renowned sculptor Horatio Greenough for the job, but apparently the two parties did not see eye to eye on certain details of the monument, and in the end the project was awarded to the sculptor Henry Kirke Brown.

On the Fourth of July, 1856, on the small triangle east of Union Square Park, New York City's tribute to George Washington was at long last unveiled. "When the covering fell, revealing the familiar lineaments of Washington, the universal burst of enthusiasm which arose from troops and citizenry in salutation almost drowned the salvos of artillery," reported the *New York Tribune*. The object that had so moved the crowd was a bronze equestrian statue (since transplanted to Union Square Park) that portrayed General Washington entering New York on Evacuation Day, November 25, 1783, at the end of the city's long occupation by British troops.

In the great flurry surrounding the new Washington monument, nobody had thought to retrieve the massive cornerstone of Pollard's Gothic tower, laid at Hamilton Square in 1847. Mysteriously, years later, when the square was cut into streets and avenues, the cornerstone never surfaced. Its whereabouts is not known. Maybe it was stolen, or perhaps it lies buried beneath the foundation of some East Side high rise.

On the one-hundredth anniversary of the *Clermont*'s 1807 voyage up the Hudson River to Albany, Cornelius Vanderbilt, William Barclay Parsons, Isaac Guggenheim, and other prominent New Yorkers founded the Robert Fulton Monument Association, with the intention of erecting a column or a statue in memory of the steamboat's inventor, interred at Trinity Church in lower Manhattan. Why stop there? asked Nicholas Butler, president of Columbia University and a member of the association. Why not build a monument *and* furnish New York City with a magnificent water gate, right on the very river Fulton had conquered with steam? Picture yachts and navy launches sailing into a grand boat basin between 114th and 116th streets, and a series of stepped terraces leading to Riverside Park, embellished with perhaps a building or two, said Butler. Here, against the backdrop of the noble Hudson and the mighty Palisades, the city would welcome presidents, kings, and other distinguished visitors, and on holidays the water gate's quays and terraces could serve as a gigantic reviewing stand for pageants, boat races, and fireworks. What better tribute to Fulton than this?

Butler's grandiose vision was yet another manifestation of New Yorkers' yearnings for the City Beautiful—the city of broad boulevards, imposing architecture, sparkling fountains, and verdant parks, born out of the White City at Chicago's fair in 1893. More than any section of New York, Butler's domain of Morningside Heights came closest to expressing those ideals, in the landscaped ribbon of Riverside Drive, in the stately massing of Grant's Tomb, and in McKim, Mead & White's handsome plan for Columbia's campus. Morningside Heights' waterfront, on the other hand, was a hodgepodge of boat houses, industrial buildings, and piers, bordered by the open tracks of the New York Central and Hudson River Railroad, a sight that by anyone's standards was far from beautiful.

While Butler's suggestion to build a water gate was clearly aimed at improving his own neck of the woods, the association's members jumped at the idea, for there would soon be a need for such a resplendent entry to New York. In 1909 the city expected thousands of dignitaries from around the

Design for a monument to George Washington. William Ross Wallace, 1847.

world to attend the Hudson-Fulton Fete, a dual celebration of Henry Hudson's historic sail in the *Half Moon* in 1609 and of the *Clermont*'s famous trip to Albany in 1807. Butler's water gate would certainly make an impressive portal to the city, so much grander than the piers and barnlike ship terminals downtown, the association members agreed, and during the fete, it could serve as the centerpiece for the long list of planned events, most of which were to take place on the Hudson River.

The association did not manage to realize the project by 1909; instead, a temporary landing stage was erected at the foot of West 110th Street. But, as it turned out, even the most magnificent water gate would have taken second billing to the Hudson-Fulton Fete, which opened on September 25, 1909, and lasted for two weeks, with a nonstop extravaganza of river pageants, parades, banquets, and pyrotechnical feats, unparalleled since in the history of New York. Wilbur Wright was on hand to thrill thousands of spectators with his rickety-looking flying machine; so were representatives of Japan, who presented the city with a gift of 2,100 cherry trees for Riverside Park. In the Bronx, busts and statues of Hudson and Fulton were dedicated amidst songs and speeches. At Battery Park, Italian-Americans unveiled a bronze statue of their hero, Giovanni da Verrazano, who had sailed into New York's harbor eighty-five years before Henry Hudson. In Brooklyn, Queens, and Staten Island, and in towns edging the Hudson all the way to Albany, the celebration was marked by carnivals, mock naval battles, exhibitions, and band concerts. But by far

the most spectacular event of the fete occurred every night after dusk, when for a few short hours New York became whiter than the White City itself had been. Strings of small twinkling lights, outlining buildings, monuments, viaducts, and bridges, set the metropolis ablaze, and above the incandescent shimmer, fireworks, searchlights, and multicolored beams danced in the sky.

After the fete, the Fulton Monument Association got back to work, announcing in late October 1909 a design competition for the water-gate project. The competition guidelines for the 564-foot-long site between 114th and 116th streets stipulated that the water gate was to include a landing stage and basin, a maritime museum, a building for the reception of guests, and, as its central feature, a tomb for Robert Fulton. As for effect, the complex was "to greet the visitor urbanely and with dignity" and convey "an impression of serene majesty."

Serving on the competition jury with association

BELOW:
The Hudson River waterfront, from the Columbia Yacht Club, at West Eighty-sixth Street, to Grant's Tomb, at West 121st Street, 1905.

OPPOSITE, TOP:
The Edison electrical plant on Blackwell's (now Roosevelt) Island silhouetted in lights during the Hudson-Fulton Fete, 1909.

OPPOSITE, BOTTOM:
Fireworks exploding over the Hudson River, 1909. In the distance is the glittering outline of the 125th Street Viaduct, and to the right is Grant's Tomb, bathed in spotlights.

Second prize, Robert Fulton memorial competition. Bellows, Ripley, Clapp & Faelten, 1910.

Third prize, Robert Fulton memorial competition. Albert Kelsey & Paul P. Cret, 1910.

First prize, Robert Fulton memorial competition. Harold Van Buren Magonigle, 1910.

members were three of New York's architectural stars, all well versed in the vocabulary of the urbane and the dignified. Among them, the jury members William Mead, Thomas Hastings, and George B. Post had designed some of the city's most august buildings, including the New York Public Library at Forty-second Street (Carrère and Hastings), the Brooklyn Museum (McKim, Mead & White), and the New York Stock Exchange (Post). Once the sixty-two competition entries were in, the architects must have been a little amused to see that many of the proposed water-gate schemes resembled versions of their own work, transplanted to the banks of the Hudson River.

By January 1910 the jury had whittled down the sixty-two entries to ten, and invited the finalists to supplement their first set of drawings with detailed plans and perspective renderings. From these, the jury would select four runners-up and one winning design, which carried with it a three-thousand-dollar award.

It was "most difficult for us to decide between the second, third, fourth and fifth prizes," Lansing Holden, the supervising architect of the competition, later said. "It was only by carefully studying the various treatments of the architectural detail and considering the fitness of the design as a practical building suggestion, that we arrived at a conclusion." The jury's dilemma was understandable, for all of the plans were remarkably similar, from the layout of the docks to the pile of steps that climaxed in a burst of monumental architecture at the crest of Riverside Park.

Nevertheless, by April 1910 the jury came to a decision. The plans of the runners-up, submitted by firms from New York, Philadelphia, and Boston, were notable chiefly for their colossal scale and dramatic effect. Next to Harold Van Buren Magonigle's winning entry, however, they looked heavy-handed and fractured, for, like most of the sixty-two schemes drawn up for the water gate, they had provided separate structures for Fulton's tomb, a museum, and a reception hall. Magonigle, by contrast, united these in an open peristyle, placing the reception hall on an axis to the north, the museum

Plan of proposed Robert Fulton memorial, Hudson River, West 114th to West 116th streets. Harold Van Buren Magonigle, 1910. The tracks of the New York Central and Hudson River Railroad disappear briefly beneath the memorial's stairs and plazas, represented in the plan by the large central square.

Harold Van Buren Magonigle, 1910.

to the south, and Fulton's sarcophagus under a triumphal arch at the center. From the water, the monument presented one sweeping horizontal line of white marble, an arrangement that was intended as much to "hide the ragged skyline along the Drive," Magonigle said, as it was designed to majestically greet visitors arriving by boat. Below the peristyle, a mountain of steps, covering the railroad tracks along the river, cascaded into a landing pool, which was framed by a pair of colonnaded piers. These

too were architectural band-aids, designed to "screen off the view of a foreshore that may be unsightly for years to come," explained Magonigle, although their ostensible use was to serve as docking facilities.

When the Fulton monument competition was over, there was a great deal of back-slapping. The participating architects congratulated the jury on doing such a fine job, and the jury praised the architects for the high quality of their work. Then they threw themselves a banquet, where undoubtedly plenty of toasting went on. The winning plans, exhibited at a gallery on West Fifty-seventh Street, drew scores of critics, who extolled "the masterly grasp of the problem" and "the well-conducted competition." But if the machinations of the competition supplied endless hours of fascinating discussion for a small inner circle of architects and aesthetes, the proposed Fulton memorial never managed to capture the imagination of the New Yorker–on–the–street, who was asked for neither an opinion nor a donation. Had the Fulton Monument Association enlisted the public's participation, it is conceivable that the water gate might have been realized. As it happened, Magonigle's plan was never heard of again.

Magonigle, however, did not fade into obscurity along with his scheme. A relative newcomer to the design world at the start of the competition, the architect went on to build a flourishing practice in New York, receiving commissions from all over the country for schools, private residences, churches, and above all, monuments. Two stand in Manhattan: the Fireman's Memorial at Riverside Drive and 100th Street (1913) and the grand *Maine* Memorial (1913) at the Fifty-ninth Street entrance to Central Park.

When it came time to lay out Central Park in the late 1850s, Frederick Law Olmsted grumbled about the extra annoyance of the two enormous walled reservoirs that were situated in the middle of the rectangular wasteland that he and his partner, Calvert Vaux, planned to mold into meadows, drives, and ponds. Both structures, built for the 1842 Croton aqueduct system, were "much too elevated . . . to form a part of [the park's] landscapes," Olmsted wrote, and his attempts to soften their presence with trees or other plantings had been frustrated by "a want of harmony between the Croton Aqueduct Board and the Central Park Commissioners." So there they sat, two huge unsightly tanks—the Yorkville Reservoir's stone embankments looming between Seventy-ninth and Eighty-sixth streets and Manhattan Lake occupying land between Eighty-sixth and Ninety-sixth streets. Together they claimed a sixth of the park's 840 acres.

In 1917 the Yorkville Reservoir, the oldest of the two cisterns, was rendered obsolete by the opening of the Catskill aqueduct system, which poured 525 million gallons of water per day into New York City's pipelines. It wasn't long before the Aqueduct Celebration Committee announced that the Yorkville Reservoir would come down, and that a monument, designed by Thomas Hastings to commemorate the new water system, would go up in its place. By "monument" the committee did not mean an inscribed granite marker of some sort. In tribute to the great engineering achievement of the Catskill system, Hastings had taken all thirty-four acres of the newly freed park space and sketched

Central Park, looking north from Cherry Hill toward the lake and the reservoirs, 1865. Manhattan Lake, the largest of the two reservoirs, lies farthest to the north, its immense waters divided by a stone embankment. The rectangular basin is the Yorkville Reservoir.

Ground plan of the monument to the Catskill Acqueduct system. Thomas Hastings, 1917.

LEFT:
Ground plan of the proposed monument to the Catskill Acqueduct system. Thomas Hastings, 1917.

out a lagoon, measuring almost five football fields in length, headed by Frederick MacMonnies's huge fountain *Columbia Enthroned* (last seen at the World's Columbian Exposition in Chicago), and surrounded it with sunken gardens. At the southern end of the lagoon, the architect placed an open-air Temple of Music, which was to seat twenty thousand people.

The plan was lost almost immediately in the upheaval of World War I, but in 1918, after the city invited designs for a war memorial on the reservoir tract, Hastings marched over to his cabinet, dusted off the old lagoon plan, made some revisions, and sent it in. The architect had a long wait ahead of him. It took the Committee on a Permanent War Memorial, appointed by Mayor John Hylan in 1918, four years to ponder the symbolic merits of various monument types—cenotaphs, triumphal arches, temples of sacrifice, and so on—before it decided on one of the sixty-seven schemes

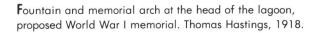

Fountain and memorial arch at the head of the lagoon,
proposed World War I memorial. Thomas Hastings, 1918.

not incidentally would have required razing the
Belvedere, Olmsted and Vaux's mock medieval castle, completed in 1872.

Park protectionists managed to fend off these
encroachments, but to their horror the winning entry
for the war memorial, announced by the committee
in June 1922, was all of this and more. The plan,
designed by Thomas Hastings, called for an enormous stadium; a mall linking the two museums; a
T-shaped, 1,300-foot-long lagoon, which was to
function as a swimming pool; underground bath-
houses; a cinder running track; playgrounds; and
sandboxes. The only semblance of a monument in
this recreational blur was the Arch of Freedom, a
peristyle at the northern end of the lagoon, generously sprinkled with somber statues of Roman
warriors. MacMonnies's fountain, featured in Hastings's 1917 plan, was replaced by a double tier of
cascading basins and figures of cavorting seahorses.

Within twenty-four hours of the plan's release,
a clamor arose from every corner of the city. "To
link the memory of those who died in the war with
a midsummer frog pond and with architecture
monstrously misplaced is not to raise a memorial
of pride and gratitude but to commit sacrilege,"
declared an angry editorial in the *New York Times*.
Why "pile more masonry on a congested little island?" protested a member of City Club, and why,
of all places, "in a rustic park?" asked representatives of the American Scenic and Historic Preservation Society. Besides which, "the city does not
need an inland Coney Island," added someone from
the Citizens' Union, who along with other opponents to the scheme envisioned hordes of bathers
descending upon Central Park, equipped with inner
tubes, picnic baskets, and beach umbrellas for a
day of swimming at the lagoon.

After enduring an entire summer of similar com-
mentary, Hastings scaled down his design to seven
and a half acres, retaining only the lagoon and the
fountain (now off limits to swimmers), and the

submitted for the memorial. Meanwhile, others
began eyeing the seven-block-long parcel of land.
In 1919 a New York socialite thought the site would
be the perfect spot to build a sports stadium in
memory of her late husband. A year later, friends
of former Mayor John P. Mitchel proposed constructing in his memory a broad, tree-lined *allée*
through the park near Seventy-ninth Street to connect the Metropolitan Museum of Art and the
American Museum of Natural History—a plan that

A long view of the lagoon, proposed World War I memorial. Thomas Hastings, 1918.

roadway between the two museums. Still, the public was not mollified. Aside from the issue of huge crowds trampling the park en route to ceremonies at the memorial several times a year, some people questioned the appropriateness of "prancing seahorses and dancing cascades" as a tribute to those who had died in World War I. "Fountains have their uses, but they speak not of the heroic dead," said William Blair of the American Institute of Architects. "Fountains speak of frivolity and joyousness, and not of the deep emotions of gratitude, of reverence, patriotism and sacrifice that should be embodied in a shrine to commemorate the war's dead."

"A war monument does not need to be a great mass of gloomy stone work," Hastings shot back. "A memorial to victory or to lasting peace which brings abundance can be designed with great charm and beauty. This is not the first design for a beautiful monument with features that are fountainlike," the architect said, and to bolster his argument he rattled off a list of similar types of work in Paris.

It was not surprising that Hastings held up Paris as an example, for the city had been his home between 1880 and 1884 while he was a student at the École des Beaux-Arts. The twenty-four-year-old graduate returned to New York an avowed Francophile—at least where architecture and design were concerned—and after working briefly as a draftsman at the firm of McKim, Mead & White, he joined his former classmate, John Carrère, to set up practice. Together the architects produced a prodigious catalog of work. Among their commissions were the Staten Island Ferry Terminals

Thomas Hastings, 1915.

(1901), Richmond Borough Hall (1906), the New York Public Library (1902–1911), and the colonnaded entrance to the Manhattan Bridge (1904–1911).

But as much as New Yorkers admired Hastings's past accomplishments (who wasn't awed walking through the marble halls of the Public Library on Forty-second Street?), they were absolutely against the war memorial. By 1924 thirty-three organizations, ranging from the Horticultural Society to the United Real Estate Owners Association, and including veterans of World War I, went on record as opposing the scheme. Nevertheless, the Board of Estimate and the Art Commission approved the plan, and in November 1925, during Hylan's waning days as a two-term mayor, $600,000 was appropriated for its construction. After trouncing Hylan for this "death-bed effort," and wryly suggesting that the whole project be moved to Prospect Park in Hylan's native Brooklyn, opponents to the monument turned to the city's mayor-elect, Jimmy Walker, and reminded him of his campaign promise. Actually, in the best tradition of politicking, Walker had never come right out and said he opposed the plan. He had merely pledged to address himself, if elected, "to the protection and preservation of every square foot of park and playground area owned by the City of New York," which was a far cry from giving the memorial the thumbs-down sign. However, once installed at City Hall in January 1926, Mayor Walker took a long look at the state of the city's financial affairs and soon decided that some of his predecessor's expenditures would have to be trimmed. One of the first casualties of Walker's budget cut was the war memorial in Central Park.

The safeguarders of Central Park were delighted by this unexpected turn of events, but they knew theirs was only a tenuous victory, for there was still the problem of how best to use the precious thirty-four acres that lay beneath the defunct reservoir. And while that was debated, they also knew they would have to be on constant alert against any number of misguided people who might seize the land for some other project, ten times more heinous than Hastings's memorial. After all, they reminded one another, in recent years various sections of the park had been suggested as a site for a music and art center (1922), twin radio towers (1923), and a replica of a French World War I battlefield, complete with trenches (1918). Given this, there was no telling what the reservoir tract between Seventy-ninth and Eighty-sixth streets might inspire.

In one of the bigger miracles in New York City's planning history, the New York Chapter of the American Society of Landscape Architects came up with a design for the site that seemed to please everyone. At the center of the seven-block rectangle, the ASLA proposed creating a huge oval lawn encircled by a broad path and flanked at Eighty-fifth Street, east and west, by a pair of children's playgrounds. Along the southern end of the site,

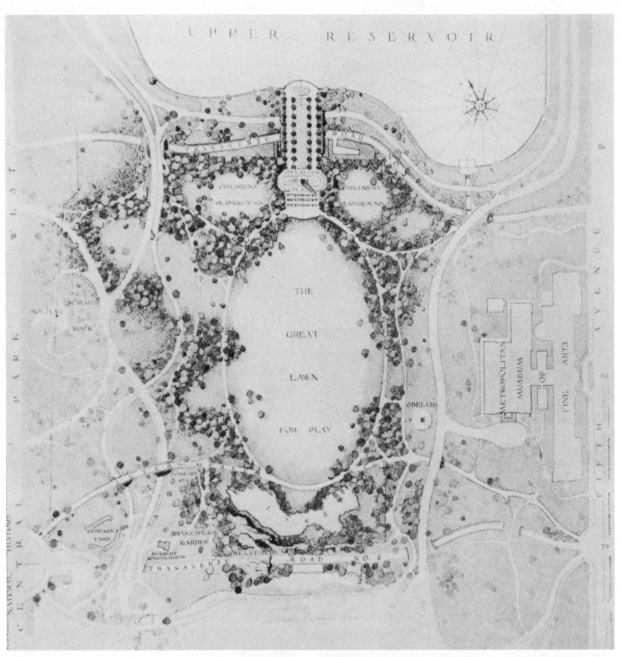

Plan for the redevelopment of the Yorkville Reservoir site. New York Chapter of the American Society for Landscape Architects, 1930.

RIGHT:
Squatters' shacks in Central Park occupy the site of the former Yorkville Reservoir, c. 1930.

the ASLA sketched out a small artificial lake, two acres in size, which was so positioned that it caught the reflection of Belvedere Castle on its craggy perch. A winding path through the park unobtrusively connected the Metropolitan Museum of Art and the American Museum of Natural History.

With the exception of a plaza and an overlook bridging the Eighty-sixth Street transverse road at the northern end of the site, the ASLA's design was adopted virtually acre for acre.

Slow drainage of the Yorkville Reservoir commenced in late January 1930. Three weeks later, in response to calls from concerned citizens, experts from the Aquarium at Battery Park rushed to the scene with nets, bait, and five-ton trucks containing tanks of water, prepared to rescue the reservoir's alleged stock of fish, which, according to some old-timers, was home to a large population of jumping trout and a magnificent salmon, whose glistening pink back could be glimpsed at midnight when the creature emerged to splash about under the moonlight. But when two days of trawling the reservoir's murky bottom in a raw drizzle produced a grand total of four mussels and a solitary bass, the fishermen packed up their gear and declared the rescue mission over.

Once the drainage was completed, the reservoir's massive retaining walls were torn down, and for the first time in Central Park's history people strolling along its leafy paths were not shaken out of their sylvan reveries by the sight of a high, stone barrier looming in the distance. Further work on the site was temporarily delayed by the Depression, but the seven-block-long parcel did not sit empty. Hundreds of homeless, espying plenty of land but no landlord, moved into the park and threw up a small town of makeshift shacks on the dried bed of the reservoir. Once settled, they quickly took advantage of the park's other bounties, hunting down birds and small animals for meals, and using the immense waters of Manhattan Lake as a laundromat and a bathtub.

The last squatters were chased off the land when development of the reservoir tract, following the general plan drawn up by the American Society of Landscape Architects, recommenced in 1933. Three years later, the meandering paths were in place, the playgrounds built, the acres of velvet sod laid, and the fruit and chestnut trees planted. In 1936, try as they might, New Yorkers sitting on the oval expanse of the Great Lawn, looking toward the tiny kingdom of Belvedere Castle and its lake, could find no vestige of the old Yorkville Reservoir.

At first, some people thought the Broadway Association's proposed monument for Times Square was a spoof. It certainly had the makings of one, from the amateurish rendering, right down to the two gargantuan palm leaves that sprang out of a thirty-foot-high pedestal, one leaf curling over Broadway, the other over Seventh Avenue. All of it was to be fashioned out of wood and plaster, including the stick figures planted on the pedestal (meant to represent statues of soldiers), and what looked like totem poles topped with bison heads (actually pylons surmounted by eagles). The ensemble of palms and sculpture was entitled "Victory Arch." One amused critic soon renamed it "Horse Feathers Sprouting From a Metronome."

As the history behind the plan unfolded during the summer of 1943, it became apparent that the monument was decidedly not a spoof. The idea to erect an arch to welcome American troops returning from the battles of World War II, still raging in 1943, had been conceived in the offices of the Broadway Association sometime in the spring. The laborious and expensive process of finding an architect or sculptor to draw up a design for the monument was circumvented when an association member stepped forward and offered the talents of his young artist daughter, Lucia Willoughby. The offer was immediately accepted, for the monument would stand only temporarily. At some future date, the association hoped to erect a more substantial

The proposed Victory Arch for Times Square, 1943.

People pack Times Square as far as the eye can see on V-J Day, 1945.

structure, something in the vein of the Arc de Triomphe, which would straddle the island north of Forty-third Street, behind the Times Tower. But until money could be raised for this major commission, it was felt that a homecoming tribute of some sort should be erected on the site, and for the time being, the Victory Arch would do nicely.

In June representatives of the association trotted the plan for the Victory Arch down to Mayor Fiorello H. La Guardia at City Hall, sailing right past the offices of the Art Commission. Since the monument was to be a temporary installation, the commission's approval was not needed.

New Yorkers didn't know whether to laugh or to cry. Giant fronds decorating Times Square, the threshold to the world's most famous entertainment district? It was "unspeakable," declared Edward Jewell, art critic of the *New York Times*. "Now is the time to protest, while silliness such as this is still on paper," he said. People hardly needed urging. After one look at the Victory Arch, appalled New Yorkers sat down to fire off letters to the editor, and nobody minced words. The proposed arch "is absurd and tasteless," said one opponent to the scheme. "It is flimsy, it is ugly, it is inept," said another. Even those who were to be

honored by the monument rejected the plan. "I'm entering the armed forces shortly," wrote one recruit. "Along with many others I expect to come back to my native New York. Tradition dictates that at some point along the roadways of my city I'll march under a victory arch. But under the proposed Willoughby thing? . . . Never!" Bombarded by dozens of equally scathing reviews, the Broadway Association packed up its plan before the summer was out.

Two years later, on V-J Day, August 14, 1945, a record crowd of more than two million people spontaneously gathered by early evening at Times Square, blowing horns, waving flags, cheering, and whistling. On the moving belt that wrapped Times Tower, the joyous news ran by them again and again, spelled out in electric lights. The war was over! All through the night a blizzard of confetti and streamers fell from windows, balconies, and rooftops onto the Crossroads of the World, as revelers celebrated amid the resurrected carnival of pulsating neon signs that had been dimmed for three long years. Times Square itself had become a victory monument; no sculptor could have created a work more jubilant.

In 1966, assured by the city of a site near Castle Clinton in Battery Park, an alliance of Jewish organizations formed the Committee to Commemorate the Six Million Jewish Martyrs and commissioned Louis I. Kahn, one of America's foremost architects, to design a Holocaust memorial. "The monument is envisioned as one which will reflect and evoke the emotional, psychological, and historical impact of the tragedy of the period," wrote David Lloyd Krieger, a member of the committee, in a letter to Kahn. "It should also deal with man's struggle to retain his dignity under the most horrendous of circumstances, and express hope for a better future, where man will not merely survive but prevail."

The Kahn commission was only the latest of

several attempts to erect a Holocaust memorial in New York City. In a somber ceremony in 1947, a simple plaque dedicated to the six million victims of the Nazi persecution had been laid in Riverside Park at Eighty-third Street, above which was to rise a pair of eighty-foot-high black granite tablets inscribed with the Ten Commandments. Lack of funds prevented the $500,000 project from being realized. A few years later the city's Jewish community rejected outright the proposal for a large stele, emblazoned with the figures of Cain and Abel, which was envisioned for the Lincoln Center area. "I'm not my brother's keeper [implies] that the murder of the 6,000,000 Jews was merely a family tragedy," protested one man, echoing the sentiments of others who objected to the proposed monument.

Model of a proposed twenty-six-foot-high Torah scroll, planned for Riverside Park at West Eighty-third Street. Nathan Rapoport, 1965.

glass piers, each eleven feet high and ten feet square, resting on a low gray granite platform, sixty-six feet square. The monument's central pier, left open to the sky, was to serve as an Ohel, or chapel, which a small group or a family could enter. It alone was to bear etched inscriptions in Hebrew and English. Explained Kahn: "The one, the chapel, speaks; the other six are silent."

The spare beauty and simple geometry of Kahn's scheme belied the months of struggle that preceded the final design. Initially Kahn had an idea for a memorial made of concrete embedded with pieces of glass, but the concrete quickly gave way to a memorial made entirely of glass, remembers the architect Marshall Meyers, who worked closely with Kahn on the project. The eventual decision to erect an all-glass monument, Kahn would later write, sprang from the central thought that the monument should express "a sense of life and hope rather than of death." Unlike stone or metal, glass would absorb the life around it, holding "the light of day and of night, the seasons of the year, the endless play of the weather, and even the sudden light of a flash of lightning." Passing figures and boats sailing in the harbor would seem to enter the monument momentarily and then dematerialize; at certain vantage points within the cluster of crystalline piers the diffused images of Ellis Island and the Statue of Liberty, America's enduring symbols of hope, would be captured like scenes in a glass paperweight.

Designing a glass monument proved to be problematic. Corning Glass Works, which consulted on the project and was to cast the piers for the memorial, was equipped with kilns large enough only to manufacture elongated blocks measuring a maximum of six feet in length and six inches in thickness. This meant, therefore, that each of the seven piers would have to be constructed of layers of glass. Kahn's sketches, interspersed with calculations and scribbled comments, give some inkling of the obstacles he encountered in devising a system of construction that would both preserve the translucence of the glass and produce piers of pleasing proportions. After exploring several alternatives, he decided to use five-foot-long pieces, tightly laid,

In 1965 the sculptor Nathan Rapoport designed two memorials for the Riverside Park site. One, a towering Torah scroll encrusted with bas-reliefs depicting episodes of the Holocaust, was rejected by the Art Commission as "excessively and unnecessarily large." The other, a figure portrayed engulfed in thorns and flames, was deemed by the Art Commission to be "of such distressing and horrifying significance" that it would frighten children in the park. It was also rejected.

Kahn's design, unveiled in 1968, neither graphically represented the atrocities of the Holocaust nor was it accusing. Conceived as "an environment of light," the monument was composed of seven

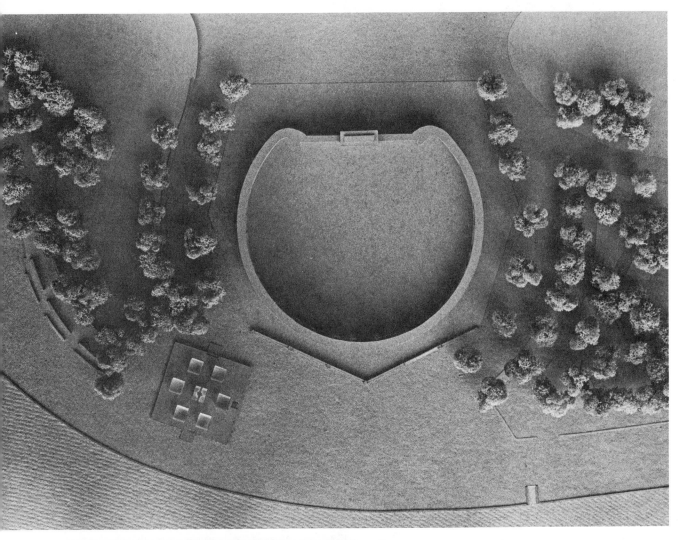

Site model of the proposed Holocaust memorial, showing the surrounding Battery Park. Louis I. Kahn, c. 1967–68. The memorial was to be located near the waterfront, just west of Castle Clinton.

LEFT:
Louis I. Kahn, c. 1967.

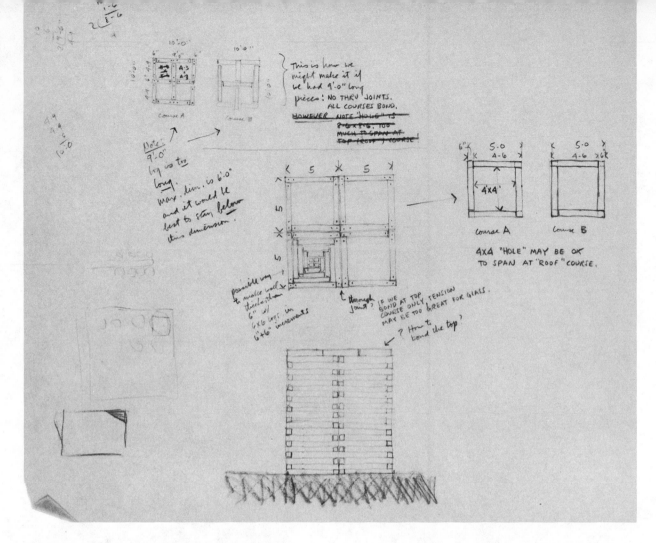

one over the other, to form ten-foot-square near-cubes that would be built "without the use of mortar, reminiscent of how the Greeks laid solid marble blocks in their temples."

Color was another problem that arose in designing the memorial. Notes made by Meyers after a visit to the Corning Glass Works read: "Clearest glass is fused silica—too expensive. Ordinary glass tends to greenish hue—not acceptable. Optical glass tends to warm straw color—more acceptable than green color." The scheme for the memorial was abandoned before color tests were run, but, says Meyers, it was thought that optical glass could be used and neutralized with another color.

The landscape architect Harriet Pattison assisted Kahn in the composition of the monument. She remembers long, difficult hours spent with Kahn drawing and redrawing cubes, shuffling them back and forth on a grid, like chess pieces, and experimenting with various numerical combinations in search of an ideal arrangement of the glass piers.

Kahn's working sketches reveal the constraints the glass blocks placed on the design of the Holocaust memorial, c. 1967–68.

They drew up diagrams for sixteen piers spaced eight feet apart, and for twelve piers spaced ten feet apart. They considered paring the design down to four fifteen-foot-square piers, and even to a solitary pier. When Kahn presented a preliminary plan composed of nine piers to the Committee to Commemorate the Six Million Jewish Martyrs, he was sent back to the drawing board with instructions to revise the design. The number nine in Jewish numerology, he was informed by rabbis and scholars who sat on the committee, represents the period of gestation. A more appropriate number was six, they suggested, for the six million martyrs.

Kahn drew up a plan for six piers spaced equidistantly apart; he was not entirely satisfied with the results. It was then that the idea of a seventh

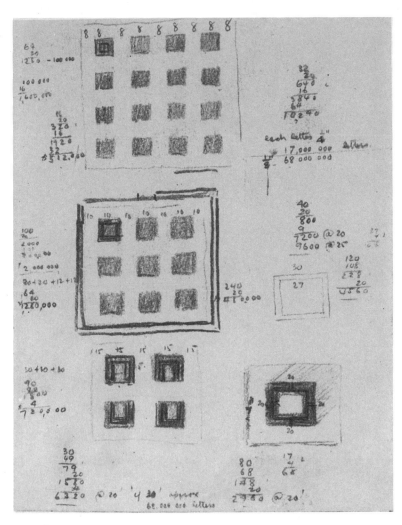

A page from Kahn's notebook, filled with some of the numerical combinations the architect considered for the glass piers in designing the Holocaust memorial, c. 1967–68.

BELOW:
This drawing by Kahn perhaps best illustrates what the architect meant when he wrote that he hoped the glass monument would give visitors both a sense of dematerialization and a sense of containment. Note the mass of the farthermost pier, which seems to float within the inscribed walls of the chapel.

pier, the chapel, was born. He placed it at the center of the memorial. "Intuitively," says Pattison, "we knew it was right."

The design for the $1,300,000 memorial was approved by the Art Commission in March 1968. Writing in the *New York Times*, the architecture critic Ada Louise Huxtable called the monument a "poetic, powerful and absolute statement of unspeakable tragedy. . . This is architecture and, at the same time, sculpture, and it is symbolism of the highest order, timeless and contemporary." Unfortunately, members of the Committee to Commemorate the Six Million Jewish Martyrs were not as unanimous in their praise of Kahn's plan. The monument was too abstract, said some; too hopeful, said others. One man, apparently failing to comprehend the potent symbolism of the glass, proposed that the monument be built in another, "less fragile" medium. Someone else suggested that the seven piers be of varied heights, "to represent persons of different ages—children, youths, men, women." Several committee members insisted that the chapel be capped with a roof.

With dissension running high among the committee's members, the dedication ceremony for the monument, scheduled for April 1968 in Battery Park, was indefinitely postponed. Kahn returned again to the drawing board. Reluctantly he added a cone-shaped ceiling to the chapel and covered the pier with a flat roof (he himself preferred the chapel without a roof). When the committee complained that the cost of the monument was too high, Kahn redesigned the piers, replacing the solid interlocking blocks with more economical glass panels set in steel frames. Other drawings by the architect show seven glass piers, all topped with pitched glass roofs.

In the meantime members of the committee had all but abandoned the fund-raising drive for the memorial. Another, more immediate cause demanded their attention, they claimed. "At this moment, the American Jewish community is confronted with the responsibility of standing by the side of Israel and Soviet Jewry, and is rendering every possible assistance to insure their survival," explained the committee member Benjamin Gebiner in a letter to Mayor John V. Lindsay. "It is incumbent upon us, therefore, to desist at present from any other major fund raising." But by the early 1970s it was evident that the committee had no intentions of undertaking a campaign to finance the memorial. Kahn's scheme was simply not what the majority of the committee had envisioned.

Had Kahn's plan for the monument been carried out, it would have been New York's only work by the architect, who died in 1974. Yet in some small measure his idea lives on. It is manifest in the Vietnam Veterans Memorial (1981), a glass-brick wall etched with excerpts of soldiers' letters that stands on Water Street, near Manhattan's financial district. It is also manifest in the design of James Stewart Polshek & Partners for a Holocaust memorial that will be built as part of the Museum of Jewish Heritage in Battery Park City. Conceived as a large, light-filled hall to be reserved for prayer or quiet reflection, the memorial is to be sited on the Hudson River, facing the Statue of Liberty and Ellis Island, and is to consist of a single, sixty-foot-square cube sheathed with glass—one of Kahn's piers enlarged, as it were. Projected for completion in late 1990, it will be the only large-scale memorial in New York City that remembers the six million victims of the Holocaust. In all, it will have taken forty-five years to build.

Plan for the Museum of Jewish Heritage and Holocaust memorial, Battery Park Place and First Place. James Stewart Polshek & Partners, 1987. Drawing by Mona Brown.

AFTERWORD

Constructed of paper and ink, daring and vision, the city that never was lies hidden behind New York's existing facade, an elusive specter of the real city. Although invisible, the two-dimensional metropolis, as old as New York itself, is linked to nearly every curve and angle of the tangible cityscape. From the seeds of Jones' Wood sprang the groves of Central Park; intertwined in the steel cables of the Brooklyn Bridge are the timber pieces of Thomas Pope's "Rainbow" invention; around the needle of the Empire State Building hover phantom, fat-bellied dirigibles.

Tomorrow, next year, and in the centuries to come, both the real city and the paper city will continue to evolve as indomitable dreamers sketch out their visions for New York. What bold schemes will they conjure up for the future metropolis: Frothy spires that dwarf the towers of the World Trade Center? Subterranian parks? Mobile bridges? Which of their plans will be incorporated into New York's cityscape and which will end up in the city that never was?

No one, of course, can accurately predict the shape that either city will take. But, with the benefit of two hundred years of hindsight, it can be said with certainty that the city that never was will forever be a constantly changing record of New York as it could look, and will continue to serve as the foundation on which it is built.

NOTES

INTRODUCTION

Page

xiii "crumbled away like sand": I. N. Phelps Stokes, *The Iconography of Manhattan Island, 1498–1909* (New York: R. H. Dodd, 1915–1928), vol. 4, p. 67.

xiii "molehill than a fortress": Ibid., p. 68.

xiii "cows and horses": Ibid., p. 124.

xiii "citizens without exception": Ibid., p. 138.

STREETS

Page

2 "incessant remonstrances": New York City, *Minutes of the Common Council*, 4 (1805–1808), p. 353.

6 "artistic manner": The Municipal Art Society of New York, Bulletin No. 5, 1904, p. 2.

6 "improvement of those cities": Ibid.

6 "perhaps destroyed": *New York Times,* August 9, 1908, part 5, p. 1.

8 "beautiful cities of Europe": New York City Improvement Commission, *Report* (New York, 1907), p. 17.

8 "monument of monotony": Louis E. Jallade, "Proposed Improvements for the City of New York," *House and Garden* 8, no. 1 (July 1905):39.

9 "lack imagination": Louis E. Jallade, p. 35.

9 "hesitate to incur": New York City Improvement Commission, *Report,* p. 17.

9 "worth its cost": *New York Times,* May 25, 1910, p. 8.

10 "loss to the city": *New York Times,* November 19, 1911, p. 12.

11 "Piccadilly Circus in London": Ibid.

11 "charitable and forbearing": *Some of Mayor Gaynor's Letters and Speeches* (New York: Greaves Publishing Co., 1913), pp. 43, 45.

11 "hearts of extravagant women": Arthur B. Maurice, *Fifth Avenue* (New York: Dodd Mead & Co., 1918), p. 265.

12 "New Yorker's heart": James D. McCabe, Jr., *New York by Gaslight* (1882; reprint, New York: Greenwich House, 1984), p. 165.

13 "in its favor": *New York Times,* June 15, 1910, p. 3.

13 "greatest drawbacks": *New York Times,* May 25, 1910, p. 18.

16 "a Colt automatic": Harvey Wiley Corbett, "Up with the Skyscraper," *National Municipal Review* 16, no. 2 (February 1927):95.

16 "that the skyscrapers breed": Ibid., p. 96.

16 "an American thing": "Skyscrapers and Traffic Congestion," *American Architect* 131 (March 20, 1927):387.

17 "municipal spaghetti": "Cities Old and New—I," *Journal of the American Institute of Architects* 14, no. 6 (June 1926):289.

17 "streets again at night": "Skyscrapers and Traffic Congestion," p. 387.

17 "to and fro": Corbett, "Up with the Skyscraper," p. 98.

17 "born there": "Skyscrapers and Traffic Congestion," p. 388.

17 "bought a new one": Corbett, "Up with the Skyscraper," p. 100.

18 "stop building skyscrapers": Ibid.

18 "double-decking must be used": Harvey Wiley Corbett, "The Problem of Traffic Congestion, and a Solution," *Architectural Forum* 64, no. 3 (March 1927):202.

20 "for all the world": Thomas Adams, *Regional Plan of New York and Its Environs*, vol. 2, *The Building of the City*, (New York: Regional Plan of New York and Its Environs, 1931), p. 309.

21 "that it may": Corbett, "The Problem of Traffic Congestion, and a Solution," p. 204.

21 "rapidly rolling vehicles": Ibid.

23 "one-level street system": Adams, p. 308.

23 "Times Square district": Ibid., p. 311.

23 "building of the city": Ibid., p. 329.

28 "that backward example": *New York Times*, December 5, 1962, p. 49.

28 "pork-barreled grab": *New York Times*, June 19, 1962, p. 37.

28 "stupid idea of a Lower Manhattan Expressway": Ibid.

28 "shadow of the expressway": New York City, Board of Estimate. "In the Matter of the Lower Manhattan Expressway." Opening statement of Charles F. Preusse on behalf of the Triborough Bridge and Tunnel Authority, December 22, 1964.

29 "dangerous for occupancy": Madigan-Hyland, Inc., *The Need for the Lower Manhattan Expressway* (July 1964), p. 21.

29 "in the United States": *New York Times*, July 22, 1965, p. 33.

30 "old Moses scheme": *Village Voice*, April 6, 1967, p. 42.

30 "who the mayor is": Ibid.

30 "for all time": *New York Post*, July 16, 1969, p. 5.

31 "whale of a success": *New York Times*, March 17, 1973, p. 30.

32 "survive in the streets": New York City, Office of Midtown Planning and Development, *Madison Mall* (October 1971), p. 17.

32 "liveable and humane": Ibid., p. 5.

32 "street-fair area": *New York Times*, March 6, 1973, p. 35.

33 "mall would create": *New York Times*, June 22, 1973, p. 53.

34 "economic existence of Madison Avenue": *New York Times*, March 6, 1973, p. 1.

34 "Madison madness": *New York Times*, June 7, 1973, p. 54.

34 "dead years ago": *New York Times*, July 12, 1973, p. 1.

PUBLIC BUILDINGS

Page

36 "of its size, in the world": *Blunt's Stranger's Guide to the City of New-York* (1817), in Charles Lockwood, *Manhattan Moves Uptown: An Illustrated History* (Boston: Houghton Mifflin Company, 1976), p. 1.

39 "this state in particular": Robert Vail, *Knickerbocker Birthday: A Sesqui-Centennial History of the New-York Historical Society, 1804–1954* (New York: New-York Historical Society, 1954), p. 23.

39 "antiquities, science and art": Robert H. Kelby, *The New-York Historical Society, 1804–1904* (New York: New-York Historical Society, 1905), p. 53.

39 "any great expense": Charles E. Beveridge and David Schuyler, eds., *Creating Central Park, 1857–1861*. Vol. 3 of Charles McLaughlin, ed., *The Papers of Frederick Law Olmsted* (Baltimore, Md.: Johns Hopkins University Press, 1983), p. 128.

39 "admirably adapted": New-York Historical Society, Executive Committee, *Minutes*, March 19, 1861, p. 319.

41 "noble undertaking": New York City, Board of Commissioners of the Central Park, *Documents*, no. 1 (February 26, 1866):2.

41 "Museum may require": *New York Times*, May 21, 1866, p. 2.

41 "with their express wishes": New-York Historical Society, *Report*, January 25, 1867, p. 88.

42 "mere freak": John Hassard, "An American Museum of Art," *Scribner's Monthly* 2 (August 1871): 409–415.

43 "effectuated measures": Winifred Howe, *A History of the Metropolitan Museum of Art* (New York: Metropolitan Museum of Art, 1913), p. 107.

43 "any other project is contemplated": Ibid.

43 "bewilder the visitor": Ibid., pp. 108, 111.

46 "a broad grin": Ibid., p. 146.

50 "a railroad station": Metropolitan Museum of Art, *The Second Century: The Comprehensive Architectural Plan for the Metropolitan Museum of Art* (New York: Metropolitan Museum of Art, 1971), p. 5.

50 "magnificent and elaborate": Howe, *History of the Metropolitan Museum of Art*, p. 176.

51 "greatest City on the Continent": New York City, Board of Aldermen, *Proceedings*, January 5, 1893, p. 16.

51 "[City Hall] site": *New York Times*, January 25, 1893, p. 10.

51 "demand its preservation": *New York Times*, January 17, 1893, p. 8.

52 "stands in the park": Ibid.

52 "would be very beautiful": *New York Times,* January 25, 1893, p. 10.

56 "wanton wastefulness": Andrew Haswell Green, *The Preservation of the Historical City Hall of New York* (1894), p. 8.

56 "names of the competitors": "The New York City Hall Competition," *Architecture and Building* 20, no. 4 (January 27, 1894):36.

56 "disgrace the City of New York": Ibid., p. 37.

56 "plans are now useless": *New York Times,* May 10, 1894, p. 8.

56 "no one knows where": *American Architect and Building News* 51, no. 1050 (February 8, 1896):58.

57 "copy of that building": *New York Times,* February 20, 1896, p. 2.

58 "ought to be": Allan Harding, "From a Tiny Cottage Church to a Temple on Broadway," *American Magazine* 98 (August 1924):48.

59 "advertisement of God's business": Ibid., p. 50.

59 "Or 5 percent": Gilbert Seldes, "Salvation and 5 Percent," *The New Republic* 44 (September 9, 1925):70.

59 "fellow man's salvation": From a promotional flyer for Broadway Temple, c. 1925.

65 "discuss Franco Spain": *New York Times,* September 25, 1985, p. 10.

65 "uses of peace": Ibid.

65 "dank and drafty": Ibid.

65 "centuries to come": Ed Allen, "Capital for the United States," *Architectural Record* 99 (March 1946):83.

65 "exchange of opinion": *New York Times,* November 30, 1946, p. 4.

67 "of all mankind": *New York Times,* November 18, 1946, p. 24.

67 "twenty square miles": *New York Times,* November 30, 1946, p. 1.

67 "All members of the United Nations": *New York Times,* December 2, 1946, p. 2.

67 "unstable ground conditions": Trygve Lie, *In the Cause of Peace: Seven Years with the United Nations* (New York: Macmillan Company, 1954), p. 110.

67 "occasional marsh odor": Ibid.

70 "bastards on the platform": William Zeckendorf, Sr., *The Autobiography of William Zeckendorf* (New York: Holt, Rinehart & Winston, 1970), p. 68.

70 "on what platform": Ibid.

70 "over the slaughterhouses": Ibid.

70 "eight and a half million": Ibid., p. 70.

70 "willing to pay": Ibid.

70 "See you soon. . . . Good-bye": Ibid., p. 71.

72 "give to the United Nations": *New York Herald Tribune,* December 12, 1946, p. 30.

72 "conduct of international affairs": *New York Times,* October 15, 1952, p. 6.

73 "fall in the same category": Walter Damrosch, *My Musical Life* (New York: Charles Scribner's Sons, 1926), p. 94.

73 "from private endowment": Ibid.

74 "note was heard": *New York Herald,* May 6, 1891, p. 7.

76 "super jitterbug": "The Duke Ellington Carnegie Hall Concerts, January 1943" (Prestige Records, 1977).

77 "violin for a juke box": *New York Times,* June 15, 1955, p. 35.

78 "Manhattan skyline": *New York Times,* August 8, 1957, p. 25.

78 "large cereal box": *Life,* September 30, 1957, p. 19.

78 "beyond our reach": *New York Times,* July 4, 1958, p. 21.

78 "will be torn down": Ibid.

78 "putting up the garage": "The Galloping Virtuoso," *Newsweek,* April 11, 1960, p. 113.

78 "rooms of the world": "Glory," *The New Yorker,* April 9, 1960, p. 32.

79 "someone like Andrew Carnegie himself": Author's interview with Raymond S. Rubinow, June 11, 1986.

79 "all love each other": Author's interview with Raymond S. Rubinow, February 27, 1988.

79 "aesthetic interest or value": New York General City Law, Section 20 (McKinney, 1968).

80 "entire civilized world": Telegram dated April 1, 1960, Carnegie Hall Archives.

80 "rooted in cultural values": Theodore O. Cron and Burt Goldblatt, *Portrait of Carnegie Hall* (New York: Macmillan Company, 1966), p. 5.

80 "bit of a miracle": "Gold That Glittered," *Newsweek,* October 10, 1960, p. 93.

TRANSPORTATION

Page

82 "disgracefully inadequate": *New York Times,* November 18, 1858, p. 4.

82 "bullies and ruffians": James D. McCabe, Jr., *New York by Gaslight* (1882; reprint, New York: Greenwich House, 1984), p. 187.

82 "echo of hell": F. Scott Fitzgerald, *The Beautiful and the Damned* (1922), in Benson Bobrick, *Labyrinths of Iron: A History of the World's Subways* (New York: Newsweek Books, 1981), p. 268.

82 "electric sewer": *New York Times,* August 13, 1984, p. 22.

85 "marble and brownstone": *New York Times,* May 17, 1865, p. 2.

85 "how changed everything is": *Harper's New Monthly Magazine* 24 (December 1861 to May 1862), p. 409.

85 "Bedlam on wheels": *New York Herald,* October 2, 1864, in James Blaine Walker, *Fifty Years of Rapid Transit, 1864–1917* (1918; reprint, New York: Arno Press, 1970), p. 7.

85 "eyelashes and . . . toenails": Reportage letter from Mark Twain to San Francisco newspaper *Alta California,* February 2, 1867, in Bayard Still, *Mirror for Gotham: New York as Seen by Contemporaries from Dutch Days to the Present* (New York: New York University Press, 1956), p. 202.

86 "street in the world": Egbert L. Viele, *The Arcade Underground Railway* (New York [1868?]), p. 7.

86 "to that of the Great Central Park": Ibid., p. 19.

88 "Millions of dollars": *Evidence Submitted to the Senate Railroad Committee as to the Practicability of the Arcade Plan, in Rebuttal* (1868), p. 12. Pamphlet vol. 52 of William Barclay Parsons Collection, Science and Technology Research Center, The New York Public Library.

88 "visionary project": *Public Papers of John T. Hoffman, Governor of New York, 1869–1872* (Albany: J. Munsell, 1872), p. 163.

90 "not done before": Viele, *Arcade Underground Railway,* p. 15.

90 "run of railway travel": *New York Times,* January 12, 1868, p. 4.

90 "mysterious rapidity": *New York Times,* October 26, 1872, p. 6.

91 "uptown fashionables": *New York Times,* October 27, 1872, p. 3.

91 "commercial calamity": *World,* October 27, 1872, p. 5.

92 "without delay": *New York Times,* November 12, 1872, p. 4.

92 "riding along the line": *New York Times,* November 12, p. 4.

95 "drive citizens entirely from it": New York City, Board of Aldermen, *Proceedings,* December 6, 1847, pp. 79–80.

98 "convince the incredulous": Alfred Speer, *Treatise on City Travel with a True Solution of Rapid Transit* (Passaic, N.J., 1875), p. 24.

98 "solution of rapid transit": Ibid., p. 23.

100 "first civilized dwelling": *New York Herald,* March 25, 1900, p. 5.

100 "past the car windows": *World,* October 27, 1904, p. 2.

100 "jeweled monster": *World,* October 29, 1904, p. 14.

100 "home-made apple pie": *World,* October 27, 1904, p. 2.

100 "the most hardy": *New York Times,* February 10, 1910, p. 6.

100 "hours of the day": *Street Railway Review,* November 1893, in *Transportation of Passengers in Greater New York by Continuous Railway Train, or Moving Platform* (New York, 1903), p. 8.

104 "their way out": *New York Tribune,* August 2, 1918, p. 6.

105 "seat on the moving platform": *New York Times,* January 29, 1922, section 7, p. 4.

105 "let's fix it right": *New York Times,* May 24, 1952, p. 26.

108 "the last minute": Jonathan Goldman, *The Empire State Building Book* (New York: St. Martin's Press, 1980), pp. 31–32.

109 "design quite unprecedented": Irwin Clavan, "The Empire State Building," *Architectural Forum* 54, no. 2 (February 1931):299.

113 "beautiful building in the world": *New York Times,* May 2, 1931, p. 7.

113 "migratory birds": Lewis Mumford, "Notes on Modern Architecture," *New Republic* 66 (March 18, 1931):121.

113 "awkwardly as a thumb": Herbert Footner, *New York, City of Cities* (London: J. B. Lippincott Company, 1937), p. 14.

113 "stars and planets": *New York Times,* April 17, 1931, p. 5.

113 "impossibly dangerous": *Dominion* (Wellington, New Zealand), May 5, 1931, in Empire State Building Scrapbook 5², Avery Architectural and Fine Arts Library, Columbia University, New York City.

BRIDGES

Page
119 "considered as extravagant": Stevens Family Papers, reel no. 14, New Jersey Historical Society, Newark, N.J.

119 "can be performed": Ibid.

119 "permanently affixed": Ibid.

120 "proper course through": Archibald Turnbull, *John Stevens: An American Record* (New York: Century Company, 1928), pp. 218–219.

122 "builder will not want": Thomas Pope, *A Treatise on Bridge Architecture, in Which the Superior Advantages of the Flying Pendant Lever Bridge Are Fully Proved* (New York: Alexander Niven, 1811), p. 282.

123 "must be lost": Ibid.

123 "never can it be": Ibid., p. 285.

123 "to its success": Ibid., p. 231.

123 "preservation of navigation": Ibid., p. 278.

126 "excellence of this invention": *Aurora General Advertiser* (Philadelphia), February 14, 1812.

126 "building & surveying": Talbot F. Hamlin, *Benjamin Latrobe* (New York: Oxford University Press, 1955), p. 419.

126 "crazy about his patent lever bridge": Ibid.

127 "voyage to Europe": Nathaniel Prime, *A History of Long Island* (Pittsburgh, Pa.: R. Carter, 1845), p. 377.

127 "stood in his way": Ibid., p. 378.

128 "around the chandelier": *New York Times,* January 24, 1867, p. 8.

128 "ruin of my life": Thomas Rainey, *Some Notes on the Life and Times of a Wanderer* (New York, 1909), p. 20.

129 "prefer the country life": Thomas Rainey, *The New York and Long Island Bridge Company* (1884), p. 7.

133 "four blocks away": Rainey, *Some Notes on the Life and Times of a Wanderer,* p. 20.

133 "archives of the past": *New York Times,* May 13, 1909, p. 1.

134 "books of fiction": *Railroad Gazette,* May 12, 1882, in George Burgess and Miles Kennedy, *Centennial History of the Pennsylvania Railroad Company* (Philadelphia: The Pennsylvania Railroad Company, 1949), p. 760.

136 "bridge cannot collapse": Gustav Lindenthal, "A Discussion of Long Span Bridges," *Engineering News* 19 (March 3, 1888):155.

141 pages of long equations: Author's interview with Hermina Wahle, October 4, 1984.

142 "jaded imagination": *New York Times,* July 29, 1921, p. 12.

142 "and the mainland": "The Hudson River Bridge," *Scientific American* 124, no. 17 (April 23, 1921):324.

143 "will be set free": "A Gigantic Bridge Over the Hudson," *Literary Digest* 30 (July 30, 1921):22.

143 "for one thousand years": *Othmar H. Ammann, 1879–1965: 60 Jahre Brückenbau* (Switzerland: Technorama Winterthur, 1979), p. 36.

147 "vehicular tunnels or bridges": American Society of Civil Engineers, *George Washington Bridge Across the Hudson River at New York, N.Y.* (New York: American Society of Civil Engineers in collaboration with The Port of New York Authority, 1933), p. 12.

147 "superhuman in perfection": *New York Times,* October 25, 1931, p. 30.

147 "seems to laugh": Le Corbusier, *When the Cathedrals Were White,* trans. Francis E. Hyslop, Jr. (New York: Reynal & Hitchcock, 1947), p. 75.

147 "skimpy": Author's interview with Hermina Wahle, October 4, 1985.

147 "most spontaneous": *New York Times,* October 25, 1931, p. 30.

151 "inconsequential errands": *New York Times,* January 26, 1939, p. 20.

151 "phantasy man has ever built": "Proposed Brooklyn-Battery Bridge," *Pencil Points* 20 (July 1939):454.

154 "on masonry piers": Triborough Bridge Authority, *The Brooklyn-Battery Bridge* (1939), n.p.

154 "noticeable in the general landscape": *New York Times,* February 17, 1939, p. 21.

154 "from an airplane": Central Committee of Organizations Opposing the Battery Toll Bridge, "An Open Letter to the President and his Advisers Requesting Further Study of the Battery Toll Bridge Project," July 14, 1939, p. 6.

154 "down on his belly": *New York Times,* February 17, 1939, p. 21.

156 "get it at all": *New York Times,* March 28, 1939, p. 18.

156 "access from the sea": Robert Moses, *Public Works: A Dangerous Trade* (New York: McGraw-Hill, 1970), p. 205.

156 "national defense": Ibid., p. 206.

156 "personal grudge": Cleveland Rodgers, *Robert Moses: Builder for Democracy* (New York: Henry Holt and Company, 1952), p. 102.

156 "best of it": Robert Moses, *Working for the People* (New York: Harper & Brothers, 1956), p. 138.

PARKS

Page

158 "might be needful": William Bridges, *Map of the City of New-York and Island of Manhattan with Explanatory Remarks and References* (New York: T & J Swords, 1811), p. 25.

161 "going out of town": *New York Evening Post,* July 3, 1844, p. 2.

161 "gay with flowers": Ibid.

161 "must be done now": Ibid.

162 "ornament of the city": New York City, Board of Aldermen, *Proceedings,* May 6, 1851, p. 33.

162 "healthful enjoyment": Ibid., p. 34.

162 "old countries of Europe": New York City, Board of Aldermen, *Proceedings,* June 3, 1851, p. 544.

163 "sale and purchase": New York City, Board of Aldermen, *Documents,* no. 5 (January 19, 1857), Appendix B, p. 80.

163 "may be obtained": Andrew Jackson Downing, "The New-York Park," *Horticulturist,* August 1851, p. 347.

163 "consulting Downing's works": George Bishop Tatum, "Andrew Jackson Downing: Arbiter of American Taste, 1815–1852," dissertation, Princeton University, 1949, p. 50.

163 "glare of brick walls": Downing, "The New-York Park," p. 347.

163 "nature and art": Ibid., p. 348.

163 "that surround them": Ibid.

164 "useless for building purposes": New York City, Board of Aldermen, *Documents*, no. 83 (January 2, 1852):146.

164 "trifling sum": Ibid., p. 157.

164 "order and variety": Ibid., p. 147.

164 "chief cities of Europe": Ibid., p. 157.

164 "the sake of convenience": Ibid., p. 140.

164 "mere luxury": *The Jones' Park Report*, June 21, 1853, in New York City, Board of Aldermen, *Documents*, no. 5 (January 19, 1857):185.

164 "air and exercise": *Central Park Report*, June 22, 1853, in New York City, Board of Aldermen, *Documents*, no. 5 (January 19, 1857):175.

167 "from the breezy river": *The Jones' Park Report, Documents*, no. 5:189.

167 "left for one": Frederick Law Olmsted, Jr., and Theodora Kimball, eds., *Forty Years of Landscape Architecture: Central Park*, vol. 2 (Cambridge, Mass.: MIT Press, 1973 [originally, New York: G. P. Putnam's Sons, 1928]), p. 28.

168 "national taste": Egbert L. Viele, *The Plan for Central Park* in New York City, Board of Aldermen, *Documents*, no. 5 (January 19, 1857):37.

168 "manly sports": Ibid., p. 39.

168 "deliberation of the topography": *New York Times*, December 12, 1856, p. 3.

169 "this magnificent Park": *New York Times*, July 9, 1856, p. 4.

169 "done in a day": "The Central Park," *Harper's Weekly*, November 28, 1857, p. 757.

169 "defects of Viele's design": Memorandum, November 1894. Calvert Vaux Papers, Rare Books and Manuscripts Division, The New York Public Library, Astor, Lenox and Tilden Foundations.

169 "memory of Mr. Downing": Ibid.

169 "person who would listen": Ibid.

169 "well-digested written description": Olmsted and Kimball, *Forty Years of Landscape Architecture: Central Park*, p. 42.

172 "success being so large": Ibid., p. 43.

172 "the Japanese lodge . . .": Plan No. 9, p. 35, in *Description of Designs for the Improvement of Central Park*, 1858.

174 "time deprived": Plan No. 5, p. 13, in *Description of Designs*.

174 "more or less sylvan": Plan No. 26, p. 25, in *Description of Designs*.

174 "and other refreshments": Plan No. 30, p. 8, in *Description of Designs*.

174 "from inverted urns": Ibid., p. 7.

174 "have been secured": Charles E. Beveridge and David Schuyler, eds., *Creating Central Park, 1857–1861*. Vol. 3 of Charles McLaughlin, ed., *The Papers of Frederick Law Olmsted* (Baltimore, Md.: Johns Hopkins University Press), p. 160.

177 "entirely original": Olmsted and Kimball, *Forty Years of Landscape Architecture: Central Park*, p. 558.

177 "some of these": Ibid., p. 562.

177 "by such hideousness": James D. McCabe, Jr., *Lights and Shadows of New York* (1872; reprint, New York: Farrar, Straus and Giroux, 1970), p. 334.

177 "fast trotters and pacers": Charles Lockwood, *Manhattan Moves Uptown: An Illustrated History* (Boston: Houghton Mifflin Company, 1976), p. 246.

177 "along the whole road": Matthew Hale Smith, *Sunshine and Shadow in New York* (Hartford, Conn.: J. B. Burr & Co., 1868), p. 360.

177 "wheelman cutting in": Charles Chapin Sargent, Jr., "A Horseman's Paradise," *Munsey's Magazine* 20, no. 2 (November 1898):198.

178 "by a policeman": *Gotham's Greater Rotten Row* (New York: The Municipal Improvement Association, 1890), p. 18.

178 "everything on Fifth Avenue": Real Estate Record Association, *Building and Architecture in New York City During the Last Quarter of a Century* (1898; reprint, New York: Arno Press, 1967), p. 92.

180 "from the water": *New York Herald*, August 4, 1890, p. 8.

181 "scheme carried out": Ibid.

181 "foreign squealers": *Gotham's Greater Rotten Row*, p. 43.

181 "disappeared from public notice": *New York Times*, April 2, 1892, p. 4.

182 "contesting in each brush": *New York Times*, April 21, 1916, p. 10.

183 "imaginative and daring": *New York Times*, May 17, 1961, p. 31.

183 "to shop and work": *New York Times*, May 25, 1961, p. 9.

183 "glittering chance": *New York Herald Tribune*, July 5, 1961, p. 18.

183 "a place of wood and fields": *New York Times*, August 18, 1961, p. 20.

183 "forget about the apartment houses": *New York Herald Tribune*, August 16, 1961, p. 6.

183 "theater, music or art": Ibid.

183 "unwise but impossible": *New York Times*, August 15, 1961, p. 31.

185 "study of the transportation problem": Ibid.

185 "country-like setting": *New York Herald Tribune Magazine*, May 16, 1965, p. 20.

185 "damaging the other": Letter to Thomas Cuite, Chairman, Finance Committee, New York City Council, March 4, 1968. Copy of letter on file at The Information Exchange, Municipal Art Society, New York City.

185 "superlative water setting": Letter to Mrs. Jacob M. Kaplan, February 6, 1968. Copy of letter on file at The Information Exchange, Municipal Art Society, New York City.

188 "significant degree by Welfare Island": *New York Times*, February 15, 1969, p. 28.

188 "firm course toward a new life": *New York Times,* February 13, 1969, p. 27.

188 "supernatural happening": *New York Times,* October 10, 1969, p. 46.

188 had already been painted: Author's interview with Robert Zion, March 18, 1986.

MONUMENTS

Page

193 "yet been accepted": I. N. Phelps Stokes, *The Iconography of Manhattan Island, 1498–1909* (New York: R. H. Dodd, 1915–1928), vol. 5, p. 1315.

193 "their fees": Ibid., p. 1505.

193 "use of man": New York City, Board of Aldermen, *Proceedings,* January 19, 1832, p. 71.

193 "copious supply of good water": New York City, Board of Aldermen, *Documents,* no. 8 (June 4, 1841):13.

193 "better planned": Robert Fleming Gourlay, *Plans for Beautifying New York and for Enlarging and Improving the City of Boston* (Boston: Crocker & Brewster, 1844), p. 3.

193 "species of improvement": Ibid.

193 "weeping willows": Ibid.

193 "Chatham square . . .": Ibid., p. 4.

194 "improvements of the city": Ibid., n.p.

194 "miserable planning": Ibid., p. 14.

194 (caption) "conjuring up something better": Ibid., p. 6.

195 "with a Flower Garden": Ibid., p. 8.

195 "termed 'The Fan' ": *New York Herald,* October 13, 1842, p. 2.

196 "now made to play": Gourlay, *Plans for Beautifying New York,* p. 6.

196 "loathsome corner": Ibid.

197 "of his Country": *New York Evening Post,* September 7, 1843, p. 2.

198 "costume of their day": A description of Calvin Pollard's plan for the Washington monument appears on a broadside issued in 1844, reprinted in Dorothy C. Barck, "Proposed Memorials to Washington in New York City, 1802–1847," *New-York Historical Society Quarterly* 15 (October 1931):79–90.

198 "National Observatory": Ibid.

198 "and a frown": *New York Evening Post,* October 12, 1847, p. 2.

198 "the republican style": *Scientific American* 3, no. 5 (October 23, 1846):38.

198 "these men meant for": *New York Evening Post,* October 12, 1847, p. 2.

198 "Fascia": *New York Daily Tribune,* July 24, 1847, p. 2.

199 "strength and permanence": Minard Lafever, *Architectural Instructor* (New York: G. P. Putnam & Co., 1856), p. 485.

199 "achieving our independence": Ibid.

199 "every American": Ibid.

200 "gold, silver and copper": *New York Herald,* October 20, 1847, p. 1.

200 "of the Edifice": Barck, "Proposed Memorials to Washington," p. 87.

200 "without appropriateness": Jacob Landy, "The Washington Monument Project in New York," *New-York Historical Society Quarterly* 28 (1969):294.

200 "very bad Gothic": *New York Evening Post,* October 12, 1847, p. 2.

201 "order and style": John Frazee, *Description of J. Frazee's Washington Monument* (J. W. Bell, 1848), p. 1.

201 "was broken": Lucien M. Underwood, *The Ancestry and Descendants of Jonathan Pollard* (Syracuse, N.Y., 1891), p. 13.

203 "salvos of artillery": *New York Tribune,* July 5, 1856, p. 1.

204 "serene majesty": "The Robert Fulton Memorial," *Architectural Review* 29 (January 1911):51.

207 "at a conclusion": "A Notable Architectural Exhibition," *New York Architect* 4 (June 1910):n.p.

209 "along the Drive": Harold Van Buren Magonigle, "The Robert Fulton Memorial," *American Architect* 97, no. 1799 (June 15, 1910):225.

209 "for years to come": Ibid., p. 226.

209 "grasp of the problem": *New York Architect* 4 (June 1910):n.p.

209 "well-conducted competition": *Architectural Review* 1 (January 1912):1.

210 "Central Park Commissioners": Charles E. Beveridge and David Schuyler, eds., *Creating Central Park, 1857–1861.* Volume 3 of Charles McLaughlin, ed., *The Papers of Frederick Law Olmsted* (Baltimore, Md.: Johns Hopkins University, 1983), pp. 205, 216.

213 "commit sacrilege": *New York Times,* June 28, 1922, p. 14.

213 "congested little island": *New York Times,* July 14, 1922, p. 12.

213 "rustic park": *New York Times,* July 1, 1922, p. 16.

213 "inland Coney Island": *New York Times,* June 29, 1922, p. 16.

214 "the war's dead": *New York Times,* April 1, 1924, p. 1.

214 "that are fountain-like": *New York Times,* April 2, 1924, p. 3.

215 "playground area owned by the City of New York": *New York Times,* November 20, 1925, p. 18.

217 "From a Metronome": *New York Times,* June 28, 1943, p. 20.

219 "still on paper": *New York Times,* July 4, 1943, section 2, p. 6.

219 "absurd and tasteless": *New York Times,* July 12, 1943, p. 14.

219 "it is inept": *New York Times,* July 4, 1943, section 2, p. 6.

219 "thing? . . . Never": *New York Times,* June 28, 1943, p. 20.

219 "survive but prevail": Letter to Louis I. Kahn, December 28, 1966. LIK #36, "Committee to Commemorate the Six Million Jewish Martyrs," Louis I. Kahn Collection, University of Pennsylvania and Pennsylvania Historical and Museum Commission, Philadelphia.

219 "merely a family tragedy": *Jewish Currents* 23, no. 4 (April 1969):39.

220 "unnecessarily large": *New York Times,* February 11, 1965, p. 1.

220 "horrifying significance": *New York World-Telegram and Sun,* February 10, 1965, p. 16.

220 "six are silent": Louis I. Kahn, statement for the press, May 3, 1968. LIK #36, "Committee to Commemorate the Six Million Jewish Martyrs," Louis I. Kahn Collection, University of Pennsylvania and Pennsylvania Historical and Museum Commission, Philadelphia.

220 with Kahn on the project: Author's interview with Marshall Meyers, March 16, 1988.

220 "hope rather than of death": "Expressing the Unspeakable," *Time* 92 (October 25, 1968):78.

220 "flash of lightning": Louis I. Kahn, statement for the press, May 3, 1968.

222 "blocks in their temples": Ibid.

222 "green color": Memorandum, September 6, 1967. LIK #36, "Committee to Commemorate the Six Million Jewish Martyrs," Louis I. Kahn Collection, University of Pennsylvania and Pennsylvania Historical and Museum Commission, Philadelphia.

225 "it was right": Author's interview with Harriet Pattison, June 6, 1985.

225 "timeless and contemporary": *New York Times,* October 17, 1968, p. 47.

225 "youths, men, women": Abraham G. Duker, letter to Louis I. Kahn, November 13, 1967. LIK #36, "Six Million American Jewish Committee Correspondence," Louis I. Kahn Collection, University of Pennsylvania and Pennsylvania Historical and Museum Commission, Philadelphia.

225 "major fund raising": Benjamin A. Gebiner, letter to Mayor John V. Lindsay, May 18, 1971. Property files, Parklands Office, New York City Department of Parks and Recreation.

BIBLIOGRAPHY

BOOKS AND DISSERTATIONS

BOOKS

Adams, Thomas. *Regional Plan of New York and Its Environs*, vol. 2, *The Building of the City*. New York: Regional Plan of New York and Its Environs, 1931.

Allen, Hugh. *The Story of the Airship*. Akron, Ohio: Goodyear Tire and Rubber Company, 1932.

American Society of Civil Engineers. *George Washington Bridge Across the Hudson River at New York, N.Y.* New York: American Society of Civil Engineers in collaboration with The Port of New York Authority, 1933.

Appleton's Dictionary of New York and Its Vicinity. New York: D. Appleton & Co., 1886.

Belden, E. Porter. *New-York: Past, Present and Future.* New York: G. P. Putnam, 1849.

Beveridge, Charles, and David Schuyler, eds. *Creating Central Park, 1857–1861.* Vol. 3 of *The Papers of Frederick Law Olmsted*, Charles McLaughlin, ed. Baltimore, Md.: Johns Hopkins University Press, 1983.

A Biographical Dictionary of American Civil Engineers. New York: American Society of Civil Engineers, 1972.

Black, Mary. *Old New York in Early Photographs, 1853–1901.* New York: Dover Publications, 1973.

Bobrick, Benson. *Labyrinths of Iron: A History of the World's Subways.* New York: Newsweek Books, 1981.

Bonner, William Thompson. *New York, the World's Metropolis, 1623–1924.* New York: R. L. Polk & Co., 1924.

Bridges, William. *Map of the City of New-York and Island of Manhattan with Explanatory Remarks and References.* New York: T & J Swords, 1811.

Browne, Junius Henri. *The Great Metropolis: A Mirror of New York.* Hartford, Conn.: American Publishing Co., 1869.

Bryant, William Cullen. *Letters of a Traveler; or Notes of Things Seen in Europe and America.* New York: G. P. Putnam, 1850.

Burgess, George, and Miles Kennedy. *Centennial History of the Pennsylvania Railroad Company, 1846–1946.* Philadelphia: Pennsylvania Railroad Company, 1949.

Callow, Alexander B., Jr. *The Tweed Ring.* New York: Oxford University Press, 1966.

Caro, Robert A. *The Power Broker: Robert Moses and the Fall of New York.* New York: Vintage Books, 1975.

Cheape, Charles W. *Moving the Masses: Urban Public Transit in New York, Boston and Philadelphia, 1880–1912.* Cambridge, Mass.: Harvard University Press, 1980.

Condit, Carl W. *American Building: Material and Techniques from the First Colonial Settlements to the Present.* Chicago: University of Chicago Press, 1968.

———. *The Port of New York*, 2 vols. Chicago: University of Chicago Press, 1980–81.

Cron, Theodore O., and Burt Goldblatt. *Portrait of Carnegie Hall.* New York: Macmillan, 1966.

Cudahy, Brian J. *Under the Sidewalks of New York: The Story of the Greatest Subway System in the World.* Brattleboro, Vt.: Stephen Greene Press, 1979.

Daley, Robert. *The World Beneath the City.* New York: J. B. Lippincott Co., 1959.

Damrosch, Walter. *My Musical Life.* New York: Charles Scribner's Sons, 1926.

Darnell, Victor C. *American Bridge-Building Compa-*

nies, 1840–1900. Washington, D.C.: Society for Industrial Archaeology, 1984.

Dickens, Charles. American Notes for General Circulation. New York: Harper & Brothers, 1842.

Diehl, Lorraine B. The Late, Great Pennsylvania Station. New York: American Heritage Press; Houghton Mifflin Co., 1985.

Downing, Andrew Jackson. Rural Essays. George William Curtis, ed. New York: Leavitt & Allen, 1856.

———. A Treatise on the Theory and Practice of Landscape Gardening, second ed. New York: Wiley & Putnam, 1844.

The 1866 Guide to New York City, reprint. New York: Schocken Books, 1975.

Fein, Albert. Landscape into Cityscape: Frederick Law Olmsted's Plans for a Greater New York City. Ithaca, N.Y.: Cornell University Press, 1968.

Ferriss, Hugh. The Metropolis of Tomorrow. Originally published 1929; reprint, Princeton, N.J.: Princeton Architectural Press, 1986.

Fischler, Stan. Uptown, Downtown. New York: Hawthorn Books, 1976.

Francis, Dennis Steadman. Architects in Practice, New York City, 1840–1900. New York: Committee for the Preservation of Architectural Records, 1979[?]

Fried, Frederick, and Edmond V. Gillon, Jr. New York Civic Sculpture. New York: Dover Publications, 1976.

Gilder, Rodman. The Battery. Boston: Houghton Mifflin Co., 1936.

Goldberger, Paul. The Skyscraper. New York: Alfred A. Knopf, 1982.

Goldman, Jonathan. The Empire State Building Book. New York: St. Martin's Press, 1980.

Goldstone, Harmon H., and Martha Dalrymple. History Preserved: A Guide to New York City Landmarks and Historic Districts. New York: Simon & Schuster, 1974.

Gourlay, Robert Fleming. Plans for Beautifying New York and for Enlarging and Improving the City of Boston. Boston: Crocker & Brewster, 1844.

Grafton, John. New York in the Nineteenth Century. New York: Dover Publications, 1977.

The Great Metropolis; or, Guide to New-York. New York: John Doggett, Jr., 1846.

Guernsey, Rocellus S. Street Openings: The Magnitude of the Subject. New York: Appeal Print Co., 1906[?]

Hays, Forbes B. Community Leadership: The Regional Plan Association of New York. New York: Columbia University Press, 1965.

Hone, Phillip. Diary, 1828–1851. Allan Nevins, ed. New York: Dodd, Mead, 1936.

Hornung, Clarence. Wheels Across America. New York: A. S. Barnes, 1959.

Howe, Winifred E. A History of the Metropolitan Museum of Art. New York: Metropolitan Museum of Art, 1913.

Huxtable, Ada Louise. When Will They Ever Finish Bruckner Boulevard? New York: Macmillan, 1970.

Jenkins, Stephen. The Greatest Street in the World: The Story of Broadway. New York: G. P. Putnam's Sons, 1912.

King, Moses. King's Views of New York, 1896–1915, and Brooklyn, 1905. New York: B. Blom, 1974.

———. Notable New Yorkers of 1896–1899. New York: Bartlett & Co., 1899.

Kouwenhoven, John A. The Columbia Historical Portrait of New York. New York: Harper & Row, 1972.

Lamb, Martha J. History of the City of New York: Its Origin, Rise, and Progress, 3 vols. New York: A. S. Barnes & Co., 1877–96.

Lightfoot, Frederick S., ed. Nineteenth-Century New York in Rare Photographic Views. New York: Dover Publications, 1981.

Lindsay, John V. The City. New York: W. W. Norton & Co., 1969.

Lockwood, Charles. Manhattan Moves Uptown: An Illustrated History. Boston: Houghton Mifflin Co., 1976.

Lyman, Susan Elizabeth. The Story of New York. New York: Crown Publishers, Inc., 1975.

Lynch, Dennis T. "Boss" Tweed. New York: Boni and Liveright, 1927.

McCabe, James D., Jr. Lights and Shadows of New York. Originally published 1872; reprint, New York: Farrar, Straus and Giroux, 1970.

———. New York by Gaslight. Originally published 1882; reprint, New York: Greenwich House, 1984.

Mandelbaum, Seymour. Boss Tweed's New York. New York: John Wiley & Sons, 1965.

Maurice, Arthur B. Fifth Avenue. New York: Dodd, Mead & Co., 1918.

Milani, Lois Darroch. Robert Gourlay, Gadfly/Forerunner of the Rebellion in Upper Canada 1837. Toronto: Ampersand Press, 1971.

Miller, John Anderson. Fares Please! New York: Dover Publications, 1960.

Mitchell, Latham S. The Picture of New York; or the Traveller's Guide. New York: J. Riley & Co., 1807.

Moscow, Henry. The Street Book: An Encyclopedia of Manhattan's Street Names and Their Origins. New York: Hagstrom Co., 1978.

Moses, Robert. Public Works: A Dangerous Trade. New York: McGraw-Hill, 1970.

———. Working for the People. New York: Harper & Brothers, 1956.

Nevins, Deborah, ed. Grand Central Terminal: City Within the City. New York: Municipal Art Society of New York, 1982.

Newton, Norman T. Design on the Land: The Development of Landscape Architecture. Cambridge, Mass.: Belknap Press and Harvard University Press, 1971.

Olmsted, Frederick Law. Walks and Talks of an American Farmer in England. New York: George P. Putnam, 1852.

Olmsted, Frederick Law, Jr., and Theodora Kimball, eds. Forty Years of Landscape Architecture: Central Park, 2 vols. Cambridge, Mass.: MIT Press, 1973. (Originally, New York: G. P. Putnam's Sons, 1928.)

Perry, John. *American Ferryboats.* New York: Wilfred Funk, 1957.

Placzek, Adolf K., ed. *Macmillan Encyclopedia of Architects.* New York: Free Press, 1982.

Pope, Thomas. *A Treatise on Bridge Architecture, in Which the Superior Advantages of the Flying Pendant Lever Bridge Are Fully Proved.* New York: Alexander Niven, 1811.

Post, John. *Old Streets, Roads, Lanes, Piers and Wharves of New York.* New York: R. D. Cooke, 1882.

Prime, Nathaniel. *A History of Long Island.* Pittsburgh, Pa.: R. Carter, 1845.

Public Papers of John T. Hoffman, Governor of New York, 1869–1872. Albany, N.Y.: J. Munsell, 1872.

Real Estate Record Association. *A History of Real Estate, Building and Architecture in New York During the Last Quarter of a Century.* Originally published 1898; reprint, New York: Arno Press, 1967.

Reed, Henry Hope, and Sophia Duckworth. *Central Park: A History and a Guide.* New York: Clarkson N. Potter, 1967.

Reed, Robert C. *The New York Elevated.* South Brunswick, N.J.: A. S. Barnes & Co., 1978.

Reier, Sharon. *The Bridges of New York.* New York: Quadrant Press, 1977.

Reps, John W. *The Making of Urban America: A History of City Planning in the United States.* Princeton, N.J.: Princeton University Press, 1965.

Rider's Guide to New York City. New York: Macmillan Co., 1924.

Rodgers, Cleveland. *Robert Moses: Builder for Democracy.* New York: Henry Holt and Co., 1952.

Roper, Laura Wood. *FLO: A Biography of Frederick Law Olmsted.* Baltimore, Md.: Johns Hopkins University Press, 1973.

Rosenwoike, Ira. *Population History of New York City.* Syracuse, N.Y.: Syracuse University Press, 1972.

Ross, Joel H. *What I Saw in New York; or A Bird's Eye View of City Life.* Auburn, N.Y.: Derby & Miller, 1851.

Sayre, Wallace S., and Herbert Kaufman. *Governing New York City: Politics in the Metropolis.* New York: W. W. Norton & Co., 1960.

Scott, Mel. *American City Planning Since 1890.* Berkeley, Calif.: University of California Press, 1969.

Silver, Nathan. *Lost New York.* New York: Schocken Books, 1967.

Simon, Kate. *Fifth Avenue: A Very Social History.* New York: Harcourt Brace Jovanovich, 1978.

Simpson, Jeffrey, and Mary Ellen W. Hern, eds. *Art of the Olmsted Landscape: His Works in New York City.* New York: New York City Landmarks Preservation Commission, 1981.

Smith, Matthew Hale. *Sunshine and Shadow in New York.* Hartford, Conn.: J. B. Burr & Co., 1868.

Smith, Mortimer. *William Jay Gaynor: Mayor of New York.* Chicago: Henry Regnery Co., 1951.

Some of Mayor Gaynor's Letters and Speeches. New York: Greaves Publishing Co., 1913.

Spann, Edward K. *The New Metropolis: New York City, 1840–1857.* New York: Columbia University Press, 1981.

Stern, Robert A. M., et al. *New York 1900.* New York: Rizzoli, 1983.

Stiles, Henry R. *A History of the City of Brooklyn,* 3 vols. Brooklyn, N.Y.: published by subscription, 1867–1870.

Still, Bayrd. *Mirror for Gotham: New York as Seen by Contemporaries from Dutch Days to Present.* New York: New York University Press, 1956.

Stokes, I. N. Phelps. *The Iconography of Manhattan Island, 1498–1909,* 6 vols. New York: R. H. Dodd, 1915–28.

Strong, George Templeton. *Diary,* 4 vols. Allan Nevins and Milton H. Thomas, eds. New York: Macmillan, 1952.

Stuart, Charles B. *Lives and Works of Civil and Military Engineers of America.* New York: D. Van Nostrand, 1871.

Tomkins, Calvin. *Merchants and Masterpieces: The Story of the Metropolitan Museum of Art.* New York: E. P. Dutton & Co., 1970.

Trachtenberg, Alan. *Brooklyn Bridge: Fact and Symbol.* Chicago: University of Chicago Press, 1979.

Trollope, Frances. *Domestic Manners of the Americans.* London: Whittaker, Tracher & Co., 1832.

True, Clarence. *Riverside Drive.* New York: Unz & Co., 1899.

Turnbull, Archibald. *John Stevens: An American Record.* New York: Century Company, 1928.

Tyrrell, Henry G. *History of Bridge Engineering.* Chicago: the author, 1911.

Vail, Robert. *Knickerbocker Birthday: A Sesqui-Centennial History of The New-York Historical Society, 1804–1954.* New York: New-York Historical Society, 1954.

Walker, James Blaine. *Fifty Years of Rapid Transit, 1864–1917.* Originally published 1918; reprint, New York: Arno Press, 1970.

Weidner, Charles. *Water for a City.* New Brunswick, N.J.: Rutgers University Press, 1974.

White, Norval, and Elliot Willensky. *AIA Guide to New York City,* second ed. New York: Macmillan Publishing Co., 1978.

Wilson, James G., ed. *The Memorial History of the City of New-York,* 4 vols. New York: New-York History Co., 1893.

Wolfe, Gerard R. *New York: A Guide to the Metropolis.* New York: New York University Press, 1975.

The World's Columbian Exposition Reproduced. Chicago: Rand, McNally & Co., 1894.

The WPA Guide to New York City. Originally published 1939; reprint, New York: Pantheon Books, 1982.

DISSERTATIONS

Frank, Fred Roy. "The Development of New York City, 1600–1900." Master's Thesis, Cornell University, 1955.

Kantor, Harvey A. "Modern Urban Planning in New York City: Origins and Evolution, 1890–1933." Ph.D. Dissertation, New York University, 1971.

Tatum, George Bishop. "Andrew Jackson Downing: Arbiter of American Taste." Ph.D. Dissertation, Princeton University, 1949.

PRINTED DOCUMENTS AND PROSPECTI

Art Commission of the City of New York. *On City Hall, in City Hall.* New York, 1984.

Description of Designs for the Improvement of Central Park, 1858.

East Island Development Corporation. *East Island: A Proposal for the Conversion of Welfare Island, New York, to a Residential Community,* 1961.

Gotham's Greater Rotten Row. New York: The Municipal Improvement Association, 1890.

Madigan-Hyland, Inc. *The Need for the Lower Manhattan Expressway,* New York, July 1964.

Municipal Art Society of New York. *Report of the Thoroughfares Committee,* Bulletin No. 5, New York, 1904.

New York City, Board of Aldermen. *Documents,* no. 83, January 2, 1852.

———. *Documents,* no. 5, January 19, 1857.

———. *Proceedings,* May–June 1851.

New York City, Board of Commissioners of the Central Park. *Documents,* no. 1, February 26, 1866.

———. *Minutes, Documents and Reports* (Two Years Ending April 30, 1859).

New York City, Board of Estimate and Apportionment, Committee on the City Plan. *Development and Status of City Planning in New York City,* 1914.

New York City, Mayor's Committee on Plan and Scope. *Plan for a Permanent World Capitol at Flushing Meadow Park,* 1946.

New York City, Office of Midtown Planning and Development. *Madison Mall,* October 1971.

New York City Improvement Commission. *Report,* 1907.

New-York Historical Society, Executive Committee, *Minutes,* 1861–1868.

New York State Urban Development Corporation. *The Island Nobody Knows,* 1969.

North River Bridge Company. *Plan for the Hudson River Bridge at 57th Street,* New York, 1925.

Port of New York Authority. *Annual Reports,* 1923–26.

———. *The Fifty-Seventh Street Bridge,* Port Information Bulletin No. 5, January 1936.

Rainey, Thomas. *The New York and Long Island Bridge Company,* 1884.

Randel, John, Jr. *Explanatory Remarks and Estimates of the Cost and Income of the Elevated Railway and Its Appendages, etc. for Broadway in the City of New-York.* New York: George F. Nesbitt, 1848.

Speer, Alfred. *Treatise on City Travel with a True Solution of Rapid Transit.* Passaic, N.J., 1875.

Transportation of Passengers in Greater New York by Continuous Railway Train, or Moving Platforms. New York, 1903.

Triborough Bridge and Tunnel Authority. *Lower Manhattan Elevated Expressway,* 1965.

Triborough Bridge Authority. *The Brooklyn-Battery Bridge,* 1939.

———. *Vital Gaps in New York Metropolitan Arteries,* November 11, 1940.

United Nations, Preparatory Commission. Compilation of documents relating to choice of site for the permanent headquarters, 1945.

Viele, Egbert L. *The Arcade Underground Railway.* New York [1868?].

———. *The Plan for Central Park.* Reprinted in New York City, Board of Aldermen, *Documents,* no. 5, January 19, 1857, pp. 36–45.

Welfare Island Planning and Development Committee. *Report,* February 1969.

ARTICLES

Allen, Ed. "Capital for the United Nations," *Architectural Record* 99 (March 1946):82–85.

Ammann, Othmar H. "George Washington Bridge: General Conception and Development of Design," American Society of Civil Engineers *Transactions,* Paper No. 1818, vol. 97, 1933, pp. 969–1035.

Bailey, Anthony. "Manhattan's Other Island," *New York Times Magazine,* December 1, 1974, pp. 32–34+.

Barck, Dorothy C. "Proposed Memorials to Washington in New York City, 1802–1847," *New-York Historical Society Quarterly* 15 (1931):79–90.

Bigelow, John. "The Tilden Trust Library: What Shall It Be?" *Scribner's Magazine* 12 (September 1892):287–300.

"Central Park and Jones Park," *Illustrated News* 1 (June 25, 1853):409.

Clavan, Irwin. "The Empire State Building," *Architectural Forum* 54, no. 2 (February 1931):229–33.

Corbett, Harvey Wiley. "The Problem of Traffic Congestion, and a Solution." *Architectural Forum* 64, no. 3 (March 1927):201–8.

Downing, Andrew Jackson. "The New-York Park," *Horticulturist,* August 1851, pp. 345–49.

"East River Park," *Architecture and Urbanism* 43 (November 1974):93–95.

"Endless Train to End New York Subway Jam," *Popular Science* 158 (May 1951):100–101.

FitzGerald, Frances. "Welfare Island: East River Loser," *New York Herald Tribune Magazine*, May 16, 1965, pp. 8–13.

Hall, Edward H. "The History of Central Park," American Scenic and Historic Preservation Society, *Sixteenth Annual Report* (1911) pp. 379–489.

Harder, Julius F. "The City's Plan," *Municipal Affairs* 2, no. 1 (March 1898):24–45.

Hassard, John. "An American Museum of Art," *Scribner's Monthly* 2 (August 1871):409–15.

Hornbostel, Henry F. "Proposed Brooklyn Bridge Terminal and City Offices," *Architects' and Builders' Magazine* 4, no. 11 (August 1903):483–89.

"The Hudson River Bridge," *Scientific American* 124, no. 17 (April 23, 1921):324, 336.

Kantor, Harvey. "The City Beautiful in New York," *New-York Historical Society Quarterly* 57 (April 1973):148–71.

Kyle, John M. "A Tribute to Othmar H. Ammann," *The Port Authority Review* 4, no. 1 (1966):3–8.

Lamb, Martha J. "Riverside Park," *Manhattan Illustrated Magazine* 4, no. 1 (July 1884):52–61.

Landy, Jacob. "The Washington Monument Project in New York," *New-York Historical Society Quarterly* 28 (May 1969):291–97.

Magonigle, Harold Van Buren. "The Robert Fulton Memorial," *American Architect* 97, no. 1799 (June 15, 1910):225–26.

Pringle, Henry F. "Billboard Preacher," *American Mercury* 18 (September 1929):79–87.

"The Proposed North River Bridge at New York City," *American Architect and Building News* 24, no. 676 (December 8, 1888):266–67.

Reed, Henry Hope. "The Vision Spurned: Classical New York—The Story of City Planning in New York," part 1, *Classical America* 1, no. 1 (1971):31–41.

———. "The Vision Spurned: Classical New York—The Story of City Planning in New York," part 2, *Classical America* 1, no. 2 (1972):10–19.

"The Robert Fulton Memorial Competition," *Architectural Review* 1, no. 1 (January 1912):1–5.

Sargent, Charles Chapin, Jr. "A Horseman's Paradise," *Munsey's Magazine* 20, no. 2 (November 1898):193–204.

"The Second Bridge Between New York and Brooklyn," *Scientific American* 44, no. 22 (May 28, 1881):335.

Silver, Robert Harold. "The Lower Manhattan Expressway," *Architectural Forum* 128, no. 8 (September 1967):66–69.

Stewart, Ian R. "Politics and the Park: The Fight for Central Park," *New-York Historical Society Quarterly* 61 (1977):124–55.

Solberg, Sara. "New York Ferryboats: Three and a Half Centuries in the Harbor," *Seaport* 16, no. 2 (Fall 1982):10–16.

"The Sunken Garden in Central Park, New York," *American Architect* 112, no. 2172 (August 8, 1917):105–8.

Wade, Herbert T. "The World's Greatest Bridge," *American Review of Reviews* 64 (August 1921):187–93.

INDEX

Abbott, Henry, 39
Abercrombie and Fitch, 32–33
Adams, Thomas, 23
Adler, Dankmar, 74
Adopt-a-Monument program, 191
airfields, 108
Allegheny Arsenal project, 126
Allen, Horatio, 195
B. Altman's, 11, 103
American Architect and Building News, 56, 57
American Institute of Architects, 39
American Museum of Natural History, 44, 46, 158
  allée for, 213, 217
  design of, 46, 50
American National Theatre and Academy, 78
American Rapid Transit Company, 99
American Scenic and Historic Preservation Society, 213
American Society for the Prevention of Cruelty to Animals (ASPCA), 90–91, 92
American Society of Civil Engineers, 136
American Society of Landscape Architects, 215–17
Ammann, Othmar H., 143, 146, 147, 149, 152, 154
Aquarium, 217

Aqueduct Celebration Committee, 210
Arcade Railway, proposed, 86–90, 95–96, 177
Arc de Triomphe, 219
Architectural League, 154
Art Commission of the City of New York, 190-91, 215, 219, 225
Arterial Highways and Major Streets plan, 24
Astor, Mrs. John Jacob, 13
Atomic Energy Commission, 65
Aurora General Advertiser, 126
Austin, Warren, 67, 70–72
Automobile Club of New York, 32
Automobile Row, 17–18
automobiles, 17–18

Badillo, Herman, 34
Baltic, 16
Baltimore & Ohio Railroad, 147
Barber, Donn, 59, 60, 61
Battery Park, 159, 167, 197, 204, 219, 225
  Brooklyn-Battery bridge, proposed for, 154, 155, 156
  Holocaust memorial, proposed for, 219–25
Battery Park Building, 155
Battery Park City, 224, 225

Beame, Abraham, 34
Beard, William Holbrook, 35, 42, 43, 44, 45
Bear Dance, The (Beard), 43
Vivian Beaumont Theater, 80
Beecher, Henry Ward, statue of, 190
Bellows, Ripley, Clapp & Faelten, 206
Belmont, August, 100, 104
Belmont family, 178
Belt Parkway, 149
Belvedere Castle, 168, 213, 217
Bennett, James Gordon, 181
Floyd Bennett Field, 108
Best & Company, 103
Bethesda Terrace, 196
bicycles, 177
Bigelow, John, 52
Biltmore mansion, 39
Bingham, Sidney H., 105
Blackwell Farm House, 188
Blackwell's Island (Roosevelt Island; Welfare Island), 128, 132, 133, 183–88, 204, 205
Blackwell's Island bridge (1877), plan for, 128–32
Blackwell's Island bridge (1894), plan for, 132–33
Bliss, Eliphalet, 129
Blodgett, William, 46
Bloomingdale Road, 3

Bloomingdale Square, 158
Board of Aldermen, 193, 195
Board of Commissioners of the
    Central Park, 39, 41–42, 44–
    46, 167, 169, 174, 175, 210
Board of Estimate, 27, 28, 34, 181,
    215
Board of Home Missions, 59
Board of Transportation, 105
Bob, Charles V., 59
Bois de Bologne, 174
Bonzano, Adolphus, 129–32, 133
Boston, Mass., 67
Boston Common, 194–95
Bowery, 11
Bowling Green, xvi
Breen, Harold, 185, 188
Breines, Simon, 77
bridges, 116–56
    cantilever, 122–26, 137
    construction of, New York City,
        116–17
    ice, 127–28
    pontoon, 118, 119–21, 142–43
    railroad, 128–41
    suspension, 126, 132, 136–39,
        142, 147, 149–50
    trussed chain suspension, 132
    unrealized plans for:
        Blackwell's Island bridge
            (1877), 128–32
        Blackwell's Island bridge
            (1894), 132–33
        Brooklyn-Battery bridge, 149–
            156
        Flying Pendant Lever Bridge,
            122–26
        George Washington Bridge,
            147, 148
        West Eleventh Street–Ho-
            boken, N.J., bridge, 118,
            119–21
        West Fifty-ninth Street–Wee-
            hawken, N.J., bridge, 139–
            140
        West Fifty-seventh Street–Wee-
            hawken, N.J., bridge, 142–
            143, 144–45, 146, 147, 148
        West Seventieth Street–Union,
            N.J., bridge, 137–39
        West Twenty-third Street–Ho-
            boken, N.J., bridge, 136–37,
            139, 140, 141
        Yonkers, N.Y.–Alpine, N.J.,
            bridge, 142
    see also specific bridges
Briere, Francois, 66
Britton, Joseph, 163

Broadway, 3, 9, 11
    elevated lines proposed for, 95–
        99
    IRT line for, 90, 100, 104
Broadway Association, 156, 217–
    219
Broadway Temple, plan for, 58–64
Bronx, 100, 103, 116, 177, 204
Bronx Borough Courthouse, 36
Bronx-Whitestone Bridge, 149
Brooklyn, 100, 103, 108, 116, 117,
    122, 123, 127, 128, 134, 149,
    156, 167, 199, 204, 215
Brooklyn-Battery bridge, plan for,
    149–56
Brooklyn-Battery Tunnel, 149, 156
Brooklyn Bridge, 137
    building of, 116, 128, 129, 132,
        137
    opening of, 116, 132
Brooklyn Daily Eagle, 200
Brooklyn Museum, 37, 207
Brooklyn Navy Yard, 156
Brooklyn Rapid Transit Company
    (BRT), 103
Brooks Brothers, 34
Broome Street, 24, 27, 29
Brown, Henry Kirke, 203
Bryant, William Cullen, 43, 161,
    162, 163, 167
Bryant Park, 13, 15, 37, 52
Buffalo, N.Y., 194
Building of the City, The, 21–23
buildings, public, 36–80
    architecture of, 36–37
    design competitions for, 51–58
    landmark protection of, 37
    proposed demolition of, 36, 51–
        52, 56, 76–80
    unrealized plans for:
        American Museum of Natural
            History, 46
        art museum, Central Park
            West, 42–43, 44, 45
        Broadway Temple, 59–63
        Carnegie Hall, 36, 76–80
        City Hall, 51–52, 54–57
        civic center, Manhattan, 57–
            58
        Grand Central Terminal, xvii
        Metropolitan Museum of Art,
            46, 48–49, 50
        New-York Historical Society,
            39–42, 46
        New York Public Library, 52,
            53
        New York State Arsenal, 39–
            42

    United Nations, 65–69
    see also specific buildings
Burgee, John, 188
Burr, Aaron, 193
Bush Terminal Building, 17
Butler, Nicholas, 203
Buttermilk Channel, 149
Byrd, Richard, 59, 63, 108
Byrd Beacon, 59

Canarsee Indians, xiii
cantilever bridges, proposed, 122–
    126, 132–33, 137–39
Cantor, Eddie, 63
Carnegie, Andrew, 73, 74, 79
Carnegie Hall, 73–80
    acoustics of, 73, 74
    building of, 73–76
    as landmark, 37
    opening night of, 76
    proposed demolition of, 36, 76–
        80
Carnegie Hall Corporation, 79
Caro, Robert, 156
Carrère, John, 215
Carrère & Hastings, 58, 207, 215
Casals, Pablo, 80
Casey, Edward P., 54–55
cast-iron buildings, 29, 31
Castle Clinton, 219, 221
Catskill aqueduct monument, de-
    sign for, 210, 211
Catskill aqueduct system, 210, 211
Centennial Exposition (Philadel-
    phia), 136
Central Park:
    acquisition of land for, 161–67
    Board of Commissioners of the,
        39, 41–42, 44–46, 167, 169,
        174, 175, 210
    boundaries of, 164
    competition for design of, 169–
        177
    design of, 158, 167–77, 210,
        215–17
    Great Lawn of, 215–17
    Greensward plan for, 86, 174–
        177
    health aspect of, 161, 164–67
    lagoon for, 212–13, 214
    as "people's park," 168
    race course for, 181–82
    reservoirs in, 165, 166, 170–71,
        210–17
    squatters in, 216, 217
    topographical surveys of, 86,
        167, 168, 169–72, 176

unrealized plans for, 159, 167, 171, 172–76, 210–15
Central Synagogue, 37
Century City, 70
Chambers Street Reservoir, 193
Chinatown, 6
cholera epidemic, 193
Christopher Street ferry, 116
Chrysler, Walter, 108
Chrysler Building, 108
Chrystie Street, 26, 27
Churchill, Winston, 76
Church of the Holy Apostles, 199
Church of the Saviour, 199
Citizens Committee for Carnegie Hall, 79
City Beautiful movement, 5, 203
City Center, 65, 79
City Club, 213
City Hall:
   building of, 36
   design competition for a new, 51–58
   proposed demolition of, 51–52, 56
City Hall (old), 197
City Hall Park, 51–57, 193, 195–196
   fountain for, 193–96
civic center (Manhattan), proposed, 57–58
Civic Virtue (MacMonnies), 196
Civil and Municipal Courthouse, 36
Clarke, Reeves & Company, 129
Clarke, Thomas, 129–32, 133
Claxton, Allen, 64
Cleopatra's Needle, 190, 191
Clermont, 121, 203
Cloisters, 185
Bird S. Coler Hospital, 183, 188
Coliseum, xvii, 36
Colossus bridge, Philadelphia, Pa., 126
Columbia Enthroned, 212, 213
Columbia University, 120, 203
Columbia Yacht Club, 204
Columbus Monument, 191
Committee on Lands and Places, 162
Committee on a Permanent War Memorial, 212–13
Committee to Commemorate the Six Million Martyrs, 219–25
Committee to Save Carnegie Hall, 77
Common Council, 161
competitions, design:

Central Park, 169–77
City Hall, 51–58
   Robert Fulton memorial water gate, 204–9
   Municipal Building, 58
   George Washington monument, 198–203
   World War I memorial, 212–17
concert houses, 73
Con Edison, 185
Conservatory Pond, 175
Coogan, Jackie, 63
Cooper, Peter, 98
Corbett, Harvey Wiley, 16–23
Corbin, Austin, 132, 133
Corning Glass Works, 220–22
Cornwallis, Charles, Lord, 199
Cottage Residences (Downing), 163, 164
County Court House (Tweed Court House), 51, 88, 89
Cox, Rachel, 121
Cret, Paul P., 206
Croton Aqueduct Board, 210
Croton Aqueduct Committee, 193
Croton aqueduct system, 52, 164, 193, 210
Croton (later Yorkville) Reservoir, 164, 165, 193, 210–17
Croton Reservoir, at Fifth Avenue and Forty-second Street, 52, 53
Croton River, 193, 195
Crouch and Fitzgerald, 34
Crystal Palace, 37
Curran, Henry, 16–18
Curtis, George William, 85
Custis, George Washington Parke, 200

Damrosch, Leopold, 73, 80
Damrosch, Walter, 73, 74, 80
Damrosch Park, 80
Dana, Charles, 181
Daniels, Howard, 174
Davies, J. Clarence, Jr., 183
Declaration of Independence, 56
Delacorte, George T., 196
de Lancey, Edward F., 51–52
demapping, 27, 28, 30
department stores, 11, 88, 103
Depew, Chauncey, 13, 181
Depew Place, 3
DeSalvio, Louis, 27, 28
deSimone, Jack, 79
dirigibles, 108–13
distemper epidemic (1872), 90–92
Dix, John, 98
Dodge, Daniel, 163–64

Douglass, David Bates, 167
Downing, Andrew Jackson, 163, 164, 167–68
Duane Street, 149
Duke, James B., 63
Duncan, Isadora, 76
Du Pont, Pierre S., 109
Dutch Kills, 116
Dutch Reformed Church of Saint Nicholas, 36
Dutch West India Company, xiii
Duveen Brothers, 11
Dyckman's Bridge, 116

Earth Week, 31, 32
East River:
   bridges for, 116, 117, 122–33
   ferries on, 116, 117, 122, 127, 128, 129
   ice bridges on, 127–28
   tunnels under, 141, 151
East River Park, plan for, xv, xvi
Eckener, Hugh, 113
École des Beaux-Arts, 39, 41, 214
Edison electrical plant, 204, 205
Eidlitz, Leopold, 180
electrical traction, 141
elevated railroads, 90–100
   building of, 97–100, 129
   electrification of, 100, 103
   endless traveling train, proposed for, 96–99
   pneumatic system, proposed for, 92–95, 98
   Viaduct Railway, proposed for, 88
Ellington, Duke, 76
Elliott, Charles, 169
Ellis Island, 220
Ellis Island, 116
Elysian Fields, 161
Embury, Aymar, II, 65, 66, 68, 69
Empire State Building, 64, 65
   mooring mast of, 108–13
   observatory of, 113
Evacuation Day, 203
Evening Journal, 113
Evening Post, 43, 161, 167, 200
Exchange Place (N.J.), 134

Family Court Building, 37
Federal Hall, 197
Federal Hall National Memorial, 197
ferries, 116–18, 121–22, 127, 128, 129, 134, 142
Ferriss, Hugh, 20, 66, 155

Fifth Avenue, 3, 10, 53, 84, 164
traffic congestion on, 11–16
Fifth Avenue Association, 33, 34
Fifty-ninth Street Bridge (Queens-
boro Bridge), 8–9, 116, 133,
141, 184, 185
Fifty-seventh Street, 74
financial panic (1893), 132, 139
Finley, James, 126
Fireman's Memorial, 209
Avery Fisher Hall, 80
Flagg, Ernest, 52, 53, 57
Flatiron Building, 6
Flower, Roswell, 56
Flushing Meadows–Corona Park,
159
Flushing Meadows Park, 66–67,
68, 69
Flying Pendant Lever Bridge (Rain-
bow Bridge), plan for, 122–26
Fort Amsterdam, xiii–xiv
fountains, 193–96, 214
Franklin Street, 6
Frazee, John, 201
Frederycks, Kryn, xiii, xiv
Fred French Building, 17
Friedberg, M. Paul, 196
Fuller, Lawson, 181, 182
Fulton, Robert:
Pope and, 123, 126
proposed memorial water gate
to, 203–9
steamboats developed by, 121,
127
Fulton ferry, 116
Fulton Ferry Landing, 117
Robert Fulton Monument Associa-
tion, 203–9

Garelik, Sanford, 34
Gavrilovic, H. E. Stoyan, 66
Gaynor, William J., 11–16
Gebiner, Benjamin, 225
Gellinoff, Abraham, 34
General Assembly Building, 69, 72
General Motors, 109
George Washington Bridge, 59
building of, 116, 122, 147
design of, xv, 142–49
towers of, 147, 148, 149
Gilbert, Cass, 147, 148, 149
Gilbert, Rufus, 92–95
Gilbert Elevated Railway, 95
Gilchrist, Huntington, 66
Gilroy, Thomas, 51, 52, 56, 57, 58
Glickman, Louis, 77, 78
Goldwater Memorial Hospital, 188
Goodyear blimps, 113

Goodyear Tire and Rubber Com-
pany, xvi, 105–7
Gordon, Bragdon & Orchard, 57
Gorham's, 11
Gourlay, Robert Fleming, 193–96
Gowanus Canal, 116
Graf Zeppelin, 109, 113
Grand Central Depot, 5, 134, 135
Grand Central Terminal:
building of, 5
proposed shuttle to, xvi, 104–7
proposed tower for, xvii, 36
Grand Prix racing track, plan for,
159
Grant, Hugh, 51
Grant's Tomb, 190, 203, 204, 205
Graves, Roswell, 173
Gray, John, 169
Graybar Building, 17
Greater New York, 8, 57, 116
Great Lawn, 215–17
Green, Andrew Haswell, 52
Green, S. William, 185
Greenough, Horatio, 203
Greensward plan, 86, 174–77
Greenwood Cemetery, 167
Griffith, D. W., 59
Gruen, Victor, 183, 184, 185
Guggenheim, Isaac, 203
Gustin, Samuel, 174

Half Moon, 203
Hall of Records, 57
Hamilton, Alexander, 56
Hamilton Avenue, 151
Hamilton Square, 158, 159, 199,
200, 201, 203
Harder, Julius, 57
Harlem Lane, 3, 177, 178
Harlem Marsh, 158
Harlem River, 116
Harlem River Drive, 182
Harlem River Speedway, 182
Harlem Square, 158
Harper's Weekly, 169, 179
Harrison, Benjamin, 137
Harrison, Wallace K., 65, 68, 69,
70–71, 72
Hartgers, Joost, xiv
Harvey, Charles T., 90, 91
Haskin, DeWitt, 135, 140–41
Hassard, John, 42
Hastings, Thomas, 207, 210–15
Haussmann, George Eugène, 8
Hawkesbury River Bridge, 139
Hayes, Rutherford, 50
Heckscher, August, 183
Heifetz, Jasha, 79

Hell Gate Bridge, 141, 143
Hewitt, Abram, 51
High Bridge, 182
Hindenburg explosion, 109
historic districts, 29, 31
Hoboken, N.J., 161
Hoboken ferry house, 120
Hoffman, John T., 88, 98
Holden, Lansing, 207
Holland Tunnel, 27, 116, 147
Holocaust memorial:
at Battery Park City, 224–25
proposed, 191, 219–25
in Riverside Park, 219
Hone, Philip, 200
Hornbostel, Henry F., 57, 58
horsecars, 85, 86, 92, 95, 99
horse racing, 177–82
Horticultural Society, 215
Hôtel de Ville, 54–55, 57
Howell & Stokes, 58
Hsu, Shuhsi, 66
Hudson, Henry, 203, 204
Hudson-Fulton Fete, 203, 204, 205
Henry Hudson Memorial Bridge,
149
Henry Hudson Parkway, 180
Hudson River:
bridges for, 116, 119–26, 134–
149
ferries on, 116, 117, 121–22,
127, 134, 142
tunnels under, 116, 121, 140–
141, 147
water gate for, proposed for,
203–9
Hunt, Richard Morris, 13, 39–42,
50, 74
Hunter College, 65
Hutton, E. F., 59
Huxtable, Ada Louise, 225
Hylan, John, 212, 215

ice bridges, 127–28
Idlewild Airport, 108
Impellitteri, Vincent, 24
Independent Taxi Owners Council,
33, 34
Interborough Rapid Transit (IRT),
11, 90, 100–107
Isaacs, Stanley, 151

Jacobs, Charles M., 132, 133, 140–
141
Jacobs, Jane, 30
Jallade, Louis, 8–9
Javits, Jacob K., 79

Jacob K. Javits Convention Center, 37
Jerome Speedway, 177
Jewell, Edward, 219
Joan of Arc, statue of, 191
Johnson, Philip, 188
Jones' Wood, 161–64, 166–67
Juilliard School of Music, 80
Juliana, 121

Kahn, Louis I., 219–25
Kaiser Wilhelm der Grosse, 16
J. M. Kaplan Fund, 79
Keep, Henry, 42–43
Kelsey, Albert, 206
John F. Kennedy International Airport, 108
Khalidi, Awny El, 66
King's Bridge, 116
King's College, 120
Kingsland, Ambrose, 161–62
Kips Bay Plaza, 70
Krieger, David Lloyd, 219

Lacarte, Julio A., 66
Ladies' Mile, 11, 103
Lafayette Memorial, 191
Lafever, Minard, 199, 200, 201, 203
La Guardia, Fiorello H., 24, 108, 149, 156, 219
La Guardia Airport, 108
landmarks, 29, 31, 37
Latrobe, Benjamin, 126
Lauchaume, J., 172–74
Lawrence, Charles B., 121
Lawrence, Cornelius, 193
Le Corbusier, 147
Lefuel, Hector, 41
Lehman College, 65
L'Enfant, Pierre, 197
Lenox, James, 39
Leone, Sebastian, 34
Lexington Avenue, 2, 104, 107
Lie, Trygve, 66, 67
Life, 78
Lincoln, Abraham, 56
Lincoln Center for the Performing Arts, 74, 77, 78, 80, 219
Lindbergh, Charles, 108
Lindenthal, Gustav:
    early career of, 136
    Hudson River bridges designed by, xvii, 136–49
    pontoon bridge proposed by, 142
    Queensborough Bridge designed by, 133

Lindsay, John V., 185, 188, 225
    proposed Lower Manhattan Expressway as viewed by, 28, 29–30
    proposed Madison Mall supported by, 31–34
"Lindsay's Loop," 28
Little Juliana, 121
Livingston, Robert R., Jr., 121–22
London, 8, 163
Long Island Rail Road, 129, 132, 133, 141
Louvre, 41
Lower Manhattan Expressway, plan for, xvi, 24–31
    demapping of, 27, 28, 30
    funding of, 24–27
    opposition to, 27–31
    population displaced by, 27, 28–29

McAdoo, William, 140–41
McClellan, George V., 5, 6, 8
McComb, John, Jr., 51
MacDonald, Charles, 139–40
McIntosh, Lachlan H., 174, 177
McKenzie, Vorhees & Gmelin, 61
McKim, Mead & White, 50, 58, 203, 207, 214
MacMonnies, Frederick, 196, 212, 213
R. H. Macy's, 103
Madigan-Hyland, 24, 27, 29
Madison Avenue, 2, 31–34
Madison Mall, plan for, 31–34
Madison Square, 85, 158, 196
Magonigle, Harold Van Buren, 207–9
Mahler, Gustav, 76
Maine Memorial, 209
Makla, Robert, 185
Manes, Donald, 34
Mangin, Joseph F., 51
Manhattan:
    commissioners' plan for, xviii–xix, 2–3, 11, 158–59
    topographical survey of, 87, 88
    views of, xiv, 7, 18, 117, 120, 123
    waterfront area of, xv, xvi, 70, 72, 134, 158, 161–62, 179–180, 182, 203–4
Manhattan Avenue, 3
Manhattan Bridge, 6, 25, 27, 116, 141, 215
Manhattan Company, 192, 193
Manhattan Lake, 170–71, 210, 217

Manhattan Square, 42–43, 46, 158, 159
"Marble Palace," 88
Marchi, John, 30
Market Place, 158
Marshall, Henry Rutgers, 10–11
Martha's Vineyard, Mass., 65
Master Apartments, 17
Mead, William, 207
Metropolis, plan for, 99
Metropolitan Life Insurance Company, 17
Metropolitan Museum of Art:
    allée for, 213, 217
    building of, 5, 39, 50
    design of, 46, 47, 48, 49
    expansion of, 185
    Fifth Avenue facade of, 39
    founding of, 43–44, 46
    original plan for, 48, 49, 50
    Wing A of, 47, 50
Metropolitan Opera House, 73, 74, 77, 80, 181
Meyers, Marshall, 220, 222
Middle Road, 3
Mile High City, 70
Miller, Michael, 174
Miller Field, 108
Millionaires' Row, 11–12, 13
Minuit, Peter, xiii
Mitchel, John P., 213
Mitchell, MacNeil, 79
Mitropoulos, Dimitri, 80
Mohansic Park, 67
monuments, 189–225
    Art Commission and review of plans for, 190–91
    design competitions for, 198–203, 204–9, 212–17
    maintenance and restoration of, 191
    unrealized plans for:
        Catskill aqueduct monument, 210, 211
        City Hall Park fountain, 193–196
        Robert Fulton memorial water gate, 203–9
        Holocaust memorial, 191, 219–25
        stainless steel obelisk, 191
        veterans' memorial (1962), 190
        Victory Arch, 217–19
        George Washington monument, 197–203
        World War I memorial, 211, 212–15
    see also specific monuments

Morningside Heights, 203
Morris, George W., 200
Moses, Robert, xvii, 65, 70
  Brooklyn-Battery bridge proposed by, 149–56
  La Guardia and, 24, 108, 149, 156, 219
  Lower Manhattan Expressway proposed by, xvi, 24–31
Mott Haven, 134
Mould, Jacob Wrey, 46, 47, 49, 50, 196
Mount Saint Vincent's Convent, 164, 165
Mumford, Lewis, 28, 183
Municipal Art Society, 5–8, 57, 154
Municipal Building, 57–58
Municipal Building Commission, 56
Murray Hill, 177
Museum of Jewish Heritage, 224, 225
museums, art, 39–50
  proposed for Central Park West, 42–43, 44, 45, 46
  see also specific museums
Music Hall, see Carnegie Hall

Nassau, 127
Nast, Thomas, 179
National System of Interstate and Defense Highways, 24–27
New Amsterdam, xiii–xiv
New Brighton, 160, 161
New Brighton Village Hall, 37
Newtown Creek, 116
New York and Long Island Bridge Company, 128, 132
New York and New Jersey Bridge Company, 137–39, 140
New York Bridge Company, 128
New York Central and Hudson River Railroad, 134, 179, 180, 203, 208
New York City:
  aesthetic goals for, 5, 6, 8–9
  British capture of, xiii–xiv
  creation of, 8, 52
  Dutch settlement of, xiii–xiv
  planning of, xiii–xvii
  population of, 8, 36, 116, 161, 193
  as site of United Nations, 65–72
  size of, xviii–xix, 85, 161, 199
  water supply for, 193, 195, 210
  see also: Bronx; Brooklyn; Manhattan; Queens; Staten Island

New York City Building, 65, 66
New York City Improvement Commission, 8–9
New York City Landmarks Preservation Commission, 29, 31, 37
New York City Planning Commission, xvi, 24, 27, 156
New York City Tunnel Authority, 156
New York Daily Tribune, 197, 198
New York Elevated Company, 95
New York Foundling Hospital, 36
New York Gallery of Fine Arts, 39
New York Globe, 13, 14
New York Herald, 74, 85, 100, 180, 181, 195, 200
New York Herald Tribune, 183
New-York Historical Society, 38, 51–52, 172
  building design for, 39–42, 43, 44, 46, 50
New York–New Jersey Bridge Company, 138
New York Philharmonic, 76–77, 78, 80
New York Public Library:
  building of, 5, 13, 15, 207
  cost of, 12
  proposed design for, 52, 53
  site of, 46, 52, 53, 193
New York State Arsenal, 39–42, 46, 164, 165
New York State Legislature, 39, 44, 46, 86, 95–96, 198
New York State Theater, 180
New York Stock Exchange, 207
New York Telephone Building, 18
New York Times, 6, 9, 13, 41, 57, 65, 67, 70, 77, 85, 87, 90, 91–92, 105, 128, 142, 147, 168–169, 181, 183, 188, 213, 219, 225
New York Tribune, 13, 85, 104, 203
New York World, 91
New York World's Fair, 28, 65, 66, 68, 69
New York Yacht Club, 13
Normandy, Eugene, 80
North River, see Hudson River
North River Bridge Company, 137, 139

Observatory Place, 158
Octagon Tower, 188
O'Dwyer, William, 24, 65, 70, 72
Office of Midtown Planning and Development (OMPD), 32

Olmsted, Frederick Law:
  Central Park designed by, 39, 86, 158, 167, 174–77, 210, 213
  as superintendent of Central Park, 169–72
omnibuses, horse-drawn, 12, 83, 85, 95, 98, 99
Oratorio Society, 73
Osborne Apartments, 73, 75

Paley Park, 185
Palmer, Timothy, 126
Pan Am Building, 36
Parade, 158
Paris, 8, 57, 174
parks, 158–88
  commissioners' allotment for, 158–59
  need for more, 161, 193
  protection of, 159
  unrealized plans for:
    Battery Park, 154, 155, 156, 159, 219–25
    Bryant Park, 13, 15
    Central Park, 159, 167–71, 172–76, 210–15
    City Hall Park, 51–57, 193–195
    East River park, xv, xvi
    Flushing Meadows–Corona Park, 159
    Flushing Meadows Park, 66, 67, 68, 69
    Hamilton Square, 199, 200, 201, 202
    Jones' Wood, 161–64, 166–67
    Manhattan Square, 42–43, 44, 45, 46
    Riverside Park, 178–81, 191, 203–9, 219
    Sara Roosevelt Park, 26
    Tivoli Gardens, Roosevelt Island, 185, 186, 187, 188
    Union Square, 190, 197, 199, 203
  see also specific parks
Parsons, William Barclay, 100, 203
Passaic, N.J., 99
PATH (Port Authority Trans-Hudson) system, 141
Pattison, Harriet, 222, 225
Pearson, Lester B., 72
Pelham Bay Park, 158
Pennsylvania Railroad, 134–41
Pennsylvania Station:
  building of, 36, 141
  demolition of, 29, 36–37

plan for curved avenue to, 10–11

subway route to, 11, 103

Philadelphia, Pa., 67, 126

Philharmonic Hall, 80

Phoenix, 121

planning, urban:

City Beautiful movement, 5, 203

commissioners' 1811 street plan, xviii–xix, 2–3, 11, 158–59

documentation of, xvi–xvii

Robert Moses, xvii, 24–31, 65, 70, 149–56

New York City Improvement Commission, 8–9

New York City Planning Commission, xvi, 24, 27

public's role in, xvi

Regional Plan Association, 18, 21–23

Triborough Bridge and Tunnel Authority, 156

Triborough Bridge Authority, 24, 25, 149, 154, 156

Welfare Island Planning and Development Committee, 185, 188

pneumatic transit system, plan for, 92–95

Pollard, Calvin, 197–98, 199, 200, 201–3

James Stewart Polshek & Partners, 225

Pomerance, Ralph, 77, 78

pontoon bridges, plans for, 118, 119–21, 143

Pope, Elizabeth, 126

Pope, Thomas, 122–26

Port of New York Authority, 143–147, 149

Post, George B., 57, 58, 207

Poughkeepsie Bridge, 139

Power Broker, The (Caro), 156

Pratt, Charles, 129

Price, Chester, 155

Procaccino, Mario, 30

Prospect Park, 86, 158

Public School 234, 37

Public Service Commission, 103

Pulitzer Fountain, 190

Putnam, George, 46

Queens, 65–69, 103, 108, 128, 129, 132, 133, 185, 204

Queensboro Bridge (Fifty-ninth Street Bridge), 8–9, 116, 133, 141, 184, 185

Queens-Midtown Tunnel, 151

Queens Museum, 65

Quill, Michael, 107

racetracks, proposed, 177–82

Rachmaninoff, Sergei, 76

Radio City Music Hall, 65

railroads:

elevated, 90–100, 103, 129

proposed bridges for, 128–140

Rainbow Bridge (Flying Pendant Lever Bridge), plan for, 122–126

Rainey, Thomas, 128–33

Rainey Park, 133

Randel, John, Jr., 2, 95

Rankin & Kellogg, 54–55, 57

Rapid Transit Commission, 95

Rapoport, Nathan, 220

Raskob, John J., 108–13

Real Estate Board, 154

Rector Street, 149

Regional Plan Association, 18, 21–23

Reisner, Christian, 58–64

Rendering Company, 91

reservoirs, 52, 53, 164, 165, 193, 210–17

Reservoir Square, 46

Richland, W. Bernard, 33–34

Richmond, Frederick, 183, 185, 188

Richmond Borough Hall, 215

Riegelman, Harold, 79

Riverside Church, 36, 59

Riverside Drive, 3, 178, 179, 180, 181, 203

Riverside Park, 158

design of, 179

Holocaust memorial proposed for, 191, 219, 220

racetrack proposed for, 178–81

water gate proposed for, 203–9

Rockefeller, John D., Jr., 59, 70–72

Rockefeller, Nelson A., 65, 70, 80

Rockefeller, William, 181

Rockefeller Center, 17, 23

Roebling, John, 128, 132, 137

Roebling, Washington, 128, 132

Rogers, Will, 63

Roosevelt, Eleanor, 28

Roosevelt, Franklin D., 65, 147, 156

Roosevelt Island (Blackwell's Island; Welfare Island), 128, 132, 133, 183–88, 204, 205

Sara Roosevelt Park, 26

Rosenthal, Abe, 65

Rubinow, Raymond S., 79

Sage, Russell, 181

Saint Hubert Air Field, 109

Saint Nicholas Avenue, 3, 177

Saint Patrick's Cathedral, 33

Saint Paul's Chapel, 37, 89

Saint-Saëns, Camille, 76

Saksin, Georgii, 66

San Francisco, Calif., 67

Schmidt, Max E., 100–103, 105, 106

Schuylkill River, 126

Scientific American, 86, 142, 198

Scribner's Monthly, 42

Secretariat Building, 72

Senate Railroad Committee, 88

Seventh Avenue, 6

Seventh Street Bridge, Pittsburgh, Pa., 136

Sherry-Netherland Hotel, 17

Shipwrights of New-York, 123

Shreve, Lamb & Harmon, 64, 109, 111

Shuttle, Forty-second Street, plan for, xvi, 104–7

sidewalks, elevated, 3, 18–23

Simon, Robert, Jr., 76, 77, 78, 79

Singstad, Ole, 151, 155, 156

Sixth Avenue, 6, 13, 94, 95

Skidmore, Louis, 65, 66, 68, 69

skyscrapers, 58, 59–64, 108–13

traffic congestion as result of, 16–18

slum clearance, 6

Smith, Al, 156

Smithfield Bridge, Pittsburgh, Pa., 136

SoHo, 29, 30–31

South Street Seaport, 117

Spanish-American War, 133

speedways, proposed, 177–82

Speer, Alfred, 95–99

Sperry Gyroscope plant, 65

Spuyten Duyvil Creek, 116, 134

Staten Island, 116, 151, 160, 161, 204

Staten Island ferry, 117

Staten Island Ferry Terminals, 215

State Office Building, 37

Statue of Liberty, 39, 220

steamboats, 121–22, 127

Steinway, William, 129, 132

Stern, Isaac, 78–79, 80

Stern, Vera, 79

Stern Brothers Building, 13

Stevens, Edwin, 122

Stevens, John, xvii
  pontoon bridge (West Eleventh Street–Hoboken, N.J.) proposed by, 118, 119–21
  steamboats developed by, 121
Stevens Institute of Technology, 122, 141
Stewart, Alexander T., 87
stock market crash (1929), 63, 109
Stokowski, Leopold, 80
Street Railway Review, 100
streets, 1–34
  commissioners' 1811 plan for, xviii–xix, 2–3, 11, 158–59
  grid pattern of, 2–3, 5, 6, 8, 9–10, 11, 95
  public squares and, 2–3, 158–159
  traffic circulation in, 3, 16–18, 24, 85
  unrealized plans for:
    curved avenue, 10–11
    diagonal boulevards, 5–10
    Lower Manhattan Expressway, 24–31
    Madison Mall, 32–34
    multitiered system, 18–23
    new avenue, 12–16
  see also specific streets
Strong, William, 56
Stuyvesant, Peter, xiii
subways:
  Arcade Railway, proposed, 86–90, 95–96, 177
  building of, 88, 90, 100
  complaints about, 11, 82, 100
  Dual System for, 103
  electrification of, 103
  Forty-second Street shuttle, plan for, xvi, 105–7
  "headless horseman," 106
  need for, 85–86, 88
  planning of, xv, 85–86, 100
  proposed moving platform for, 100–3, 105, 106
  Roosevelt Island link for, 185, 188
Sulzberger, Arthur Hays, 65
suspension bridges, 126, 137, 147
  plans for, 136–40, 142–47, 149, 150–56
  trussed chain, proposed, 132
Sweeny, Peter "Brains," 177–81
Szell, George, 80

Taylor, Joseph, 167
Tchaikovsky, Peter Ilyich, 74
Temple of Dendur, 185–88

Third Avenue, 177
Third Avenue Bridge, 129
Thomas, John R., 54–55, 57
Throgs Neck Bridge, 149
Tibbett, Lawrence, 77
Tiffany & Company, 11
Tilden, Samuel J., 52
Tilden Trust, 52
Tilden Trust Library, plan for, 52, 53
Times Square, 19, 217–19
Times Tower, 219
Tivoli Gardens, proposed, 185, 186, 187, 188
Tompkins, Daniel D., 123
Tompkins Square, 158
Topographical Atlas of the City of New York (Viele), 88
Torah scroll monument, plan for, 191, 220
trains, *see* railroads; subways
Transit Authority, 105–7, 185
transportation, public, 85–113
  complaints about, 82
  horse-drawn, 12, 82, 83, 85, 86, 90–92, 95
  light-rail, xvii
  traffic congestion and, 82, 85, 88
  see also elevated railroads; subways
Transport Workers Union, 107
Treatise on Bridge Architecture, A (Pope), 122–25
Treatise on the Theory and Practice of Landscape Gardening, A (Downing), 163
Triborough Bridge, 149
Triborough Bridge and Tunnel Authority, 156
Triborough Bridge Authority, 24, 25, 149, 154, 156
Tribune Building, 39
Trinity Church, 87, 197
trolleys, electric, 85
Trump, Donald, xvii
trussed chain suspension bridge, proposed, 132
Tuthill, William B., 74, 75
Twain, Mark, 85
Tweed, William Marcy "Boss," 88, 178, 179
Tweed Court House (County Court House), 51, 88, 89

Union Ferry Company, 128
Union Square, 85, 158, 190, 197, 199, 203

United Nations, 65–72, 105
  donation of site for, 72
  General Assembly of, 65, 66, 67, 72
  proposed design for, 66–67, 68, 69
  Security Council of, 65
United Nations Headquarters Committee, 65, 66, 67, 70
United Real Estate Owners Association, 215
United States Custom House, 36, 154, 155
Urban Development Corporation (UDC), 188

Van Cortlandt Park, 158
Vanderbilt, Cornelius, 203
Vanderbilt, William, 181
Vanderbilt family, 12, 124, 135, 178
Van Wyck, Robert, 100, 133
Vaux, Calvert:
  Central Park designed by, 39, 86, 158, 167, 169, 172, 174–177, 196, 210, 213
  museums designed by, 46–50
Venturi and Rauch, xv, xvi
Verrazano, Giovanni da, 204
Verrazano-Narrows Bridge, 117, 149
veterans' memorials, 190, 211, 212–15, 225
Viaduct Railway Company, 88
Victory Arch, plan for, 217–19
Viele, Egbert Ludovicus:
  Arcade Railway designed by, 86–90, 95–96, 177
  Central Park designed by, 167–172, 174, 176–77
Vienna, 8
Vietnam Veterans Memorial, 225
Villard Houses, 33
V-J Day, 218
von Bülow, Hans, 73

Wagner, Robert F., Jr., 24, 28, 79, 183
Walker, Jimmy, 113, 215
Wallace, William Ross, 201, 202
Wall Street, xiv
Warner Brothers, 59
Warren, H. Langford, 54–55
Warren & Wetmore, 58
Washington, George, 56, 121, 174, 197
  proposed monument to, 197–203

Washington Monument Association of New York City, 197–203
waterfront, xv, xvi, 67, 70, 72, 127, 134, 158, 161–62, 179–180, 182, 203–4, 221
water gate, plan for, 203–9
Weber, Hamilton, 108
Weber, P. D., 57
Weehawken ferry, 116
Welfare Island (Roosevelt Island; Blackwell's Island), 128, 132, 133, 183–88, 204, 205
Welfare Island Planning and Development Committee, 185, 188
Westchester County Planning Commission, 67
West Eleventh Street–Hoboken, N.J., bridge, 118, 119–21
West Fifty-ninth Street–Weehawken, N.J., bridge, 139–40
West Fifty-seventh Street–Weehawken, N.J., bridge, 142–43, 144–45, 146, 147, 148

West Seventieth Street–Union, N.J., bridge, 137–39
West Side Highway, 25, 27, 149, 151
West Street, 134
West Twenty-third Street–Hoboken, N.J., bridge, 136–37, 139, 140, 141
Westway, xvii
White City, 4, 5, 204
Whitman, Walt, 200
Whyte, William, 31
Williamsburg Bridge, 27, 116, 117
Willis Avenue Bridge, 129
Willoughby, Lucia, 217–19
Willson, Hugh B., 85–86, 88
Wood, Fernando, 167
Woodring, Harold, 156
Woolworth Building, 17, 18, 146, 147
Working for the People (Moses), 156

World's Columbian Exposition (1893), 4, 5, 8, 100, 101, 212
World War I memorial, plan for, 211, 212–15
Wright, Wilbur, 204

X City, 70–71, 72

Yonkers, N.Y.–Alpine, N.J., bridge, 142
York and Sawyer, 50
Yorkville, 177
Yorkville Reservoir, 210–17
Young, John, 200
Younger, K. G., 66

Zeckendorf, Marion, 70
Zeckendorf, William, Sr., 67–71, 72
Zion, Robert, 185, 188

PHOTOGRAPH SOURCES

The author gratefully acknowledges the use of photographs from the following sources. Photographs not listed here are from the author's private collection or are in the public domain.

American Society of Civil Engineers. *Transactions,* Paper No. 1818, vol. 97, 1933 (pages 138–139)

Margot Ammann (page 146 left)

Architectural Record (pages 10, 17, 66, 211 bottom, 212, 214)

Archives of Ontario, Toronto, Canada (page 194 right)

Collection of the Art Commission of the City of New York, City Hall, New York (page 195)

Avery Architectural and Fine Arts Library, Columbia University, New York City (page 71)

Fabian Bachrach (page 72 left)

Broadway Temple-Washington Heights United Methodist Church, New York City (pages 58, 60, 61, 62, 63, 64)

Mona Brown (page 224)

Carnegie Hall Corporation Archives, New York City (pages 74 left, 76)

Courtesy of Con Edison, New York City (page 205)

Seymour B. Durst (page 182)

Helmut Jacoby (page 77)

Photograph copyright Robert C. Lautman (page 221 bottom)

Prints and Photographs Division, Library of Congress, Washington, D.C. (pages 87 bottom, 201)

John V. Lindsay (page 32)

Mariners' Museum, Newport News, Virginia (page 121)

Metropolitan Museum of Art, New York City (pages 46, 47, 48, 49)

The Municipal Art Society of New York (page 6)

Museum of the City of New York (pages 1, 13, 19 top, 54, 55, 84 bottom, 104, 112, 123, 134, 168, 175, 178, 180 left, 192 top, 196, 197, 210, 216 bottom)

Courtesy of National Parks Service, Frederick Law Olmsted National Historic Site, Brookline, Massachusetts (page 172 bottom)

New York City Department of Parks and Recreation (page 176)

John B. Bayley/New York City Landmarks Preservation Commission (page 29)

New-York Historical Society, New York City (pages 37, 38, 40 top, 41, 43, 50, 75, 84, 91, 94, 117, 120, 162, 163, 166, 173, 180 right, 198, 202, 204)

Eno Collection, Miriam and Ira D. Wallach Division, New York Public Library, Astor, Lenox and Tilden Foundations, New York City (page 165)

I. N. Phelps Stokes Collection, Miriam and Ira D. Wallach Division of Art, Prints and Photographs, The New York Public Library, Astor, Lenox and Tilden Foundations, New York City (pages xiv, 127)

Stuart Collection, Rare Books and Manuscripts Division, The New York Public Library, Astor, Lenox and Tilden Foundations, New York City (page 40 bottom)

Map Division, The New York Public Library, Astor, Lenox and Tilden Foundations, New York City (pages 170, 171 bottom)

U.S. History, Local History and Genealogy Division, The New York Public Library, Astor, Lenox and Tilden Foundations, New York City (pages 3, 18, 53 top, 179 top)

The New York Times Company. Reprinted by permission. Copyright © 1943 by the New York Times Company (page 218 top)

Passaic Public Library, Passaic, New Jersey (pages 96–97, 98, 99)

Reprinted from *Pencil Points,* July 1939, with the permission of Reinhold Publishing (page 155 bottom)

George Pohl (page 221 top)

Reprinted from *Popular Science* with permission © 1951, Times Mirror Magazines, Inc. (pages 106 bottom, 107)

Queens Library, *Herald Tribune* Morgue (page 78)

Regional Plan of New York and Its Environs, vol. 2, *The Building of the City* (1931), reprinted by permission of the Regional Plan Association (pages 19 bottom, 20, 21, 22, 23, 216)

Frederick W. Richmond (page 184)

Reprinted with permission. Copyright © 1921 by Scientific American, Inc. All rights reserved, August 13, 1921 (page 143); June 25, 1921 (pages 144–145); June 4, 1921 (page 146 left)

Courtesy of *Scientific American,* February 9, 1867 (page 87 top); April 13, 1872 (page 93); May 13, 1905 (page 102); May 28, 1881 (pages 130–131); February 23, 1895 (page 133); May 23, 1891 (page 137); May 2, 1896 (page 140); Supplement, February 12, 1881 (page 191); October 23, 1847 (page 199)

Shreve, Lamb & Harmon Associates, P.C. (page 111)

Courtesy of the Society for the Preservation of New England Antiquities, Boston, Massachusetts (page 172 top)

South Street Seaport Museum, New York City (page 128)

Staten Island Institute of Arts and Sciences (page 160)

Sterling Memorial Library, Yale University, New Haven, Connecticut (page 194 left)

Courtesy of Triborough Bridge and Tunnel Authority, New York City (pages 24, 25, 26, 27, 150–151, 152–153, 154)

Copyright 1977 Louis I. Kahn Collection, University of Pennsylvania and Pennsylvania Historical and Museum Commission, Philadelphia (pages 222, 223)

UPI/Bettman Newsphotos (page 30)

Venturi, Rauch and Scott Brown (page xv)

Wide World Photos, Inc. (page 218 bottom)

Samuel C. Williams Library, Stevens Institute of Technology, Hoboken, New Jersey (pages 118, 119)

Zion & Breen Associates, Inc., Imlaystown, New Jersey (pages 186, 187)